Institutions of the English Novel

Institutions of the English Novel

From Defoe to Scott

Homer Obed Brown

PENN

University of Pennsylvania Press

Philadelphia

Copyright © 1997 University of Pennsylvania Press
All rights reserved
Printed in the United States of America on acid-free paper

10 9 8 7 6 5 4 3 2 1

Published by
University of Pennsylvania Press
Philadelphia, Pennsylvania 19104-6097

Library of Congress Cataloging-in-Publication Data

Brown, Homer Obed, 1933–
    Institutions of the English novel: From Defoe to Scott / Homer Obed Brown.
        p.   cm.
    Includes bibliographical references and index.
    ISBN 0-8122-3383-2 (alk. paper)
    1. English fiction—18th century—History and criticism.   2. English fiction—
19th century—History and criticism.   3. Literature and society—Great Britain.
4. Literature and history—Great Britain.   5. Canon (Literature)   I. Title.
PR851.B75   1997
823.009—dc21   96-47118
                                                                                                    CIP

This book is dedicated to the most important institution,
my family
Brown, Graham, and Press

to my children, Alexandra, David, and Katharine,
my brother John Graham Brown,
my mother-in-law Sylvia Press,
and
in memory of
my parents H.O. and Jacqueline Graham Brown
and my father-in-law Alexander Press

And to Harriet, with all my love

Contents

Preface

MY TITLE CONCERNS SOME OF THE institutions associated with English prose fiction—fiction we have come to name "novels"—in the eighteenth and early nineteenth centuries and with the uncertain, inchoate, and multiple institutions (in the active sense of that slippery word) in this time period. Uncertain, because none of the "founding" novels were given that now revered generic name by Defoe, Richardson, or Fielding, who authored and authorized them by different names. The name "novel," in any case, had different semantic values then from those it took on during the nineteenth and twentieth centuries as what I am going to call an "institution." Inchoate and multiple, because, whatever their influence on the way "the novel" came to be thought of in the next two centuries, and there were a lot of variations and differences in such thinking, no one of them can be accepted as the "first" or originary novel. No one of them is sufficient to represent what later became "the novel," given not only the radical differences of narrative form and thematic content among them, but also their radically different "addresses" and levels of social life they "represented," in all senses of that term. Nor, despite Ian Watt's hope, are they in their differences from each other a "recapitulation" of the variety of forms taken by the later novel unless any difference is taken to symbolize difference as such.[1] The fictions of Defoe, Richardson, and Fielding, it could be argued, only become "the novel" by means of retrospective histories that made them seem inaugural and exemplary at once.

In other words, I see "the novels" of Defoe, Fielding, and Richardson as separate institutions in the plural; generative "moments" at best; each a new beginning (of what, in principle, it might be difficult to trace, except in that vague Whiggish sense that everything that happens occurs with the eventual purpose of producing us); and each with separate "genealogical lines," always imagined retrospectively, usually without recognition of the overdetermination of the notion of genealogy as the major concern of such narratives as *Tom Jones*. In short, they are legitimized retrospectively by later institutions at a point *after* the novel has already achieved the status of institution.

Among other things, an "institution" is always a claim on entitlement by a significant past of something at work in the present. When is that "moment" of the novel's institution? There are probably many. One important moment is in the second decade of the nineteenth century with the novels of Austen and Scott and the latter's criticism,[2] a moment, significantly, following three decades of great (and much maligned) novelistic and romance production. Another important institutional conjuncture is the controversial "aesthetic" elevation given the novel by Henry James and his argument over the nature of the novel with H. G. Wells, among others. In this moment the novel "began" for the modernist New Criticism, and this event is the enabling, foundational origin in one of what seems to me the most crucial institutional histories of the novel. For it was this history that legitimated the New Critical appropriation of the novel for intensive close reading in university classes during the large postwar expansion of American university enrollments.[3] Watt's *Rise* in 1957 effectively combined historical with formalist considerations to recuperate the eighteenth-century novel as a *modern* form of literary art.[4] Watt implied that not only was the novel of Defoe, Richardson, and Fielding modern, it also played a major role in the invention of modernism as such. That Watt's intervention came at a decisive moment in the institutionalization of the novel in America can be demonstrated by a glance at a few contemporary publications of novel theory.[5]

What I am arguing is that it is as necessary to "historicize" the discourse of the novel, particularly the discourse of the origins of the novel, as it is to historicize the novel itself, given the implicitly transhistorical nature of the object as it is presented in most histories of its origin. I also think it would be a mistake to underestimate the significance for the institution of the novel of this particular moment of the late 1950s, which called it to the attention of a newly emerging and powerful academic discipline that gave it new intellectual, aesthetic, and institutional legitimation by viewing it in terms of its relevance to contemporary concerns. At the same time, this is a decisive moment for another institution—the American university—in which the novel plays an important role in the formation of a newly professionalized and disciplined study of English and American literature, across developing and ever more finely tuned disciplinary lines defining historical period, genre, and a canon of authors. Moreover, I also believe that historical accounts of the rise or origin of the novel, whatever their value as histories, have as part of their effect—intended or not—the establishment of protocols for reading novels and these extend to determining what is important to read in novels and which novels can be read "seriously," or even given the privilege of the now curiously esteemed title instead of one of its déclassé and plebeian hyphenated forms.

Insistence that the novel fully realized its generic identity—that it was "institutionalized"—by 1750 is based on a misconception of institution, implying not only an untenable confusion of intentionality with fully received acknowledgment but also the ideological seventeenth- and eighteenth-century political problematic of genealogical determination.[6] The premise is this: what an institution was in its beginnings it must always be; what an institution can become is fully present in its origins (or at least according to the way those "origins" are conceived retrospectively). Aside from the tautology of this claim in principle, in this particular case it sets a definite ideological limit on what kind of novel can claim entitlement and, for that matter, on the definition of the very culture that produces and is produced by this increasingly effective narrative shaper of cultural and social desire.

To suggest that the novel fully achieves its identity by 1750 presupposes that the identity of *the novel* is defined by its *contextualization* at this particular moment. It also serves to discount the massive change in meaning undergone not only by the term *novel* but also by the particular texts of Defoe, Richardson, and Fielding in the next two centuries, and especially the crucial next seventy years.[7] It ignores later historical contexts that actually make possible the readings given by Watt and McKeon, for example, the development of notions of "realism." In this sense, Watt's *Rise* and McKeon's *Origin* seem chapters in the pre-history of the novel and might more aptly be called by Paul Hunter's title, *Before the Novel*.[8] I will return to this knotty problem of historical contextualization later on. I regard such work as absolutely necessary, as I hope the chapters which follow amply demonstrate. It is also work that never ends, however, and we must guard against the supposition that the meaning of any genre or institution, or even any text and, for that matter, any utterance, is manifest in any single historical moment or context. On the contrary, the novels of Defoe, Fielding, and Richardson actually change in meaning as they are historicized at later vantage points.

If it is part of the business of an institution to attempt to control its own proper contexts, institution also, as Bourdieu has pointed out, institutes or legitimates a difference, an exclusion.[9] Watt's and McKeon's institutions of the novel seem set to allow them to use a sort of generic cleansing to exclude it from any contamination by the curiously dreaded term "romance." That Fielding and Richardson both attack Romance and reject its title I do not question. They also both include "novel," in its contemporary meaning, in this attack and reject that term as well. But even if these authors' attacks on romance were not more ambiguous than Watt and McKeon allow for, their attack and its determined negation of romance would incorporate its structure and themes, not to mention names of characters such as Pamela, as necessarily inherent in the identity of their own texts.[10] More important, however, is the fact that it is the term "romance" that will govern the multifarious "novelistic" experimentation and publication over the next sixty or seventy years.[11]

It is interesting and, I think, institutionally significant that not long ago we tended to give the American novel, which has its beginnings during this later period, the generic title romance. This identification was academically institutionalized in the American university at the same time as Watt's *Rise*, by the publication the same year of Richard Chase's *The American Novel and Its Tradition*. This generic difference was seen by American critics as a response to desired, if not always felt, constitutive differences between English and American cultures, not only in the colonial period, but continuing on into the present. Might it not be significant in this regard, then, that American academics—a category that includes Ian Watt—are the most vociferous in insisting on a more or less discrete and complete mid-eighteenth-century origin of the English novel? Does not this insistence on the "national" difference equally insist on a relationship similar to the one suggested earlier about the mid-century English novel's banishment of romance? What are the implications for linear history of the possibility that the "later" experience of the novel by Americans seems to have produced romance, the novel's at once more primitive and more aristocratic predecessor? Another location, however, must also be triangulated with these crossing binary oppositions.

The "revival of romance" in the second half of the eighteenth century makes it foolhardy to assume that the term "romance" has any more stability than the term "novel." Romance, at that time, also had a special importance for a Scottish and even British sense of national identity. Scotland's position within a larger British Anglophone community was not entirely different from that of Anglo North Americans: it was neither exactly a colony nor exactly a separate nation, and it certainly had not been brought (nor for that matter invited) to merge identities with England completely on an equal basis in their 1707 Union. Mutual economic interests and problems connected them with the American colonies. Romance tradition as it was reconstructed gave them priority over the English in terms of their relationship to the origin of "British" national identity. The romance read as a tale about the origin of the nation held a special appeal for Americans, just as did the social and anthropological ideas about the origins of societies held by theorists in the Scottish Enlightenment, who in turn based many of those theories on what could be described as the American experience.[12] As, among other things, theorists of concepts of subjectivity, personal identity, national language and literature, and particularly culture and its institutions, they had a major impact both on the novel and on a new understanding of the significance of romance, from which in fact, they partially derived those theories. As I argue, what is occluded by these recent histories of the "origins" of the novel is the refiguring of the romance and its role in the "institution" of the novel.

What then is instituted in and by these foundationally obsessed "novels" I read in the chapters which follow? First of all, it must be said that what is instituted in them is institution itself, as question, as problem—institution interrupted, deferred, and aborted. As I worked on and taught these texts over the years, I was struck with the recurrence in them of questions of patriarchy and genealogical order, and, with the latter, disturbances or errances of historical and narrative order. Such disturbances included destabilization of inheritance, often misdirected or displaced, and aberrations or monstrous crossings of generation or genre, including, for example, the creation of "new species." Also related were problems of identity or identification and legitimacy, along with persistent questions of proper names and naming. Finally, questions of education and development—*bildung*, in its fullest sense—and their efficacy and order seemed always to be invoked. These last two categories, naming and educational development, would seem especially prominent given the basic biographical or autobiographical form and eponymous way these texts are known. These questions, moreover, each seemed to have institutional dimensions, since they touched on basic issues of social organization.

I first became aware of these issues and their involvement in questions of historicity in the most perverse and aberrational form in reading *Tom Jones*, particularly in relationship to Scott's *Waverley*, a surprise given the former's apparently happy, natural normality and "perfect plot." Since Fielding seemed still to survive at the beginning of the nineteenth century as *the* progenitor of the novel, let me discuss it briefly as it affected the development of my principal institutional concerns.

Two problems with *Tom Jones* puzzled me from the beginning. First was Fielding's explicit placing of this *History* of a young man's journey toward manhood and recognition or legitimation of identity and inheritance in the context of the 1745 Jacobite Rebellion. There are many explicit references to this historical "event" and even more allusions to its political and constitutional issues and its prehistory, yet there had been little mention, let alone explanation or even discussion, of it in critical readings of this "foundational" novel, except as a means of establishing a circumstantially specific "calendar" for the events of the story. This issue seemed even more intriguing, and the silence even more puzzling, given Fielding's known political involvement in these events and issues on the government's side, both during the rebellion, when he published satirical pamphlets and *The True Patriot*, and a little later (just before writing the novel), at the time of the trial of chief conspirators, when Fielding published another serial satirical attack, *The Jacobite's Journal*, also commissioned by the government.

The other problem was historical and contextual in another way, although it had its resonances in the Jacobite story as well. This problem is Tom's illegitimacy, which is not erased by his recuperation or "elevation" at the end of the novel, and which, by English law in force at the time, would bar him from any inheritance of any kind, except by an act of Parliament. There are also references to this law—the *filius nullias* law—in the novel. Yet Tom's inheritance is not only not explained in the book, it also goes unnoticed by any modern reader of the book. The complaint against the "stain" of Tom's illegitimacy is traditional in earlier readings of the book. Scott mentions it in his essay on Fielding, seeing it as a tribute to his first wife, who also was a "natural child" (*Lives*, 63–64). John Colin Dunlop questions it in 1814 in his *History of Prose Fiction* (II, 575). Dunlop pointed out that Fielding would have caused no difficulty for readers if he had merely "supposed" that Tom's "mother had been privately married to the young clergyman." Planting this supposition, he says, would not only have had the advantage of removing "the stain from the birth of the hero, but, in the idea of the reader, would have given him better security for the property of his uncle Allworthy." In support of this contention, he goes on to recall "a miserable continuation" of Fielding's novel written by an unnamed, "wrongheaded author (of whom Blifil was the favorite)" and who "made his hero bring an action against Tom after the death of Mr. Allworthy, and oust him from his uncle's property" (575).

Scott takes up an analogous problem, which supplements the issue in Fielding, in the last volume of *The Heart of Midlothian*, when he has the English Sir George Staunton risk arrest for his crimes as George Robertson by returning to Scotland, the scene of those crimes, to look for his son, who was lost and supposed murdered immediately after his illegitimate birth at the beginning of the novel. Now he is led to believe his son is alive. Since George has returned to his true identity and inherited station in society, and has elevated and married the child's mother, he desires an heir. Scott has him suppose that if he can find the son, "let him but prove worthy of his father's protection" and "Sir George Staunton was at liberty to adopt him as his heir if he pleased, without communicating the secret of his birth; or an act of parliament might be obtained, declaring him legitimate, and allowing him the names and arms of his father. He was, indeed, already a legitimate child according to the law of Scotland, by the subsequent marriage of his parents" (*Heart*, 486). (Scottish law was based on Roman law, but English law was not.)

These problems—the relevance to the novel of the 1745 Jacobite Rebellion and the problematic nature of Tom's inheritance, given his illegitimacy—seem to me to be related. Both involve a break or disruption in patriarchal, genealogical descent, the double transference from patriarchal to matriarchal and from son to nephew. Both involve questions of legitimacy linked to that disruption of lineal descent; one is the legitimacy of the Hanoverian succession and sovereign authority, the other has to do, obviously, with Tom's illegitimacy and the problem of his legitimation and of his right to assume and rule Allworthy's estate. The question of Tom's illegitimacy in relation to the question of Jacobite rule should remind us here of the Exclusion Crisis and the attempt to legitimate Charles's illegitimate son, the Duke of Monmouth, in order to substitute him for Charles's brother James in succession to the throne, and Monmouth's subsequent unsuccessful and bloody rebellion after his father's death—events alluded to in Tom's encounter with "the Man of the Hill," who had joined Monmouth's forces in that rebellion. And finally, linked with the question of Tom's legitimacy is that of "the new species of writing" that Fielding is trying to legitimate in this novel.

In my reading of *Tom Jones*, I attempt to show not only that these issues are related, but also the way the genealogical absolutism of Jacobite ideology, a theory of history in itself, both "contaminates" and is undercut by the narrative of Tom's history. This latter constantly "wanders" from incidental and errant "example" comically by means of accident and misinterpretation to unintended and unexpected effects. Where others felt that its controlling logic was providential, it seemed to me to be that of chance and accidental in all the senses of that term, providence being the fictive claim of Romantic "authors." I could not help but feel, as I worked on this novel, how much more like *Tristram Shandy* it is than it is usually understood as being.

I have gone on at length about the "problems" and their logic that served as my point of departure for the *Tom Jones* chapter because it seems to register the greatest number of issues, thematic and formal, shared by the other texts I write about in this volume. It also gives the simplest, most complete, and direct version of the analogy made between Jacobite patriarchal absolutism on the level of the State and private life.

As I have indicated, my general thesis, presented explicitly in the Introduction and the final chapter, argues that what we now call "the novel" didn't appear visibly as a recognized single "genre" until the early nineteenth century, when the essentially heterogeneous fictional prose narratives of the preceding century were grouped together institutionally under that name. I argue here against received notions of an early to mid-eighteenth-century "origin" of "the novel" elaborated by scholars such as Watt and McKeon. Rather, I believe those earlier fictional narratives we now call by the name "novel" were diverse, inchoate, singular acts of institution that could only much later be seen and instituted collectively as a more or less integral genre. In other words, I wish to claim that these earlier narratives are designated novels by a more modern cultural and literary institution as precursors in its own retrospective legitimating institutional history. In the chapters following the Introduction, I attempt to demonstrate how some of these earlier narratives are involved in the institution of political and cultural concepts such as self, personal identity, the family, history in a play of concepts and problematics that contribute to the possibility of what later will be called the novel.

While there are obviously thematic resonances between my readings in these chapters, I have avoided explicitly linking them together in any developmental way because I want to insist on the multiple and discrete moments of their institutions. Developmental, teleological narratives are the retrospective political business of later moments of institution which seek to legitimize particular kinds of present texts.

In the first chapter, "The Errant Letter and the Whispering Gallery," I run through the whole history of the novel, analyzing recurrent examples of figures for writing and speech as private letters (usually misdirected or purloined) and gossip, used as form or theme or even plot resolution and, by implication at least, characterizing the narrative's own nature or origin. Chapter two reads Defoe's "novels," principally *Robinson Crusoe*, as attempts to institutionalize a writing of an authentic self, but which can only "realize" that self as a series of displacements and disguises. Chapter three offers a reading of *Tom Jones* in relation to the 1745 Jacobite Rebellion, which Fielding is at pains to present as the background of the more domestic events of his narrative. This insistent context seems never to have been considered extensively. I trace the links in terms of issues and formal complications of displaced identities and historically recovered proper names. These issues here impli-cate questions of genealogy and its disruptions and therefore of narrative history, the family, and the legitimate authority of state rule. Chapter four advances these issues a step farther by investi-gating *Tristram Shandy*'s radical development of questions of per-sonal identity, family, and genealogy through Tristram's traumatic "institutional" moments—his parents' pre-nuptual contract, his conception, birth, baptism, circumcision, puberty, education, and so forth. Here I focus on the reading of Yorick's sermon at the moment of his birth. The trials and accidents of the text of this sermon, repeatedly misplaced or lost and then found and finally returned to the ghost of its author, are seen as a parable of the quasi-material changes necessarily suffered by any text continually re-marked with the stains of the historical accidents of its various and varying occasions or contexts of its readings as it journeys through time, a fable of the inescapable historicity of any writing the instant it is dropped from its author's hand.

Finally, in the last two chapters, I move to an author who was actually outside the *English* narrative tradition proper—we have not really recognized this for a long time—but whose intervention into that tradition, I argue, ironically did more to institutionalize the *English* novel than the work of any other single individual. I speak of Sir Walter Scott. In chapter five, I analyze Scott's novels concerning the 1715–45 Rebellions, events more consequential in Scottish history than for England. I concentrate especially on *Waverley*, Scott's first novel, which can be read as a reappropriation and revision of Fielding's *Tom Jones*, since it too places a young Englishman on the road in search of his identity during the '45 Rebellion. Scott, however, sets his hero on the road *to* Scotland as a means of reintroducing its culture to its sister kingdom. In his essay on Fielding, Scott saw his novels as being so narrowly English as to be "untranslatable" by Scottish and Irish readers. Clearly, Scott aimed to create instead a truly *British* national iden-tity by way of a novel that one recent critic has called the first genuinely multicultural novel, a project in itself possibly doomed to failure in his own time, although it may speak to ours. He was, however ironically, successful in instituting the English novel as it became known in the nineteenth century and as we know it today. In chapter six I argue that, by collecting and editing the narrative fiction of the previous century, a melange of heterogeneous forms; by giving the extensive critical introductions (following Mrs. Barbauld's slightly earlier endeavor, but considerably more comprehensively); and by the vast international success of his own *Waverley* series, Scott gave the "genre" of "the novel" material substance, identity, and a proper name. This production was met with extensive serious confirmation by a rising literary-critical discourse that now found "the novel" worthy of that respect. From this point, I follow the history of the varying reception of Scott's favorite, Defoe, whose works he also edited, independently of his novel collection, as the institution of the novel developed in the course of the nineteenth century and into the twentieth, a history not unlike Tristram's story of the travails befalling Yorick's sermon.

Acknowledgments

As I look back on my debts for assistance on this book, I realize its and my dependence from the beginning on an intellectual community, an institution. It seems to me that I always loved the novel, but I am grateful for the wonderful teachers who started me off on the quest of its elusive nature—Victor Elconin, Roy Male, Earl Wasserman, and, especially, J. Hillis Miller, who is now also my colleague.

It took me a long time, however, to begin to reflect on the implications of the necessity and nature of the institutional context "always already" presupposed by any such questioning. Early and essential encouragement for the developing argument came from the late Eugenio Donato, Edgar Dryden (I've done little since graduate school I haven't first discussed with him), Nancy Armstrong, Leonard Tennenhouse, John Rowe, Edward Said, Michael Wood, Ronald Paulson, Josué Harari, Bill Sisler, and Hillis Miller, and later from Deidre Lynch, Bill Warner, and Eric Halpern. I also received a great deal of support and suggestions from colleagues in the period in the English departments of SUNY Buffalo and UC Irvine—among them Leslie Fiedler, Dave Tarbet, Jim Bunn, Roy Roussel, Tom Kavanagh, Robert Folkenflik, and Richard Kroll, as well as colleagues "at large" in the field, particularly Joe Riddel, Max Novak, and Paul Hunter.

I am particularly indebted to the astute readings of chapters and the whole manuscript, by Eugenio Donato, Ed Dryden, Nancy Armstrong, John Rowe, Hillis Miller, and Renee Dye. I also have to thank the formidable insistence of the "junta" formed by Armstrong, Harari, and Rowe, with Rey Chow, that I finally have done with it. For bibliographic assistance and help in finding hard to locate texts, I want to thank Eddie Yeghiayan and Cathy

Palmer and the staff of the UCI Libraries and all my "helpers" at the UCI Bookstore. Finally, no real idea of the institution could be given without acknowledgment of the major part played by students, graduate and undergraduate, in the development of any critical argument. This has truly been a corporate enterprise.

I also want to mention a particular intellectual debt to Jacques Derrida, happily, my colleague and teacher, the importance of whose work in general, it seems to me, is currently too much ignored by cultural critics and historians. In particular, his insight into the importance for historical thinking of among other things, the "iterability" of language as the basis for any sense of "historicity" as such, had a major influence on my development of the argument of this book.

My largest debt of all is for the help, encouragement, and inspiration of my family to whom this book is dedicated and without whom it never could have been imagined, let alone written, and especially to Harriet, my wife, best friend, and co-conspirator, without whose readings, encouragement, and selected moments of impatience it might never have been finished.

Versions of parts of this book have previously appeared in print or have been presented at conferences or in lectures at other universities. An early version of its argument was presented on an MLA panel in Los Angeles in 1982 and in a lecture at The Johns Hopkins University in 1988. A somewhat later version appeared in my review article "Of the Title to Things Real: Recent Argument over the Origins of the English Novel," in *ELH: A Journal of English Literary History* 55 (Winter 1988). Its argument was also presented for discussion at a meeting of The Bay Area Friends of the Eighteenth Century at UC Berkeley in 1994. Parts of that argument from the Introduction are also in my essay "Why the Story of the Eighteenth Century Origin of the (English) Novel Is an American Romance" in *Cultural Institutions of the Novel*, ed. Deidre Lynch and William Warner (Duke University Press, 1996). An earlier version of Chapter One appeared in *Genre* 10 (1977). Chapter Two appeared in a slightly different version in *ELH* in

1971 and has been reprinted in two or three anthologies. Chapter Three appeared in *Revisions of the Anglo-American Tradition: Part I*, a special issue of *boundary 2* (1979). Chapter Four was presented in a slightly different version at the 1984 "Colloquiam les correspondances: les figures de l'épistolaire" at the Centro Internationale di Semiotica e Linguistica, Urbino, Italy and later that year as an essay in *MLN* 99, a special issue dedicated to the memory of Eugenio Donato, to whom I rededicate it here. The earliest version, very different, of Chapter Five was presented for discussion at an MLA panel in Houston in 1980. A somewhat shorter version of Chapter Six appeared under the subtitle "The Contribution of Defoe," in *Novel: A Forum for Fiction* (Spring 1996). I am grateful for the permission of editors and publishers of these journals or books to print these versions here.

Financial help in the form of post-doctoral or summer research and travel from Columbia University, the University of Illinois Center for Advanced Study, the State University of New York, and the University of California have greatly assisted my research. I also want to express my gratitude for the interest, care, and patience of Eric Halpern and Alison Anderson at the University of Pennsylvania Press.

Introduction: Beginning with No Beginning

> Romance and real history have the same common origin. . . . A moment's glance at the origin of society will satisfy the reader why this can hardly be otherwise. The father of an isolated family, destined one day to rise into a tribe, and in farther progress of time to expand into a nation, may, indeed, narrate to his descendents the circumstances which detached him from the society of his brethren, and drove him to form a solitary settlement in the wilderness, with no other deviation from truth, on the part of the narrator, than arises from the infidelity of memory, or the exaggerations of vanity.
> —Sir Walter Scott, "Essay on Romance"

> I would prefer to call them rites of consecration, or rites of legitimation, or, quite simply, *rites of institution*—giving this word the active sense it has, for example, in expressions like "*institution d'un heritier*" ("appointing an heir").
> —Pierre Bourdieu

GIVEN THE TRADITIONAL IDENTIFICATION of institution solely with either origins or mature cultural formation, if not its ossification, one must begin by examining the word and concept "institution" and, especially, by drawing out some of the implications regarding literature or the novel as institutions.

Literature, which only took its modern meaning in the late eighteenth century, has been called (or thought of as) an institution at least since Hippolyte Taine in the mid-nineteenth century. Poetry had been considered an institution in the Scottish enlightenment and at least as far back as Vico's *New Science*,[1] although, as his modern English translators point out, Vico used the Italian equivalent of the term only once, and that in the ancient legal sense of naming an heir (the same sense described by Pierre Bourdieu in the epigraph to this introduction).[2] In the more or less modern meaning of the term "institution," literature and the novel were referred to even during the New Criticism in this country as "institutions."[3] These usages considered literature (or the novel) as a whole, more or less organized unit functioning in society but, like other institutions, autonomous and affected by other social elements or forces externally as an institution. This concept was part of a developing sociology of institutions, which thought of society as organized by such institutions.

According to Thomas Goddard Bergin and Max Harold Fisch, in their introduction to Vico's work, it was something like this usage of the word *istituzione* in Italian political discourse of the early eighteenth century that made Vico eschew use of it in any of its noun, verb, or participle forms, although he could be considered as a founder of modern social-cultural theory and its articulation of the social role of literature. As Bergin and Fisch point out, in Latin and the Romance languages, the cognates of "to institute" and "institution" "all imply deliberate contrivance, artifice, choice, will, intent"—characteristics, interestingly enough, that we attribute to great "authors" in the modern institutions of literature. "One of their chief senses," Bergin and Fisch continue, was as "formal education—planned systematic instruction—as distinguished from uncontrolled learning" (li). These translators felt they were now able to translate various terms Vico used by forms of "institution" because this "rationalistic theory of the origin and nature of institutions," at least partly because of Vico's work, began to lose its status as "the accepted theory."

But Vico made another change in the theory of institutions that is relevant to my purposes here. It concerns the effects rather than the origins of institutions:

The rationalistic theory assumed that the institutions of society were made by "men," in the sense of human beings who were already fully human, in whom the humanity of Vico's "age of men" was already fully developed. What Vico wanted to assert was that the first steps in the building of "the world of nations" were taken by creatures who were still (or who had degenerated into) beasts, and that humanity itself was created by the very same processes by which the institutions were created. Humanity is not a presupposition, but a consequence, an effect, a product of institution building. (lii)

This point must serve as a caution for current convictions concerning the institution/origin (leaving aside the ambiguous relationship between these terms for the moment) of the novel, produced as they must be from within the culture that the novel has produced or made possible. This danger of what might too simply be called "anachronism," but which could be understood in the Freudian term *nachtraglichkeit*, is also a danger of the word *institution* in any of its uses. Perhaps too familiar a word in common discourse, it seems part of its function to make the strange, unusual, or singular, or if you will, the "novel," seem familiar, even common—legitimate and "authorized." There is another kind of ambiguity about "institution"—does it name a thing or an act, an act or an activity? Raymond Williams called it "a noun of action or process," and it is interesting to note the way the term always seems to require a narrative when Williams goes on to describe it as "a noun of action or process which became, at a certain stage, a general and abstract noun," describing something apparently objective and systematic; in fact, in the modern sense, an institution.[4]

Institution, then, designates at once an act, an action, a process and the product of that action or process—at once, action and stasis, lingering effect, or remainder as such. From the Latin *instituare*, institution means literally to cause to stand or stand up, to move something to standing, or at least the illusion of standing, in (one) place. That "something," which almost always is or involves an assembling of collective acts or practices, is also of some social importance, acknowledged in that "standing," both figurative and literal. Moreover, there is a kind of reification at work in the term, an effect of the happening it names that makes the happening—institution—appear as something in itself. This effect perhaps explains why when we think of institutions we almost always think of buildings: church, school, and bank are all names of common institutions, but also names of the material buildings in which they are housed and with which they are often confused. The building sites and situates the institution. An "edifice" gives it not only an imposing presence, but also a past and future, an appearance of duration and continuity. And while it shelters, guards, and arranges the practices and people it houses, seemingly guaranteeing the unity and coordination of all therein, the building also stands for and declares the institution's anteriority and alterity, its transcendance of any particular person or practice it maintains. The particular people or practices are made to seem accidental to the institution that names them and grants them distinction, while the notion of material "house" is made to seem of the essence of institution. The history of the words edifice and edification captures this seeming reversal. They both come from the Latin *aedificare*: *aedes*—a temple or building—and *facere*—to make or build. Thus, to edify meant to build or establish before it meant to instruct or improve. All this suggests the operation of a powerful social imaginary which institution establishes and relies on for its own authority—its seemingly material presence, wholeness, and integrity.

Without letting go of the sense of institution associated with reification, I am also using the term in the active sense mentioned by Raymond Williams, with the added richness given it more recently by Mary Douglas, Pierre Bourdieu, and Jacques Derrida.[5] There is a paradoxical sense of the word institution that must be heard in all its contrariety in my use of the term. While it implies an origin, the establishment of something new for "the first time," institution, as an establishment, also implies reception, acceptance, recognition, acknowledgment, and legitimation. The institution of the novel takes place between a necessarily fictive (in a double sense) origin, or first time, and that time of legitimation and acknowledgment. The institution of the novel is still happening now in those institutional histories of its "origin"— particularly in Bourdieu's sense of institution as "consecration," the bestowal of symbolic distinction, or capital by means of a title (125–26). With this paradox in mind, it might be instructive to return to the conclusions of Watt's and McKeon's histories to look in more detail at their characterization of what follows "the institution of the novel in 1750."

Ian Watt's conclusion demonstrates the reductive awkwardness of teleological solutions that respond in part, to the demand for closure. He adduces "the example of Sterne" to demonstrate that "the two major differences in narrative method between the novels of Richardson and Fielding are by no means manifestations of two opposite and irreconcilable kinds of novel, but merely rather clearly contrasted solutions of problems that pervade the whole tradition of the novel and whose apparent divergences can in fact be harmoniously reconciled" (*Rise of the Novel*, 296). Here Watt's "harmonious" solution to the differences between these "novels" brings him home to another story of the novel—the first serious novelist for both the New Criticism and F. R. Leavis's *The Great Tradition*, Jane Austen, who is said to merge Fieldingesque and Richardsonian novelistic modes. Both stories—the resolution of difference as telos and that of the originator of the "great tradition" of the novel—are assembled by the allegory of natural growth and development: "Indeed, the *full maturity* of the genre itself, it can be argued, could only come when this reconciliation had been achieved, and it is probable that it is largely to her succesful resolution of these problems that Jane Austen owes her eminence in the tradition of the English novel" (296, my emphasis). And a little later Watt admits that "compared with Jane Austen, or with Balzac and Stendhal, Defoe, Richardson, and Fielding all have fairly obvious technical weaknesses" (301). Historically, however, he grants them "two kinds of importance: the obvious importance that attaches to writers who" helped to create "the dominant literary form of the last two centuries," a tautological argument, "and the equally great importance" that comes with their status as essentially independent innovators," and the fact, therefore, that "their novels provide three rather sharply de-

fined images of the form in general, and constitute a remarkably
complete recapitulation of the essential diversities in its later tradition" (301).

This conclusion is oddly echoed more recently in Michael
McKeon's reworking of Watt, when he reverses the temporality of
Watt's term ("recapitulate") to make an even grander claim. For
Watt, the Richardson-Fielding-Austen trio serves as a "recapitulation" of all the possibilities enjoyed by the novel to come in the
next two hundred years. For McKeon, *Tristram Shandy* provides
the last novelty, and after him, "it may be said, the young genre
settles down to a more deliberate and studied *recapitulation of the
same ground*, this time for the next two centuries" (*Origins of the
English Novel*, 419, my emphasis). If for Watt the whole complicated history of the development of the nineteenth century and
modern novel lies before it, he at least recognizes the difference.
For McKeon, one difference turns all other differences into versions of the same; the novel realizes its mature identity in the "institutionalization" of the conflict and a dialectical *rapprochement*
between Richardson and Fielding.

Well, almost. "If we distance ourselves from the details of this
rapprochement," McKeon says, "we may catch a glimpse of where
the novel goes after its origins." But where it goes, according to
McKeon, is not very far. After "the implications of the formal
breakthrough of the 1740s are pursued with such feverish intensity
over the next two decades, what follows is "the young genre" set-
tling down to recapitulate "the same ground . . . for the next two
centuries." All McKeon grants to the apparently non-"feverish intensity" of the next sixty years (let alone, two centuries) is the
bland anachronism that "by the end of the eighteenth century,
romance idealism *will have emerged* from the long process of positive revaluation that issues in the romantic movement and in the
ascendancy of the secularized, human spirituality of the aesthetic"
(418–19, my emphasis). In both these cases, there seems to be a
strange hiatus in the latter part of the eighteenth century (unless McKeon is referring to the romance revival by his "positive
revaluation" from whose "long process" "romance idealism will

have emerged"). Except for this strangely predestined awakening of Sleeping Beauty, for McKeon, this hiatus extends through the novel's whole future history. When their histories close, so does history as such. By the early nineteenth century, the novel is *history*. But, of course, I want to argue, contrary to this sense of the word, that the novel really *is* history.

I don't dispute the "novelty" of what Defoe, Fielding, Richardson, and Sterne accomplished—far from it. I just don't think the concept of "recapitulation" gets us very far. I accede to the claim Richardson and Fielding each made for a "new species," except to note that they were competing "species" that generated heterological "evolutionary" lines of descent.[6] I dispute neither their influence on the nineteenth-century novel nor the role they played as chosen precursors for various later novelists. I am simply insisting that they exerted their influence at different times and on different writers. While each had his day, then, it was seldom the same day. Richardson perhaps had his greatest influence in the second half of the eighteenth century. But in 1824, when Scott's edition of Ballantyne's Novelist's Library reprinted the novels of Fielding and Richardson, the reviewer for *Blackwood's Edinburgh Magazine* wrote, "Who reads Richardson?"[7] And while Fielding's influence was intensifying, Defoe's was scattered, as *Robinson Crusoe* was about to be relegated to children's inspirational literature or social theory until perhaps the early twentieth century.

The point of all this is to suggest that it was not the combination of Defoe-Richardson-Fielding that set a paradigm for the development of the novel as institution in the eighteenth or nineteenth centuries. As I argued earlier, each represented a different, incomplete beginning, yet each had a place, although an unequal one, in the early nineteenth-century institution of the novel.

When and how does an institution actually begin—actually become instituted? Does the Christian church as institution begin as such when Jesus names (renames?) Peter? In a mystical sense, perhaps, but one which I doubt historical scholars of the novel would be willing to grant the naming of the novel as genre. Or does it begin when the narrative of that naming is circulated and wins more than immediate recognition? As Derrida points out, the paradox of any invention is that on the one hand it depends on absolute novelty, a break with the law and convention, and on the other, it begs for social recognition, usually official, by the law and institutional forms of legitimation, such as patents or titles. Would we insist on the generic entitlement Novel for *Clarissa* or *Tom Jones*, an entitlement not claimed by them, without the meaning given that title by the great institution of the Victorian novel, without Austen or even Scott? Can there be generic status, and in this sense, *institution*, before general recognition?

Referring to a historical constitutional revolution crucial to the novels I discuss in the essays that follow, namely the once hotly contested "accession of the *Prince of Orange*" to the throne of England, David Hume said that the legitimacy of this accession "ought not now to appear doubtful, but must have acquired a sufficient authority from those three princes, who have succeeded him upon the same title." Hume then went on to state the maxim:

Princes often *seem* to acquire a right from their successors, as well as from their ancestors; and a king, who during his life-time might justly be deem'd an usurper, will be regarded by posterity as a lawful prince, because he has had the good fortune to settle his family on the throne, and entirely change the antient form of government. . . . Time and custom give authority to all forms of government, and all successions of princes; and that power, which at first was founded only on injustice and violence, becomes in time legal and obligatory. Nor does the mind rest there; but returning back upon its footsteps, transfers to their predecessors and ancestors that right, which it naturally ascribes to the posterity, as being related together, and united in the imagination.[8]

Not irrelevantly, this maxim comes toward the end of a long disquisition on the legitimation of property and sovereign authority. An important theme in eighteenth-century fiction, as in its politics, and an ancient meaning of "instituting," as Bourdieu reminds us, is the naming of an heir. As we have seen, discourse about the origin of the novel is rife with genealogical notions and language, but with the history of the novel, as with the history of Princes, the legitimation of institution works in reverse. The child legitimates the father. But even those terms betray the strict genealogist. In Hume's whimsical but in 1740 still charged example, the situation is more complicated. It is worth recalling that William of Orange, the prince who "had the good fortune to settle his family on the throne," had no surviving children to succeed him. The "three princes" referred to by Hume were, of course, Anne (his sister-in-law and cousin) and the first two Georges of Hanover (very distant cousins).

In these terms, it might be useful to look at the question of the novel from the vantage point of the early decades of the nineteenth century. It is Scott rather than Austen who will give us that vantage point. The choice between them is in part a choice between two different histories of the development of the novel, two different genealogies. As I said earlier, Austen became the pivotal figure for modernists in the twentieth century, who also thought that the novel in general only matured to a state deserving serious aesthetic consideration with Flaubert and James.[9] Watt chooses Austen for his pivotal figure and doesn't even mention Scott, because, while he is implicitly writing against Leavis's downgrading of the eighteenth-century novelistic tradition, these "New Critics" are the readers whose attention he solicits. One might hazard a suspicion that genre-based novel historians will always wind up choosing one kind of novel from a range of generic deviations.

I would argue that this neglect of Scott creates a confusion between the history of an institution and institutional history. The first is the history of the way an institution defines itself; the second is simply one of those fictions, the most recent history. No historian of the institution of the novel can afford to ignore the Scott phenomenon that occurred at the beginning of the nineteenth century. At any rate, although Austen had already begun to publish her novels with moderate success before the first appearance of the Waverley novels in 1814, Scott quickly dominated the field and stood as the giant precursor for both the English and American novel for most of the rest of the century. He also gave Austen's novels their first serious critical attention in print. For their contemporaries, Scott was thought to have either restored or originally established the novel as a major, serious, English and even European cultural institution. Scott's novels set the model for the great nineteenth-century English novel and, for that matter, the European and American novel, or more precisely the novel of the Americas, as well.

In order to understand Scott's new novel-romance as a displacement of the earlier novel, including the displacement of its history into the history of romance, it is necessary to rehearse some contemporary notions about the status of narrative fiction and its past. It is possible to say that by 1814, Scott shared several assumptions about the novel with a number of other critics and historians: It had existed in one form or another at all times and all places. If there were a distinction to be made between the romance and novel it was not so much a generic as a "generational" difference—in Scott's words, "In its first appearance, the novel was the legitimate child of the romance."[10] That is to say, there was continuity in the difference. Romance and novel were also analogous in their social importance and power as both expression and producer in the formation of individuals, culture and nation. If the chivalric romance served as the "epic" of ancient Britain, the modern romance or novel should perform the same function. It was not performing this function because the novelistic resources it inherited from the eighteenth century were "exhausted" and the contemporary romance/novel had been largely appropriated by "female writers" writing for female readers.[11] While this last charge had been the complaint of many critics, including feminists, Scott's account of the exhaustion of earlier modes of fiction had explicit reference to the heritage of Fielding.

The notion of the exhaustion of that heritage is suggested in Scott's 1815 review of Jane Austen's *Emma*.[12] Austen's novels, he says, "belong to a class of fictions which has arisen almost in our own times, and which draws the characters and incidents introduced more immediately from the current of ordinary life than was permitted by the former rules of the novel." This earlier fiction, "the legitimate child of the romance," he goes on to explain, though "the manners and general turn of the composition were altered so as to suit modern times," generally "remained fettered by many peculiarities derived from the original style of romantic fiction" (227). The two "novels" cited by Scott as examples of this problem are *Tom Jones* and *Peregrine Pickle*, and the problem they posed was not so much a problem for readers contemporary to Fielding and Smollett as it was for Scott's contemporaries, although it was an inherent problem, implicated in the strengths of these authors. Here Scott's argument is a somewhat subtle one, involving a sense of historicity. These authors and others like them, Scott writes, no doubt appealed to "that obvious and strong sense of interest" which comes from a "curiosity" induced by improbable adventures, "violent changes of fortune," and exaggeratedly idealized sentiments. In this respect, these earlier fictions "differed from those now in fashion, and were more nearly assimilated to the old romances" (229). On the other hand, the problem is that, "strong and powerful as these sources of emotion and interest may be, they are, like all others, capable of *being exhausted by habit*" (230, my emphasis).[13] In other words, the problem consists in the iterability of such stories, both in the repeated readings of these narratives throughout the intervening century and in their imitability over that period by less talented writers, an imitability, ironically, guaranteed by their initial success. Such "materials," Scott says, "(and the man of genius as well as his wretched imitator must work with the same) become stale and familiar." The "novelty" of such narratives is no longer novel and, to the extent that their appeal is based on such qualities, Fielding's novels are likely to be read as wornout romances. Why then, by this logic, would not all novels, after a period of time, be subject to this fate? How about Austen's novels, or Scott's, for that matter, especially since he has so often been likened to Fielding? Part of the answer obviously has to do with his suggestion of differences of that earlier fiction from what is now in "fashion," interestingly reminiscent of Scott's implied explanation in his introductory first chapter of *Waverley* of its subtitle, " 'Tis Sixty Years Since," as a period of the past which is too recent either to be regarded as ancient or to have become fashionable. A better answer,

however, is a little more convoluted. The appeal of Fielding had
to do with "the combination of incidents new, striking and wonderful *beyond the course of ordinary life*" (229, my emphasis). In
contrast, Scott praises Austen for "the art of copying from nature
as she really exists in the common walks of life, and presenting
to the reader, instead of splendid scenes of an imaginary world,
a correct and striking representation of that which is daily taking
place around him" (239). Moreover, "keeping close to common
incidents, and to such characters as occupy the ordinary walks of
life, she has produced sketches of such spirit and originality, that
we never miss the excitation which depends upon a narrative of
uncommon events" (231). By implication, over the passing of time
such representation, successfully accomplished, could come to be
read historically and hence as having become sufficiently different
from, while enough related to contemporary concerns as to provoke new "excitements."

In his later essay on Fielding for Ballantyne's Novelist's Library, reprinted in his *Lives of the Novelists*,[14] Scott, paradoxically,
seems to praise Fielding's fidelity to the ordinary English life of his
time, improbable adventures aside, but actually finds that fidelity
a limitation, too culturally local and insular. Scott reveals in this
essay another agenda for his history of the novel, and, by implication, also his own plan for his own novels. In Scott's essay, the implication is that Fielding is "the first of British novelists" only by
default, since his accomplishment is in fact more narrowly based.
It is true that Scott avers that when Fielding wrote *Joseph Andrews*
he "engaged in a mode of composition which he retrieved from
the disgrace in which he found it, and rendered a classical depart-
ment of British literature" (56). It is also true that Scott says that
Fielding, in the prefatory chapters of *Tom Jones*, demonstrated that
he "considered his works as an experiment in British literature"
(67). Despite his detailed admiration for Fielding's artistry, however, Scott is more circumspect when it comes to naming what is
actually produced. When Fielding published *Tom Jones*, according
to Scott, "the first *English* novel was given to the public, which
had not yet seen any works of fiction founded upon the plan of

painting from nature" (63, my emphasis). At the close of the essay, Scott salutes Fielding as "father of the English Novel; and in his powers of strong and national humour, and forcible yet natural exhibition of character, unapproached as yet, even by his most successful followers" (70).

Indeed, Scott marks this more narrowly "national" emphasis from the very beginning of the essay, where he uses the terms "English" and "England" eight times in the first paragraph. He begins with the claim that "of all the works of the imagination, to which *English genius* has given origin, the writings of Henry Fielding are, perhaps, most decidedly and exclusively her own" (46, my emphasis). Lest we fail to feel the force of the limitation, Scott "localizes" the difficulty even more pointedly in the second sentence. Fielding's writings, he says, "are not only altogether beyond the reach of translation, in the proper sense and spirit of the word, but we even question whether they can be fully understood, or relished to the highest extent, by such natives of Scotland and Ireland as are not habitually and intimately acquainted with the characters and manners of Old England." One would think that the lack of such "reach" as might include Scotland and Ireland might diminish the imperial "British" achievement of Fielding's work. Scott's allusion to the problem of translation suggests a linguistic idiom perhaps difficult to capture in another European language. But this is not at all what he has in mind. The shocker comes with the mention of Scotland or Ireland, which implies that Fielding's idiom cannot travel across ethnic boundaries within Anglophone culture. Finally, one realizes that what is involved in Scott's notion of "translation" is temporal or historical as well as cultural translatability. Translation, in all these senses, might properly designate Scott's own project in his writings.

The case that follows for Fielding's incarnation of the English genius is itself comically redundant. His comic characters "are personages as peculiar to England as they are unknown to other countries," but then, too, the major "actors, whose characters are of a more general cast, as Allworthy, Mrs. Miller, Tom Jones himself, and almost all of the subordinate agents . . . have the same

cast of nationality, which adds not a little to the verisimilitude of
the tale" (46). And then he goes on to make sure we understand
their Englishness, paradoxically, as a limitation. "The persons in
the story live in England, travel in England, quarrel and fight in
England, and scarce an incident occurs, without its being marked
by something which could not have happened in any other country" (46). After saying that "this nationality may be ascribed to the
author's own habits of life," Scott adds insult to injury by explaining that by Fielding's slide down "from the high society to which
he was born, to that of the lowest and most miscellaneous kind to
which his fortune condemned him . . . he acquired the extended
familiarity with the English character, in every rank and aspect,
which has made his name immortal as a painter of national manners" (46). Here then, Scott describes his requirements for a truly
"British" novel in terms of what is *missing* in Fielding's "painting"
of "national manners." For Scott, the role of the novel is that of the
romance and the epic before it: the foundation of a nation and a
national identity that represents *Britain's* "natural" heterogeneity.

In his 1824 "Essay on Romance," Scott provided a fable of the
origins of romance which could serve as well for his history of the
novel and its relationship to romance. This form of narrative, he
said, had developed in pace with society. In fact, he argued, "Romance and real history have the same common origin":

A moment's glance at the origin of society will satisfy the reader why this
can hardly be otherwise. The father of an isolated family, destined one
day to rise into a tribe, and in farther progress of time to expand into a
nation, may, indeed, narrate to his descendents the circumstances which
detached him from the society of his brethren, and drove him to form a
solitary settlement in the wilderness, with no other deviation from truth,
on the part of the narrator, than arises from the infidelity of memory, or
the exaggerations of vanity. (134–35)

According to Scott, these "deviations" from the truth in the
story of the origin of the tribal patriarch (itself a story of an originary "deviation") are then multiplied by "the vanity of the tribe"
and "the love of the marvellous, so natural to the human mind"

as "the tale of the patriarch is related by his children, and again by his descendants of the third and fourth generation." Finally, there are further turns of deviation from "a third cause": "the king and the priest find their interest in casting a holy and sacred gloom and mystery over the early period in which their power arose." Hence, a great paradox. While the authority of a family, tribe, or nation is authorized by a story of its original "fathering," the power of its present authorities, including the control over the interpretation of the story itself, depends on the mystification of the processes of transmission of both the narrative and the authority it makes possible—in short, of institution as such. Moreover, this mystification is also a main source of the "fictiveness" of the "tales of the patriarchs." I must pause for a moment over Scott's own mystification of origin in his account, for if Scott's story of the origin of Romance as the story of the origin of society is apparently always a story of the father/narrator's double deviation from the origin— from both his father and from the "truth" of that deviation, Scott's account is itself also deviant in a number of ways.

First, I want only to underline the way it echoes without acknowledgment and changes the narrative founding the authority of Judeo-Christian culture—the story of Yahweh's call to Abraham to leave his roots and set out for the wilderness to start a new nation, the story that begins the second major part of Genesis known as "the Story of the Patriarchs":

Now the Lord said to Abram, "Go from your country and your kindred and your father's house to the land that I will show you. And I will make of you a great nation, and I will bless you, and make your name great, so that you will be a blessing." (Genesis 12:1-2, RSV)

Repeating with deviation, repeating deviation, Scott's story thus performs or reenacts exactly what it describes. Moreover, it also performs a double effacement of authority since Scott leaves out both the attribution to the prior story and that story's attribution of the origin of the patriarch's break with his past to God's command.

What is the meaning of this transformation? Is Scott's version merely a secularization of the sacred story? On the one hand, Abram leaves his father's house by divine command, becoming Abraham in the process, while on the other, the arbitrariness of the departure of Scott's patriarch-to-be is unexplained. Might it stem from some unspecified "wandering inclination"? Does not the narrative of Robinson Crusoe, among other eighteenth-century fictions, break apart between these choices? Scott's more secular version of this story clearly echoes the nature of the genealogical issues of the eighteenth-century novel. His story of the origin of romance as the story of the father can itself serve as a "first" version of the romance of the novel. In the chapters that follow, we will look to the novel and to the story of the novel for what Scott sees as the role of romance—the construction of culture, a story of institution, story as institution. For Scott, romance both chronicles and shapes the institution of modern culture—that is to say, romance is a story of institution that itself becomes institutional. In order to make this paradox clearer, I need to pursue the effects and implications of these deviations in Scott's account of the history of the Romance and the birth of the novel.

Deviation seems to be the rule (to think, for the moment, as if "deviation" and "rule" might be kin) throughout Scott's essay on Romance. He begins the essay be deviating from Dr. Johnson's classical definition of romance in its opposition to "the kindred term *Novel*." In effect, Scott identifies romance as deviation as such. He does so first by singling out of Johnson's definition its "only essential ingredient"—"wild adventures." This reduction is all the more emphatic in that it is at the expense of Johnson's identification of romance with the chivalric social order of the middle ages, which Scott will spend most of the essay detailing. After redefining romance as "a fictitious narrative . . . the interest of which turns upon marvellous and uncommon incidents," an editor's footnote refers to a passage from the *Quarterly Review* stating that "novels are often *romantic*, not indeed by the relation of what is obviously miraculous or impossible, but by *deviating*, though perhaps insensibly, beyond the bounds of probability or consistency" (latter emphasis mine). But an even more dramatic swerve is taken when Scott next asserts that "The word Romance, in its original meaning, was far from corresponding with the definition now assigned. On the contrary, it signified merely one or other of the popular dialects of Europe, founded (as almost all these dialects were) upon the Roman tongue, that is, upon the Latin" (130–31). In other words before "Romance" named a mode of narrative, it named the language in which that narrative was sung or written, and even in this curiously indeterminate way it names not just a language of origin but a deviation or variation upon one— "one or other of the popular dialects of Europe . . . founded upon" the classic language of the father, Latin. But it is also a dialect which deviates so richly from the Roman conqueror that as "early as 1150 it plainly appears that the Romance Language was distinguished from the Latin, and that translations were made from the one into the other." And so this story of a national father's break from his father and brethren to start a new family is also the story of the language in which it is told.

The "wild adventures" of romance, the language, will continue to haunt and perhaps to shape Scott's account of the rise and decline of romance, the narrative, and of the social order that was both mirrored and produced by it. I want to pause for a moment on this story of a language that must have had a special, if overdetermined, meaning for Scott, his novels, and the context of their writing. Romance is not simply the name of a national language, but precisely the precondition of several, each differing from the other as much as any one of them differs from their Latin original. Scott is charting here the beginning not only of the vernacular, but also that of "natural" or national languages as a story of rebellion and exile. As Scott indicates, romance is the general name for the various European languages that developed out of Latin. "The name of Romance was indiscriminately given to the Italian, to the Spanish, even (in one remarkable instance at least) to the English language" (131). This last example is most remarkable, in Scott's terms even laughable, because he will argue the poverty of English when it comes to romance. For even though the term has this general sense, "it was especially applied to the compound language of France; in which the Gothic dialect of the Franks, the Celtic of the ancient Gauls, and the classical Latin, formed the ingredients" and this special language of Romance has a special kinship to the "British" (Celtic) sources of one of the two main branches of Romance narratives. British, as opposed to English. In Scott's terms, the once and future nation.

Like the generality of his initial use of the linguistic term Romance, and like the simple Ur-narrative of the national father with which I began, Scott's account of the history of Romance as narrative begins as generalized view of a repeated way of beginning: "The European Romance, wherever it arises, and in whatever country it begins to be cultivated, had its origin in some part of the real or fabulous history of that country; and of this we will produce, in the sequel, abundant proofs. But the simple tale of tradition had not passed through many mouths, ere some one, to indulge his own propensity for the wonderful, or to secure by novelty the attention of his audience, augments the meagre chronicle with his own apocryphal inventions" (148). Originally, Scott reasons, these were ballads or "national" songs which celebrated "the early valour of the fathers or of the tribe" (148):

But neither with these romantic and metrical chronicles did the mind long remain satisfied. More details were demanded, and were liberally added by those who undertook to cater for the public taste in such matters. The same names of kings and champions, which had first caught the national ear, were still retained, in order to secure attention; and the same assertions of authenticity, and affected references to real history, were stoutly made, both in the commencement and in the course of the narrative. Each nation . . . came at length to adopt to itself a cycle of heroes like those of the Iliad; a sort of common property to all minstrels who chose to make use of them, under the condition always that the general character ascribed to each individual hero was preserved with some degree of consistency. (150)

The background and resources for this new view of both romance and novel came from more than a half-century of Romantic research and publication, fictional and historical. Romance was far from being dead at mid-eighteenth century. A half-century later, the terms "novel" and "romance" were still being used interchangably, and not only by Scott. Moreover, what had been written, much of it under the title of romance, by writers such as Inchbald, Burney, Edgeworth, Smith, or Radcliffe, for example, could hardly be called "recapitulation." It could, however, be described as experimentation not only with narrative form and romance, but also with the concepts of person, identity, and legacy in ways very different from the fiction of midcentury. In fact, this was a time so known for its "romantic" pursuits—that is, not only for its antiquarian ballad and romance research, but also for its exploration of such "romantic" subjects as sensibility, sentiment, and gothicism, that it has sometimes been called anachronistically "pre-romantic." But is this term any more anachronistic than "eighteenth-century novel?" In fact, "romantic," like its sometime associate "gothic," is itself a synonym for "anachronistic." "Romance" in various ways is also a synonym for "history," but it is especially so in its combination with "revival," as the name for the antiquarian enterprise of collecting and editing the old ballads and romances and researching the culture that produced them. That last phrase suggests just how much is at stake with the subject of romance. For this increasingly "historicist" research opened on to a search for native, national origins and originarily native poetic forms. If these forms were at first seen as parallel with early classical forms, such as the Homeric epic, they were soon apprehended as more appropriate models for modern British, as sometimes opposed to English, literary forms. But what also emerged was a historicist notion of native, national culture.

Arthur Johnston, in *Enchanted Ground*,[15] still the best introduction to this movement, says about Richard Hurd's *Letters on Chivalry and Romance* (1762) that "Hurd, for example, accepted that literature was the product of a particular type of society, and took its form from the predominant interests of that society. This long established view enabled critics to explain literature in terms of society, and to deduce a society from its surviving literature— whether the epics of Homer, the poems of Ossian, or the plays of Shakespeare. Holding to this doctrine, Hurd argued that the spirit of romance was born of the ages of chivalry, which were in turn the product of the feudal organization of society, a particular attraction for many eighteenth-century writers" (52).

Johnston's exposition of this research into what amounts to literature's relationship to historical culture and of the developing and consequential study of medieval romance by Thomas Percy, Thomas Warton, Joseph Ritson, George Ellis, and Sir Walter Scott demonstrates some of the struggle of emerging notions of "culture." The significance of the peculiarly nationalist aspects of this research for the romantic novel and particularly for a writer such as Scott cannot be overestimated. Although the scholars who want to dissociate the novel from the romance may do so because, understandably, they associate romance with aristocratic culture and reactionary politics as well as with the opposite of realism, it is its connection with the present of eighteenth-century England that is important here. Johnston concludes his study with this statement, quoting Carlyle: "Those who theorized about the origin of romance were looking for the starting point of 'modern' literature. And it was not to Greece and Rome that the more rigorous theorists looked. The Romance scholars from Percy to Scott left as their legacy the realization that the middle ages originated or perfected 'nearly all the inventions and social institutions whereby we yet live as civilized men'" (197).

In summary, several different though related implications are involved in this "Revival." The medieval romance offered possibilities for the revitalization of the modern poetic imagination because it was the originary native spring for poetry in *this place* (Britain) and because it was the natural (proper) expression of the culture and society rooted in this place at an originary and foundational moment in their own historical past, in contrast with the neoclassical Greek and Roman past. "Modern" literature is both what started and what should continue to start in this place. Moreover, though romance had been (and continues to be) identified with the imagination in the sense of its fictional extravagances, its departures from historical truth, those extravagances are now

seen to belong to the culture the romances portray and not just
to the genre, although, as Scott will say, romances also *fed* that
culture's ancient extravagances. As I have indicated earlier, Scott's
thought was that the romance not only portrayed a culture but,
indeed, produced it. Those "extravagances" belonging to the institutions of Chivalry, the cultural/social system of the society repre-
sented/produced by the romance, can also now be understood as
the foundation for modern British (and European) civilization,
its institutions, and its "manners." This is the sense of Johnston's
quotation from Carlyle, a claim also made by Scott and others.

In short, in the origins of romance, we can find the origin of
a specifically national literature and culture and the basis for a specifically national identity. Romance, then, becomes the name for
the native imagination, always in both its good and bad senses,
the name for native fictions of origin and, by the same stroke, the
name for history and the historical, the name for past and parent
or for their traces in their felt absence. Yet it also, in complicated
senses, becomes the name for difference and deviation, deviation
from origins, from the parent, from history and the truth, from
and within culture, and hence from proper identity or identification, deviation and difference from and within identity, and even
difference and deviation from and within language.

All these emergent concerns about significant fictional narrative as an "expression" of a native culture, as a means of producing
national identification as well as a sense of personal identity, could
not *not* affect the way "the novel" of Defoe, Richardson, or Fielding came to be read and represented. To insist that the novel had
fully matured into an institution earlier is not only to confuse beginnings with establishment—the paradox of institution—but it
is also to fall into the trap of institution and to think that novels
or the novel can only be understood in one context. We have seen
the way Scott was able to understand, and lead his audience to
read, romance in a very different way, and in terms of a different
temporality, from the way that Defoe, Richardson, and Fielding
might themselves have understood it. Scott recoupled romance

and novel in a new way that worked retroactively. He also recognized in those texts what the rules of circumstantial or formal realism were unable to register. They are no longer merely documentary. They are *documents*—as if self-historicized. They are historical, history, historicity itself.[16]

I

The Errant Letter and the
Whispering Gallery

Who shall tell what may be the effect of writing? If it happens to have been cut in stone, though it lie face downmost for ages on a forsaken beach, or "rest quietly under the drums and tramplings of many conquests," it may end by letting us into the secret of usurpations and other scandals gossiped about long empires ago: — this world being apparently a huge whispering gallery. Such conditions are often minutely represented in our petty lifetimes. As the stone which has been kicked by generations of clowns may come by curious little links of effect under the eyes of a scholar, through whose labours it may at last fix the date of invasions and unlock religions, so a bit of ink and paper which has long been an innocent wrapping or stop-gap may at last be laid open under the one pair of eyes which have knowledge enough to turn it into the opening of a catastrophe. To Uriel watching the progress of planetary history from the Sun, the one result would be just as much of a coincidence as the other.
— George Eliot, *Middlemarch*

In weaving these mystic utterances into a continuous scene, we undertake a task resembling in its perplexity that of gathering up and piecing together the fragments of a letter which has been torn and scattered to the winds. Many words of deep significance, many entire sentences, and those possibly the most important ones, have flown too far on the winged breeze to be recovered. If we insert our own conjectural amendments, we perhaps give a purport utterly at variance with the true one. Yet unless we attempt something in this way, there must remain an unsightly gap, and a lack of continuousness and dependence in our narrative; so that it would arrive at certain inevitable catastrophes without due warning of their imminence.
— Nathaniel Hawthorne, *The Marble Faun*

TRADITIONALLY, TWO OF THE WAYS THE novel has had of at once disguising and validating itself have been as letters and as gossip.[1] Both ways differ from the mask many novels take on as "true histories," establishing or putting into question their authority while at the same time underlining certain essential characteristics of narrative fictions. As letters, there are, of course, novels such as *Pamela*, *Clarissa*, and *Humphrey Clinker*, and there are the novels which claim or imply an origin in gossip such as *Vanity Fair*, *Wuthering Heights*, several of Hawthorne's novels, and perhaps Trollope's Barsetshire chronicles. Beyond their uses as form or validation, letters and gossip figure in many other novels as plot devices, themes, perhaps even emblems, within the novel of its own nature, genesis, both its lie and its feared truth about itself. One thinks of the misdelivered letter that contains the secret of Tom Jones's true parentage, the letters of "Nemo" sought after in *Bleak House*, the delayed letter that reveals the mystery of the check in *The Last Chronicle of Barsetshire*, the letter that initiates Raffle's blackmail of Bulstrode in *Middlemarch*, Poe's "Purloined Letter," the letters of "The Aspern Papers," Becky Sharp's revelation to Amelia of Osborne's letter to her or the fact that Becky enters society through her usefulness as a scribe for others, the amount of time and importance given to the writing and reading of letters as indices of character in Austen's novels in general, and all the associated documents and wills endlessly lost and discovered that haunt novel after novel. As for gossip, there is the chorus of opinions that accompanies the actions of Tom Jones, Lady Dedlock, the Podsnaps and friends, the Crawleys (particularly Becky) and the Steynes, the Pyncheons and Hester, or the chatter that provides the major community activity in Austen's villages and that becomes maniacal over the lapse in Dr. Crawley's memory and the mystery of the purloined check in *The Last Chronicle of Barsetshire*. One would, in fact, be hard put to say whether Trollope's Barsetshire novels are about or *are* gossip.[2]

It is probable that part of the pleasure we derive from the

classic novel is similar to that derived from gossip. Here is Jane Austen's description of Miss Bates in *Emma*: "She was a great talker upon little matters, which exactly suited Mr. Woodhouse, full of trivial communications and harmless gossip."[3] It seems punningly just that Miss Bates's chatter usually has as its pretext a letter from "Jane."

If letters are usually private communications, gossip is communal and, in fact, according to some anthropologists, both constitutes and regulates a community. Hillis Miller has noted a pattern in the lives and work of five Victorian novelists who "escape from exclusion," from being isolated outsiders, "by playing the role of a narrator who coincides not with a god and not with any individual person, but with the general mind of the community."[4] One aspect of this "collective mind," this voice of the *sensus communis*, of *endoxa*, resembles nothing so much as the "idle talk" of the "they" (*das Man*) or an impersonal "we" (as in *Nostromo*) of Heidegger, which

communicates rather by following the route of *gossiping* and *passing the word along*. What is said-in-the-talk as such, spreads in wider circles and takes on an authoritative character. Things are so because one says so. Idle talk is constituted by just such gossiping and passing the word along—a process by which its initial lack of grounds to stand on [*Bodenständigkeit*] becomes aggravated to complete groundlessness [*Bodenlosigkeit*]. And indeed this idle talk is not confined to vocal gossip, but even spreads to what we write, where it takes the form of "scribbling" [*das Geschreibe*]. In this latter case the gossip is not based so much on hearsay. It feeds upon superficial reading [*dem Angelesenen*]. The average understanding of the reader will *never be able* to decide what has been drawn from primordial sources with a struggle and how much is just gossip. The average understanding, moreover, will not want any such distinction, and does not need it, because of course, it understands everything.

The groundlessness of idle talk is no obstacle to its becoming public; instead it encourages this. Idle talk is the possibility of understanding everything without previously making the thing one's own.[5]

Some novelists and readers, of course, would reject the more negative elements of this description. Some would reject it altogether, and some would accept it in toto. It should be noted that Heidegger prefaced the passage by saying that he did not mean the "inauthenticity" of this everydayness of *Dasein* in any pejorative sense; it is no less real than what he will call "authentic" *Dasein*; it is the manner of being most people begin with—it is the loss of "primary relationship of Being toward the entity talked about" (or else such a relationship has never been achieved). "Idle talk" does not communicate in such a way as to let this entity be appropriated "in a primordial manner." Some novelists and readers, perhaps the novel as such, might simply contest this notion of *authenticity* or of "primordial appropriation" or, in a more complicated way, see the relationship between idle talk and authentic being as a problem posed by and in novels in a "primordial way."

At any rate, it seems clear that part of the pleasure readers derive from novels is similar to the pleasure of listening to or reading gossip, of participating, in silence and solitude, in a special way that both conserves and supplements silence and solitude in an illusion of company or community. They are entertained by the chatty, confiding tone of a narrator (what used to be thought of the baggy-pants chatter of the omniscient author) who tells them about the private goings on of people who come to be known with an intimacy (apparent) that exceeds what can be known about others in actual life. Even novelists, when they are not defending the Art of novels, often describe their pleasure in reading in a similar way. Here, for example, is Proust defending Balzac:

The truth of Balzac's situations—a truth somehow contingent and personal so that one remembers so many of the situations in terms of those who take part in them, as for instance, that of Rastignac marrying the daughter of his mistress Delphine de Nucigen, or Lucien arrested on the eve of his marriage with Mlle. de Grandlieu, or Vautrin inheriting from Lucien de Rubempré whose fortune he had tried to make, like the Lantrys' fortune, founded on a cardinal's love for a eunuch, the little old man to whom all pay their respects—is here striking. And there are those subtle truths, gathered from the surface of fashionable life and all with enough general applicability for one to be able to say long afterwards: How true that is![6]

And here is Diderot's praise of Richardson:

In the space of a few hours I had undergone a vast number of situations, scarcely available throughout the length of the longest life imaginable. I heard genuine discussions about the passions; I watched self-interest and self-esteem played and judged in a hundred different ways; I became the spectator for a multitude of incidents; I felt that I had acquired experience. . . .

I still recall the first time that Richardson's works fell into my hands. I was in the country. How delightfully this reading moved me! I felt my happiness was curtailed with each such page. Soon I underwent the same sensation that men in an excellent business must feel, having lived together for a long time, when they are about to separate. When I finished, it seemed to me suddenly that I was all alone.[7]

Both Diderot and Proust, at opposite ends of the modern era, testify to the reader's sense of actual experience of the private feelings, motives, desires of other people. Moreover, Diderot captures that feeling of having been in virtual, intimate company with another mind realized by the reader's bereaved shock of sudden loneliness at the moment the book is finished.

Part of the defensiveness of novelists about the high seriousness of their craft, their need to disclaim the fictional nature of their works under the guise of documents and history, might very well have come from received opinion about the gossipy pleasure, the trivial, personal level of discourse. Concurrent with the early use of the term "novel" for fictional narratives in prose, the word also (as it still suggests) meant news, tidings of what is new. Gossip is as much a fear of the novel as a recurrent theme within it and an occasionally asserted source of its narrator's information. It takes a John Barth to allow a character to make the essential point:

"Nay, out with your story, now, and yours as well, sir, and shame on the both o' ye thou'rt not commenced already! Spin and tangle till the Dogstar sets i' the Bay—nor fear I'll count ye idle gossips: a tale well wrought is the gossip o' the gods, that see the heart and hidden point o' life on earth; the seamless web o' the world; the Warp and Woof... I'Christ, I do love a story, sirs! Tell away!"[8]

Some novelists (or narrators) openly identify the sources of their stories as gossip. Edgar Dryden, in an admirable discussion of the importance of gossip to Hawthorne's *The House of the Seven Gables*, notes the narrator's avowed reliance on "popular belief" and "popular rumours," "chimney-corner tradition," "traditions about the ancestor, and private diurnal gossip about the Judge, remarkably accordant in their testimony. It is often instructive," Hawthorne adds, "to take the woman's, the private and domestic, view of the public man." Dryden explicates the meaning of these claims in the following way:

Gossip, it seems, is both informative and evaluative; not only does it "preserve traits of character with marvelous fidelity" but it places them in the context of a shared morality. In some ways it may be regarded as the true voice of the community since it transcends self-interest by being associated with no identifiable source and by having existed prior to the involvement of any single individual. Moreover, it appears to be the channels of gossip rather than a dialogue between an I and Thou which prompt communication and preserve communial unity. To participate in gossip, therefore, is to affirm one's membership in a community.[9]

On the other hand, this theme of Hawthorne's narrator with its emphasis on the anonymity of gossip, as Dryden points out, remains in tension with the insistent self-assertiveness of the narrator who also "sometimes skeptically discredits the products of the popular imagination that shape the world of the fiction":

This skepticism implies the recognition that the novel is a novel, that this world is not as groundless as the gossip that shapes it. These elements of the "anti-novel" call into question the authenticity of the chimney-corner tradition, since any emphasis on source and process causes gossip to founder. The channels of gossip remain open only as long as the source remains hidden. And once the channels are closed, each I is forced either into solitude or to direct confrontation with a Thou. (316)

While noting the justness of this reading, one needs also to recall that a similar tension appears whenever the motif of gossip appears. Trollope's "chronicles" seem equally insistent on creating an environment of gossip and on his own notoriously intrusive inventiveness. One thinks also of Fielding's playful reliance on irony concerning the chorus of gossip and opinion in *Tom*

Jones. Thackeray's claim that the source of his information about his characters was the dinner-table gossip at Pumpernickel or the whisperings of Tom Eaves is matched by his opening and closing claim of being "the stage manager" of a "puppet-show" of his own invention.[10] If these claims are contradictory in the literal sense of the word, it is because of a *paradox* built into the notion of *endoxa*. Gossip is anonymous, yet *somebody* starts it. Its uncertain status is an essential characteristic. It is made up, in uncertain mixture, of information, speculation, and invention. If it is groundless and self-constituting, it is because communities are so. It establishes an authority without an author. This ambiguity of gossip is emblematic of its riddle of narrative voice (and perhaps of language itself): who (or what) speaks (writes)? Is it Thackeray or "Thackeray," and what is "Thackeray" or any other narrator but a web of conventions. received ideas, and inventions—personal, communal, traditional? Socrates said that the problem of all writing is that it is parentless:

And once a thing is put in writing, the composition, whatever it may be, drifts all over the place, getting into the hands not only of those who understand it, but equally of those who have no business with it; it doesn't know how to address the right people, and not address the wrong. And when it is ill-treated and unfairly abused it always needs its parent to come to its help, being unable to defend or help itself.[11]

It is precisely this parentless drift, this unresolvable ambiguity that the novel has "inherited" from gossip, which is, "before" all, speech. In the *Phaedrus*, Socrates prefers speech to writing because of writing's inability to explain itself. The Platonic dialogues begin typically with opinion, *endoxa*, and move dialectically toward truth. That is, they are represented as doing so in writing. The notion that Western Culture is a footnote to Plato points up what has to be the self-conscious irony of Plato's inscription of Socrates' complaint.

The "parentlessness" that writing shares with gossip is "primordial" or "original." The ambiguously anonymous drift of writing matches the drift of meaning of the word "gossip," which originally meant "godparent": "one who has contracted spiritual affinity with another by acting as a sponsor at a baptism" (O.E.D.). It is a contracted relationship both to the parents and to the person baptized—"spiritual," that is to say, a relationship that substitutes for biological relationship. As a verb, it means "to be a gossip or sponsor to; *to give a name to*" (my italics) before it comes to mean "to talk idly, mostly about other people's affairs; to go about tattling."

As speech, gossip upholds the authority of the community and community values not through its truth but in its *process*—it takes place within *ear-shot*.[12] It requires and establishes the presence together of those who gossip, though not, of course, those gossiped about. It is a spiritual mimesis of a biological relationship because it is exogamous (the basis for community) as well as familial (familiar). As written or read in the novel, while it may represent the lonely individual's desire or nostalgia for community, for "news," it also points up an essential puzzle about the *authority* of fiction (in all its senses) and all the broken or substitute genealogical relationships that haunt the novel in both form and content.[13] Rather than mediating between the individual and society, both in its story and as object, the novel *locates*, is the medium of both the overlapping and the break. Valery says that poetry (literature) is a communication between someone who is not the author and someone who is not the reader.[14]

On the other hand, while the letter is sometimes the bearer of gossip, news, "good news," or Gospel as read along with the Epistles of the Mass, to those who are absent—the medieval definition of the letter was "sermo absentio ad absentem"[15]—its importance derives more usually from the fact that it is a *private* communication rather than a public one. As the anthropologist Max Gluckman notes, "where the passing of information becomes the central theme of the conversation or letter, we pass over the border of gossip and are confronted with something that might be called 'privileged communication.'"[16] To use Dryden's formula above, the letter is a "confrontation" between an "I" and a "Thou" in solitude. Rather than a contract binding a community, the letter is a pact between individuals in isolation. Rather than the presence "within ear-shot," it presupposes the isolation and distance between individuals. It is always important that what the letter says can't be *said* in any other way, can't be spoken. Instead of the endless round of speculation that is gossip, the letter gives answers (information); its emphasis is on *revelation*. The letter is a message to be delivered, gossip is *received*. As opposed to the private revelations of the memoir or journal, the letter always is double, for it requires and presupposes an I *and* a Thou, an I-for-a-Thou, and a Thou-for-an-I. Yet while the emphasis is on private revelation, the information of the letter is usually incomplete—it represents the feelings of the moment, uncertain of the moment's issue. So, it represents a curious play of immediacy-mediacy, presence-absence —a play quite different from that of gossip. The letter is always *in medias res* and *in medias personae*. Although Henry Fielding, not surprisingly, wrote that "sure no one will contend, that the epistolary Style is in general the most proper to a Novelist, or that it hath been used by the best Writers of this Kind,"[17] he noted that it has one advantage, "that by making use of Letters, the Writer is freed from the regular Beginnings and Conclusions of Stories, with some other Formalities, in which the Reader of Taste finds no less Ease and Advantage, than the Author himself." While he found nothing to praise in the *private* letters of *private* persons— "Love-Letters, and Letters of Conversation, in which last are contained the private Affairs of Persons of no Consequence to the Public, either in a political or learned Consideration, or indeed in any Consideration whatever" (132)—in the letters of the great he found an importance that adds another characteristic to my discussion:

These have been always esteemed as the most valuable Parts of History, as they are not only the most authentic Memorials of Facts, but as they serve greatly to illustrate the true Character of the Writer, and do in a manner introduce the Person himself to our Acquaintance. (131)

To the letters of those who have played a role in history, he adds those "between Men of Eminence in the Republic of Literature," letters which have "equal Authority" to those in "the political World" (132). What Fielding underlines here is the documentary nature of the letter as Memorial, a text that establishes authority of the person, of the *moment*, a text part of the meaning of which is that it can be read *later*. This characteristic, as we shall see, has significance for the writer himself, as well as for other fictional writers and readers "of no consequence." The letter is a record, for later, of the moment. Collections of letters show passage, and their closeness to the moment raises expectations of truth. Fielding's comments on letters reveal his preference for history as a model for the novel. Letters are valuable only in the degree of their value as supplementary documents, supplementary perspectives on historical (already known) events or personages. Supplementary only, because unlike Richardson, he believes that letters can *lie*.

One is reminded of Alexander Pope's attention to this supplementary value in the way he saved, edited, revised, and published his own letters. Also interesting is Rousseau's use of his own letters, in packets of appendices, in the *Confessions* where letters and gossip are important themes. They are particularly important in Book IX, a complex narrative of his entanglement in intersecting networks of gossip and scandal, crossing letters, both simple and duplicitous, complicated and multiple love-affairs—not returned but not unrequited—the narrative of the time he begins, in a strangely crowded solitude, his own epistolary novel while simultaneously himself embedded in a number of other ones. Both Pope and Rousseau demonstrate the potential of the letter for a desire to reveal a carefully designed private view of the self to some party or public not originally addressed and to do it in a form so confidential that it testifies to the authenticity of the revelation.

The same characteristics of the letter or packet of letters that draw Fielding's conditioned praise and make possible Pope's and Rousseau's constructions after the fact offer also a risk, a danger to which Pope and Rousseau were possibly responding. Thackeray's narrator in *Vanity Fair* points out:

Perhaps in Vanity Fair there are not better satires than letters. Take a bundle of your dear friend's of ten years back—your dear friend whom you hate now. Look at a file of your sister's: how you clung to each other till you quarrelled about the twenty pound legacy! Get down the round-hand scrawls of your son who has half broken your heart with selfish un-dutifulness since; or a parcel of your own, breathing endless ardour and love eternal, which were sent back by your mistress when she married the Nabob—your mistress for whom you now care no more than for Queen Elizabeth. Vows, love, promises, confidences, gratitude, how queerly they read after a while! There ought to be a law in Vanity Fair ordering the de-struction of every written document (except receipted tradesmen's bills) after a certain brief and proper interval. Those quacks and misanthropes who advertise indelible Japan ink, should be made to perish along with their wicked discoveries. The best ink for Vanity Fair use would be one that faded utterly in a couple of days, and left the paper clean and blank, so that you might write on it to somebody else.[18]

Authentic testaments to the moment, mirrors or "vanities," let-ters also contain everything one wants or should want to forget and leave forgotten. What both Thackeray and George Eliot in her epigraph to this chapter emphasize is the necessary *difference* in meaning of the letter when read later or by someone other than the one addressed. Of all written documents, the personal letter seems to be the most vulnerable, the most susceptible to this drift of meaning. Unless destroyed in the moment for which it was written, it is in its nature to wander.

As sacred or secular text, the letter can provide the basis for community, as in the Epistles of the New Testament, the letters of the historically great and associated documents such as the Tablets of Moses, the Twelve Tables of the Romans, the Declara-tion of Independence, or even the letters from Jane that are the source of gossip at Miss Bates's, or the Letter that flits through the pages of *Finnegans Wake*. ·But to become Novel or to play a role in the novel, letters must be read by someone other than the one to whom they are addressed. They must be Purloined.[19] They must become *literally* a communication between someone who is not the writer and someone who is not the reader.

In the epistolary novel, all the motifs I have associated with
the letter come into play: the pact between individuals; the isolation, distance, privacy, privilege, substitution for presence, supplement of solitude; the revelation of secrets or the passing of
information; the fact that what is written cannot be said in any
other way; the emphasis on the uncertainty of the moment; the
interplay of mediacy-immediacy, presence-absence; and the possibility of meaning changing later. All these elements are present
but with additional complications. At first it would appear that
the letters of, say, *Pamela* are simply reports, representations of
actions that take place *outside* the book and her feelings and fears
about them. But it quickly appears that the characters of an epistolary novel are involved in at least one other novel, and more
often more, outside the letters before us and that those letters are
the intersections of those other stories. Moreover, in an essential
way the letters themselves, the spaces between them, the distances
they presuppose, the interrelationships of the letters—all take on
an active role, become *actors* in multiple dramas. Pamela's first letter not only begins the novel, the writing of it *initiates the action* of
the story and, throughout, the letters themselves, more than even
the principal acts of the novel, are the principal *actors*. They are
at once subject and object, actors, acted upon, signifiers of desire,
and the desired signified. Mr. B＿＿ is as obsessed with reading her letters as with penetrating her body, and both actions are
transgressions, violations, of her privacy, her "privates," her propriety, what is proper to her. Body-person-text become identical
in this way. The physical shock of threatened bodily rape is carried
over to the forced seizure of her private writings and innermost
thoughts and feelings. In this complex figuration, body, person,
and text become involved in a series of exchanges.

What surprises Mr. B＿＿, with the suddeness of an over-
powering desire, is the shock of her resistance to his casual advances—her insistence on her integrity of person, on "proper distance," on the fact that she is person, *in propria suum*, not his
property as a servant—*and* the discovery that she writes letters.
Both actions are signs of an unmasterable interiority, otherness.

Moreover, since her letters come to be most frequently hidden in her dress, the disrobing of the body is involved with the revelation of the letter. The same identification is made with even more intensity in *Clarissa*, so that the notion of *aletheia*—unveiling—becomes powerfully eroticized.

In this way, not only the writing of letters becomes an important action in the epistolary novel, but also the *reading* of them, preferably (but not exclusively) by someone other than the one to whom they are addressed. And it is the multiple and repeatable reading of the letters that brings about the dénouement or catastrophe. This is as true of *Pamela* as it is of *Les liaisons dangereuses*, and, in a quite fundamental way, of *Clarissa*. It is by his reading of her purloined letters that Mr. B———— becomes convinced of Pamela's sincerity and value and marries her; that is, it is by violation of her, his *and* ours, that her identity is attained. In fact, it is only by her own later rereading of her letters that Pamela herself can be sure of her identity ("honesty"). If it is true that her sense of self is initiated by having been taught to read other texts by Mr. B————'s mother, if it is true that she creates herself by the writing of letters, as Roy Roussel notes,[20] and imposes that self on all the readers both inside the novel and since, it is because that self exists as the body of a text, a repeatable past that imposes its name on and through an anonymous reader.

The motif of exposure, involved in this question of becoming text, is basic. It is the discovery that Pamela writes letters outside his household that threatens Mr. B———— with a form of exposure in the beginning, but his incomplete name, another "letter," is also significant in this regard. Besides suggesting the mysterious cipher he is for her through most of the novel, it seems only an innocent convention, an effect of the real. But what that convention suggests is that he has a real place in society, a status, that to *name* him would be an unsupportable exposure. He is literally unrepresentable. As a servant, Pamela is from the beginning only a representative—her exposure or exposability is socially taken for granted. She does have a last name—Andrews—but we quickly forget it, a fact to which I will return. She is or becomes simply Pamela. The name of the novel consisting of the letters by which she creates her self and insists on her singularity carries the paradox; she comes only to represent herself without surname—*Pamela*, the name of an individual *sui generis*—and the name of a text.

The question of the importance of the interposed recipients that ultimately leads to us as readers of the novel involves another basic transformation. Most of Pamela's letters are addressed to her parents, even when she knows they can no longer be delivered and, in some senses, she is writing only for herself, her own future definition. The fact that they are written for another is required for the creation of an identity and opens a path toward otherness that gradually leads to us. It acknowledges that opening. But the particular other to whom they are addressed is also a way of defining herself biologically, naturally, and genealogically—similar to her identification of self with body and text. Her letters represent her desire both to return to her familiar source and her hesitancy, since they are letters, in doing so, although she will later try to return. The threat of her letters to Mr. B———— comes from a different idea of "family." As his servant, to the extent that Pamela is not to be regarded simply as a useful household appliance, she is also ambiguously a member of *his* family. The opposition is stated in the postscript Pamela writes to her first letter which Mr. B———— catches her trying to hide in her bosom:

O how ashamed I was!—He took it, without saying more, and read it quite through, and then gave it me again;—and I said, Pray your honour forgive me!—Yet I know not for what: for he was always dutiful to *his* parents; and why should he be angry that I was so to *mine*? And indeed he was not angry; for he took me by the hand, and said, You are a good girl, Pamela, to be kind to your aged father and mother. I am not angry with you for writing such innocent matters as these: *though you ought to be wary what tales you send out of a family*.[21]

The seeds of anger are planted, however. If she is vulnerable to the exposure to gossip to the degree that she stays on— she claims—because of her need for a reference, the cipher of his name testifies to his much greater social vulnerability. Shortly he will demand that she "not write the affairs of my family purely for an exercise to her pen, and her invention" (22–23) and accuse her of taking "freedoms . . . with my name" (25). The opposition between different notions of family is further underlined when Mr. Williams intercedes for Pamela, after her abduction, with Lady Darnford and Sir Simon

"who [says] to his lady in my presence, Why, what is all this, my dear, but that our neighbour has a mind to his mother's waiting-maid! And if he takes care she wants for nothing, I don't see any great injury will be done her. He hurts no *family* by this": (So, my dear father and mother, [Pamela interposes] it seems that poor people's honesty is to go for nothing). (138)

What is at stake here is a class distinction, but not simply that. As his servant, Pamela is a member of his family metaphorically and socially, and he is her master. Because of his social position, because he is magistrate, he has a metaphoric "parental" authority over her that is almost absolute. She doesn't dispute that authority or the social paternalism for which it stands, but insists on her rights under it, although she actually has few legal rights. So she is placed initially between two kinds of authority to which she refers by letter—that of her biological parents and that of society, based on the model of the family. By insisting on her distance from both, by in a sense refusing and resisting both, as she creates the identity of a singular name, by and through her writing, she is literally orphaned, as is the text that bears her name. She becomes the embodiment of Socrates' complaint against writing I quoted earlier: "getting into the hands not only of those who understand it, but equally of those who have no business with it; it doesn't know how to address the right people, and not address the wrong. And when it is ill-treated and unfairly abused, it" (she) has no parent to come to her help.

Whether she or her writing is "unable to defend or help itself" is another question, but that can clearly be said of Clarissa Harlowe. Pamela, through her writings, is saved. She takes on a last name, albeit a letter than cannot be exposed-completed, by being violated-read, by the apparent replacement of the biological chain by a social one that will initiate a new generation. She is, in a sense, saved from the exclusive integrity that will lead to Clarissa's self-willed death, but it is also clear that, more important than her power to bear children, what is really necessary to her marriage with Mr. B——— is that she continue to generate texts for him to read.

Clarissa is more radical in its recognition of the nature of the text, as Clarissa is a more radically insistent individual.[22] She rejects all forms of sexual generation, past and future, all links other than written ones, denies her body to the point of death, its genealogical link with the past and her family, its power to generate a future, and insists on her own spiritual integrity and identity. If she defers to a spiritual "father" it is only ambiguously and deceptively (figuratively) in a letter which she must later decode for Belford, who must in turn interpret it to Lovelace.[23] She lives, writes, dies to become an "example." The fact or existence of the book bearing her name depends on, requires, and expresses her death. As exemplary text what she requires, what she generates, is an endless future of interpretative texts—exegesis, commentary.

Epistolary novels such as *Pamela* and *Clarissa* demonstrate the significance of the production and appropriation of texts (under the guise of simply presenting them as *already there*). In a quite complicated and affecting way the letters of Pamela and Clarissa carry with them a sense of the encroaching circumstantiality of texts, their occasions, what was lost and what was gained in their becoming texts—their costly struggle to come into being, their dependence on others and on several different orders of signifying chains, their recognition of anteriority and exteriority, and also what is created *by* texts.[24]

What happens when this form of the letter and its properties become absorbed into another "document," the novel? A quick answer would be that, in one way or another, letters *name* the source or provide the answer to the novel's puzzle. A letter or document can be the "source" of the story, as in Hawthorne's essay "The Custom-House," which prefaces and grounds *The Scarlet Letter*. It can also be a source in two other senses: in the way that it is the misdelivery of the letter that contains the truth of Tom Jones's birth (his "source") that makes necessary his exile or journey from Paradise Hall, or Tulkinghorn's observation of Lady Dedlock's shocked recognition of Nemo's handwriting that motivates his search for documentation, ultimately letters, that will implicate her in a former hidden life and lead to the discovery of Esther Summerson's origins. In both cases, a letter contains both source and solution. There are novels, however, that apparently use the letter more simply as solution, such as Trollope's *The Last Chronicle of Barsetshire*, in which the long-delayed answer by letter clears up the mystery of the apparently purloined check and establishes the innocence of Mr. Crawley, or *Finnegans Wake*, in which the Letter is supposed either to (but never quite does) explain the nature of HCE's crime or establish his innocence. There are also all the letters, casual or tangential, accidental or part of another apparently different causal series, such as Raffle's discovery of Bulstrode's letter in *Middlemarch* or the failed delivery of Tess's letter of confession to Angel, part of a chain of accidental events in Hardy's novel that leads us to the apparently predestined doom of his heroine.[25] My difficulty in categorizing these uses of letters indicates that they bear with them significant complications. I have alluded to them earlier, and I want, in a moment, to go into some "examples" in more detail.

There are two other points to be made initially. (1) There is always a curiously accidental sense surrounding them or they appear as almost mechanical devices of the plot, a novelistic version of the *deus ex machina*. They are fortuitous or gratuitous, and they are almost always supplementary and repeat in one way or another information found elsewhere in the novel or other motifs or themes found in a different form in any particular novel. The letters are identified with a secret or other kind of information that one "stumbles on" or that comes from "outside" (the form or *as* form) to save or destroy the hero or heroine or justify that salvation or damnation to the reader. Letters are thus often used to bring about change or to provide an object of conflict. (2) The letter, or the information it contains, is usually now doubly *purloined*—in the sense I used that term with the epistolary novel. What was revealed to the reader there, but withheld from some of the characters, is now what is withheld from the reader as well, who takes the place of Mr. B——— or Lovelace and assumes or is captured by their desire. To the extent that the reader knows about the letter, it raises the expectation of a final "truth," an expectation otherwise raised by the puzzle it will eventually solve if he knows nothing of the letter, or it slips past his attention as in *Tom Jones*.

As "true" answer, it is usually a truth associated with the past, the truth as it was known by someone in the novel's projected past that is at stake in the discovered or delivered letter. Even the letters found by Hawthorne in a symbolically moribund Custom-House, which stand as the source of his novel, simply point to another mystery concerning a letter—the Scarlet A (adultery-mixed, impure origin or origin as transgression—Alpha—Aleph—the letter as such).[26] In other words, this "source" is an enigma that the text of the novel will try to explicate, draw out, prolong (the etymological cognate of "purloin"), though fail finally to solve. In this sense, the letter contains a "story," the withholding of which makes possible the "plot."[27]

What about gossip? In the epistolary novel, it was connected with the fear of exposure which informed the letters or against which they were intended to provide some kind of defense. In one way or another, it is the purpose of the letter, by providing a "true" answer, to close the round of speculation that is gossip—to replace the substitute parent with a parent-Truth. In the traditional novel, as letter moves into the background and away from a recipient, gossip moves forward and takes form and body. The fear takes on a name. One is tempted to adopt the formula from information theory used by Margot Norris in her lucid account of style and technique of *Finnegans Wake*: gossip is the "noise" (etymologically, "rumor") that interferes with (delays) the "message" or information the letter contains.[28] The fact that in the same theory this interference is compensated for normally by sufficient redundancies in the transmission of the message can be associated with, but does not explain, the usually supplementary nature of the letter in the novel.

It is an attractive formula, and it indicates some important meanings of the relationship between the letter and gossip in the novel, but it does not exhaust their potential for meaning. The letter and gossip are nothing if not multiple and overdetermined. There is also a countersense to the relationship.

If the letter is in the novel as some kind of shadowy reminder of its genesis in the writing of one individual to another, as a kind of double to signature (however enigmatic) or as answer-response (however spurious), gossip is a shadowy reminder of its end—a textual discourse of a communal or group consciousness, the replacement of a private connection between two individuals by a network connecting a community or culture, a substitution or an establishment of connections that is, not incidentally, the typical format of a Dickens novel.

At any rate, the letter collects-condenses information, answers, and solutions. Gossip stands for the delay of the letter, or in place of the letter. It is by nature displacement, association, and affiliation. But it is also dispersion or diffusion. If the letter stands for what is connected with the past, origin, genealogical source, and parent, then gossip comes to suggest everything that is disseminative, almost in the sense Derrida uses this word—playing on the figure for an act that is like the production of meaning or the illusory act that (non) produces the mirage of meanings that can never be organized into even a polysemic totality, that can never be returned to any father.[29] Finally, no distinction between letter and gossip can escape blurring because what is always at issue in the novel is the *waywardness* of the letter, which is precisely what mars the possibility of all distinctions. While the letter suggests vestigial concerns with documentation and something held back or in reserve, its always supplementary nature also suggests its inability to return, the hidden possibility of the novel's inability to close, or that any closure is only illusory. The wandering (errant-fictional) letter and gossip meet as the sign of the sign, the capacity of language for interminable drift.

Two examples: In *Tom Jones*, it seems a simple and mechanical device of plot that the letter containing the truth of Tom's birth reaches the wrong person—the absolutely *wrong* person. The Blifil-devil comparison is by now commonplace, but it is worth noting that Coleridge's comments on this novel include the remark that "Devil, *Diabolus* means slanderer." [30] The fact that the letter arrives at a moment of turmoil—that all the people who have the information it contained are brought together, intersect paths, but are properly kept apart, particularly in the Inn at Upton, so that the information is not divulged until the end—can be thought of as Fielding's marvelous management of the most perfect novelistic plot. Yet this "management" has implications and raises problems that affect all other factors in the novel. For example, the author's problem is similar to Tom's but more successfully handled. It is a question of a certain reserve, an economic and sexual holding back, rather than "spending" everything at once or going for immediate gratification—an economy that Tom doesn't learn until (presumably) the end of the novel. The notion of immediate gratification also suggests the possibility of incest, which is also raised by his lack of knowledge of his identity or the wrong idea of his identity, which in turn is prolonged by the displacement of the letter, its misapprehension. And that displacement is paralleled by a series of other displacements or substitutions. Besides his wandering exile, or as part of it, there are the women who stand in place of the Sophia (wisdom) whom he desires and for whom he searches, one of whom is Mrs. Waters, the false mother, that is, a substitute for his real mother. A similar displacement could also be suggested in the language of the book—for example, the use of the word *Honour* in all kinds of senses—serious, casual, as an oath, and for all kinds of purposes, including its totally irrelevant use as the name of a character. [31]

Revelation comes in an unexpected way at the end of the novel, in a flurry of crossing letters, confusions and misapprehensions of acts and their authorships, disputed and mistaken authority (familial and other kinds), tale-telling, a virtual contagion that masks two facts: (1) that the letter is never actually delivered; and (2) that Allworthy's reconciliation with Tom and naming him as heir in replacement of Blifil does not confront the fact that he is still an illegitimate heir, a bastard, besides being only a nephew. First, the truth is brought to Allworthy, after the shock of the reputed incest, by the false mother herself—Mrs. Waters. It is then verified by the lawyer Dowling, who has been involved in machinations against Tom and other evasions of the truth. In other words, truth is offered by the (bad) woman and the (agent of the) Law—both of which, figuratively and actually, have been given to a good deal of sliding throughout the novel. Woman is the unknown, invisible, or absent agency or source; man is the Law, and also agent, power of representation, and (thought to be) the regulator of her fecundity.

Allworthy demands of Blifil that he produce the actual letter from the dead but real mother, but there is no sign that he does or can. There are also other supplementary testimonies to Allworthy of Tom's goodness in both speech (gossip) and letter, but the solution is grounded by Allworthy's original inclination toward him that was there before all the misapprehensions. Second, no one questions the right of Allworthy, who is childless, to name Tom Jones (or anyone else) as heir in the novel, nor will I question it here. I simply want to note that it takes place in the midst of Squire Western's questions about the "government" of his daughter and his parental "authority" over whom she will marry. And in turn, the question of the relationship of paternal authority to the Jacobite Rebellion, which literally intersects both the path of Tom Jones and the pages of the book is never explicitly addressed.[32] The Rebellion is based on the Stuarts' claim of the absolute authority of genealogical succession and the divinely transmitted and absolute authority of the monarch. The novel abounds with references to the *event*, the sentiments of various parties, and the texts on which the ideological dispute is based. Moreover, the other texts of Fielding from the time of the writing of the novel were interventions in that dispute. The question I'm raising is, in effect, what are the limits or edges of *this* text? What is its status as an event? What are its relationships with what is external to it, textual and otherwise? Where can one draw a halt to the lines leading away from its pages?

Similar questions have been and should be raised about *Middlemarch*. I return to the epigraph of this chapter, chosen with the hope that its suggestiveness would resonate throughout my consideration of its figures and the problems they pose. It states its issues in a grand way with its talk of an inscription in stone that "may end by letting us into the secret of usurpations and other scandals gossiped about long empires ago." The last phrase is almost a syllepsis and transfers a spatial to a temporal sense, without losing the spatial sense. It suggests both the empires of the "usurpations" and the "long empires" of time between those "scandals" and their present (accidental) deciphering. The grandness is continued:

As the stone which has been kicked by generations of clowns may come by curious little links of effect under the eyes of a scholar, through whose labours it may at last fix the date of invasions and unlock religions, so a bit of ink and paper which has long been an innocent wrapping or stop gap may at last be laid open under the one pair of eyes which have knowledge enough to turn it into the opening of a catastrophe. To Uriel watching the progress of planetary history from the Sun, the one result would be just as much of a coincidence as the other.[33]

"Uriel," the allusion to *Paradise Lost*, the trained "eyes of a scholar," "catastrophe," "planetary history," "the date of invasions," and the unlocking of "religions"—the idea is staged in terms of great events, terrible catastrophes, and important knowledge. One would think the passage would refer to (for it certainly echoes) the high ambitions of Casaubon or Lydgate or even Dorothea. Certainly it would have some connection with one of the major plot threads of the novel! But, of course, it is precisely the "clown" who has picked up the significant "stone" rather than kicking it away. It is the very unknowledgeable, very minor character John Raffles who, upon entering the novel casually at this late point, finds a folded piece of paper discarded by his stepson, another minor character, Joshua Riggs "Featherstone." Raffles uses the paper to tighten the leather covering around his brandy flask, the filling of which and a sovereign are the prices he exacts to go away and leave his stepson alone.

The folded paper is an innocent letter to Riggs "Featherstone" from Mr. Bulstrode. By the largest kind of "coincidence," Raffles has the right eyes for it—he is the one person who can use it to tie the self-righteous Bulstrode to a sordid past of "usurpations and other scandals gossiped about long empires ago." The narrator underlines very pointedly the discrepancy between the language of the prefacing generalization and what it prefaces, between the terms of the "comparison" and the person and action it is meant to illustrate. She follows the passage I have quoted with this statement: "Having made this rather lofty comparison I am less uneasy in calling attention to the existence of low people by whose interference, however little we may like it, the course of the world is very much determined." How the "lofty comparison" makes the narrator "less uneasy" about the "coincidence" or the insignificance of the action it describes is not actually very clear. Nor is how drawing the reader's attention to it in this way, "not lightly giving occasion to" the existence or interferences of "low people," will greatly "help to reduce their number." But Raffles's discovery is certainly one of the openings of the catastrophe(s) of the novel. It leads, though decidedly not in any linear fashion, to Ladislaw's discovery of his heritage and affects certain decisions he makes, to Raffles's own death, perhaps murder, which in turn leads to the downfall of Bulstrode, which implicates Lydgate and contributes to his ruin, which attracts Dorothea's sympathy and so, in some way or another, aided by other equally accidental series, ultimately brings her together with Will, and so on.

Raffles's discovery is one of the points of intersection between the structure of the plot and one of the important themes of the book, a theme named in the narrator's comment. It is one of those little accidents, nameless acts, "minute causes" that contribute to the determining of "the course of the world." There is an unclosed question in the final line of the passage. From the angelic perspective and in terms of planetary history, who can say that one act is more or less significant than another, more or less of a "coincidence" than another?

There is also another question raised in the passage under the form of an apparent assertion: "Such conditions are often *minutely represented* in our *petty* lifetimes." What *is* the relationship between great and "petty" or "minute"? What is the relationship between the terms of a comparison, between representation and what is represented? These are questions the passage seems to take for granted. In two essays important both for a theory of the novel and a reading of *Middlemarch*, Hillis Miller has shown the way the various patterns, themes, and threads of the novel refuse to close into a coherent totality.[34] In one essay, he demonstrates the way the novel seems to take recourse to a metaphysically enclosed concept of history (certainly one of its concerns), but at the same time "deconstructs" that system. In the other, he argues lucidly that there are three "totalizing metaphors, or rather families of metaphors" which the reader is invited "to use as a paradigm by means of which to think of the whole," and that "each group of metaphors is related to the others, fulfilling them, but at the same time contradicting them, cancelling them out, or undermining their validity."[35] In the other essay, he alludes to other questions which are related to the one I raise here.

Miller points out that "the relation of Middlemarch to English society is . . . that of part to whole, or that of a sample to the whole cloth . . . synecdochic. . . . In *Middlemarch* a fragment is examined as a 'sample' of the larger whole of which it is a part, though the whole impinges on the part as the 'medium' within which it lives, as national politics affect Middlemarch when there is a general election, or as the coming of the railroad upsets rural traditions" (126). These questions can and should be prolonged, both in terms of the narrative "structure" (itself a "totalizing metaphor") and in terms of the question of representation raised in many ways throughout the novel, for example, in Rome in the discussions of art between various characters and in the figure of

Rome itself. What is the status of the synecdoche as a means of representation, a question Miller is right in raising? Ultimately the questions would have to be extended outside the margins of the novel, for in the historical context in which it locates itself, the question of "representation," of "sample," of a part standing for a larger part, of the full "representation" of unique and psychologically "complete" individuals, all these terms have multiple references. On the one hand, they figure in the political debate surrounding the Reform movement which "crosses" the pages of the novel, and on the other hand, they are questions of aesthetic "realism." Ultimately one would also want to question all the kinds of equivalences suggested by the questions I have just asked and the passage I have cited from *Middlemarch*. The questions I have raised about *Tom Jones* and *Middlemarch* suggest another puzzling question: the status of fictions as "illustrations" or "examples" of historical or philosophical events or ideas.[36]

Without such questions, one with the eyes of Uriel might assume a "history" of the form of the novel, of fictional narrative, in which at some point in its development the letter stopped returning: that it, like Tess's misdelivered confessional note, slipped under (into) the carpet (text/textus—woven fabric), or that it was burned as in *Bleak House* by a kind of spontaneous combustion, or lost in a kitchen middenheap/battleground as in *Finnegans Wake*; that at some point, the letter is shredded, becomes the missing eighteen minutes, explodes into the "Fragmentary Sentences," which is the title of the chapter in Hawthorne's *The Marble Faun* from which I have taken my other epigraph. Without resort to the stiff Barthesian demarcation between the classic "readerly" text and the modern "writerly" text[37] and the somewhat silly debate surrounding it, some such idea of the "history" of the form is attractive and inevitable although impossible to locate or mark without the creation of another "fictional" narrative or allegory of a second order. The tension was "always, already" there. One would continue to ask, was not the letter always, already "exploded," and whether or when it had already opened the possibility of truth without closing it, begun a play in which we were implicated and continually forced to locate both the letter and its explosion and ourselves, its circumstances and our own?

In weaving these mystic utterances into a continuous scene, we undertake a task resembling in its perplexity that of gathering up and piecing together the fragments of a letter which has been torn and scattered to the winds. Many words of deep significance, many entire sentences, and those possibly the most important ones, have flown too far on the winged breeze to be recovered. If we insert our own conjectural amendments, we perhaps give a purport utterly at variance with the true one. Yet unless we attempt something in this way, there must remain an unsightly gap, and a lack of continuousness and dependence in our narrative; so that it would arrive at certain inevitable catastrophes without due warning of their imminence.[38]

There is, of course, no "letter" in *The Marble Faun* except this figurative one, although the whole novel is taken up with the questions of representation and interpretation,[39] the creative, transgressive, or copying acts of a group of characters living a "romance" in Rome (which has given "romance" and one form of the novel its name.) The novel is, however, structured by enigmas and an impending sense of "catastrophe," by an anticipation of a final revealing "truth."

There are actually two enigmas. The first has to do with the relationship of Donatello to "the Faun" of Praxiteles, whether he is actually a Faun or not (that is, his animal/human, genealogical status). It is this question, in the form of a representation, that the narrator tells us late in the novel is the source of his interest in the stories of the characters. Kenyon's final attempt to capture the meaning of Donatello in a statue is left unfinished, half emerging from the crude stone, because it both represents and poses "the riddle of the soul's growth" (368). The narrator says, "It was the contemplation of this imperfect portrait of Donatello that originally interested us in his history, and impelled us to elicit from Kenyon what he knew of his friend's adventures" (368).

The other enigma is the one described in the passage I have used as an epigraph, the puzzle of the past of Miriam, the terrible thing from which she seems to be fleeing, and the identity/nature of the strange "model" who haunts her and the power he seems to have over her. The "Fragmentary Sentences" refer to the bits of conversation overheard between Miriam and the model—fragments that intensify but in no way clarify the puzzle.

Neither riddle is, of course, resolved. The first question no one really expected to have answered, and Hawthorne was right to be a bit huffy about it in the conclusion he added to the fourth printing of the novel, although it was a "false" problem and his response distracts from, or rather points to, more basic issues. The other question is more basic to the plot structure, and convention would demand its answer. The scene near the end in which Miriam reveals her identity to Kenyon is described in this way:

And she revealed a name, at which her auditor started, and grew pale; for it was one that, only a few years before, had been familiar to the world, in connection with a mysterious and terrible event. The reader—if he think it worthwhile to recall some of the strange incidents which have been talked of, and forgotten, within no long time past—will remember Miriam's name. (414)

The reader will remember the name, that is, if he lives completely within the fiction and shares its own fictional memory.[40] At the beginning of the last chapter (first printing), the narrator asks to be thanked for avoiding "tedious," "minute elucidations" (439). The reader, he trusts, "is too wise to insist upon looking closely at the wrong side of the tapestry, after the right one has been sufficiently displayed to him"—"Kindly readers" will accept "this pattern . . . at its worth, without tearing its web apart, with the idle purpose of discovering how its threads have been knit together." For, after all, "the actual experience of even the most ordinary life is full of events that never explain themselves, either as regards their origin or their tendency."

In the added conclusion the narrator returns again to Kenyon and Hilda for answers to the readers' questions. Hilda knows, but mysteriously cannot tell as long as she is in Rome. The power of the church/state is hinted at as a reason, but Rome is Romance and that border cannot be crossed by answers. As a substitute,

Kenyon's speculations satisfy some of the narrator's questions, but
when he asks again "Miriam's real name and rank, and precisely the
nature of the troubles that led to all those direful consequences,"
he receives a repetition of the answer he has already offered the
reader:

> "Is it possible that you need an answer to those questions?" exclaimed
> Kenyon, with an aspect of vast surprise. "Have you not even surmised
> Miriam's name? Think awhile, and you will assuredly remember it. If not,
> I congratulate you most sincerely; for it indicates that your feelings have
> never been harrowed by one of the most dreadful and mysterious events
> that have occurred within the present century!" (450)

The epigraph and these passages I have quoted from *The
Marble Faun* do not simply confirm the current notion that the
reader is a participant in the production of meaning in a literary text. They do not simply imply that, for a "writerly" text, the
reader "must undertake a task resembling in its perplexity that of
gathering up and piecing together the fragments of a letter"—
re-remembering it, inserting his "own conjectural amendments,"
either for the pleasure or the bliss of the text, or even so that there
should not "remain an unsightly gap."

Rather, the questions these passages indicate are ones of the
"memory" or reference, before or outside, necessary to any representational text,[41] questions of the status of fictional "truths"
around, during, or at the end of narratives, questions of our need
for the revelation of the true "fictional" name at the catastrophe as
the end of reading. Indeed, they raise the question of the meaning
and necessity of the whole structure of problem or lack—delay,
deferral—of revelation and release I have been posing throughout
this chapter.

2

The Displaced Self in the Novels of Daniel Defoe

A fine Story! says the Governess, "you would see the Child, and you would not see the Child: you would be conceal'd and discover'd both together."

—*Moll Flanders*

Speech was given to man to disguise his thoughts.

—Talleyrand

I. Names

NAMES, FALSE NAMES, AND ABSENCE OF names seem to have special importance for Daniel Defoe's novels.[1] None of his fictional narrators, with the exception of Robinson Crusoe, tell their stories under the names they were born with.[2] The Narrator of *A Journal of the Plague Year* is anonymous, signing his account at the end with the initials "H. F." In the other novels, the narrators receive their names in something like a special christening. Bob Singleton is given his name by one of the series of "mothers" through whose hands he passes after being kidnapped from his true parents. Colonel Jack receives the name "John" from the nurse who is paid to take him by his real parents, who are unmarried "people of quality." Unfortunately, all three of the nurse's "sons," one of them really hers and the other two paid for, are named "John."

Moll Flanders's real name is too "well known in the records, or registers, at Newgate and in the Old Bailey," so she chooses to write under the alias "Moll Flanders" and begs the reader's patience "till I dare own who I have been, as well as who I am." It is by the revelation of this true name (to Moll but not the reader) that Moll recognizes her real mother, who had also adopted an alias, and discovers that she has married her own brother. "Moll Flanders" is the name she takes during her time as a thief in London, when, though already a middle-aged woman, she falls under the tutelage of a woman who refers to her as "child" and whom she calls "mother."

The title page of *Roxana* is a veritable catalog of her aliases throughout her career. Curiously, the name "Roxana" is the name she bears for the shortest time and one she did not give herself. She received it, in the presence of the king, from the spontaneous cry of a group of men at a masked ball in appreciation of the costume she was wearing. But Roxana is a special case, for the reader does learn at least her true Christian name because it is also the name of her daughter, who pursues her through the last part of the book.

At the moment of narration, few of Defoe's narrators are living under the name by which they "sign" their stories. Secrecy seems to be an absolute precondition of self-revelation. Or, to put it in a less perversely contradictory way, these narrators seem under a double compulsion to expose and to conceal themselves. Certainly it is a literary convention, a premise of fictional narration, aimed at convincing the reader of their veracity, since Defoe published all these books as the "real" memoirs of their narrators. But it is a curious convention, since it goes beyond a mere premise of narration and becomes an important theme in the narration, an event in the story itself.

Moreover, literary convention cannot explain this practice of concealment in the life of the true author of these fake memoirs, Daniel Defoe, which was not, of course, his real name. Before and even after he took up the writing of these books at the age of sixty, Daniel Defoe served as the agent of various interests, parties, and governments, writing and acting under innumerable

assumed names and points of view, to the extent that it is difficult to separate fact from fiction in our knowledge of his own life,
and impossible to go beyond certain limits in ascertaining what
he actually wrote.

Robinson Crusoe is a somewhat special instance of Defoe's
habit of concealing the true names of his narrators. Robinson has
purportedly related the events of his own life under his own name
through two volumes—he at least has committed no crime and
requires no secrecy. In the Preface to the third volume, however,
Robinson hints that if the events he has narrated are not strictly
true, they are allegorically true and that perhaps Robinson Crusoe
is not his real name. Many readers have taken this hint to mean
that Defoe had written his own spiritual autobiography under the
metaphor of the shipwrecked and isolated Crusoe. The question
has never been decided. The double project of revelation and concealment of this least sophisticated of novelists was successful. The
"real" Daniel Defoe has disappeared into the absence of an irre-
coverable time.

We can only probe for the meaning of the double compulsion
in the written world of his novel and perhaps ponder the relationship of that compulsion to the project of writing lies that look like
truth. Our hopes are limited: if we are reduced to a search for the
meaning of the name he withheld from us, we also know that in
the end we will have to content ourselves with no more than the
name alone.

What will we find to explain this curious game of names? In
a sense it cannot be completely explained or understood because
the only real evidence lies in the books themselves and also because, since it is a literary convention, we are touching upon a
cultural symptom as well as a personal one, and all such symptoms are overdetermined. Two provisional explanations, however,
will emerge from an examination of Defoe's fiction. One has to
do with a strong fear of the menace of other wills, a pervasive
fear in these novels. Another explanation has to do with the way
the self becomes somebody else in conversion. In this discussion I
will place special weight on Robinson Crusoe, for while it provides

less mystery about names than the other novels, it offers itself as a kind of myth to explain the fear of exposure, detailing the consequent strategies of the self. In order to discuss this impulse at the source of Defoe's fiction, I will have to defer consideration of the intense fascination with the factual, the most pervasive and already much discussed characteristic of Defoe's writing—defer it, I would hope, only to recover it in a new light.

These provisional explanations might help also to illuminate what is involved in the constitution of imaginary novelistic characters.

II. The Myth of Singleness

> In my youth, I wandered away, too far from your sustaining hand, and created of myself a barren waste.
> —Augustine, *Confessions*

Defoe's novels are based on a notion of radical egocentricity. Robinson wonders why his isolation on the island was "any grievance or affliction" since "it seems to me that life in general is, or ought to be, but one universal act of solitude":

The world, I say, is nothing to us as it is more or less to our relish. All reflection is carried home, and our dear self is, in one respect, the end of living. Hence man may be properly said to be alone in the midst of the crowds and hurry of men and business. All the reflections which he makes are to himself; all that is pleasant he embraces for himself; all that is irksome and grievous is tasted but by his own palate.

What are the sorrows of other men to us, and what their joy? Something we may be touched indeed with by the power of sympathy, and a secret turn of the affections; but all the solid reflection is directed to ourselves. Our meditations are all solitude in perfection; our passions are all exercised in retirement; we love, we hate, we covet, we enjoy, all in privacy and solitude. All that we communicate of those things to any other is but for their assistance in the pursuit of our desires; the end is at home; the enjoyment, the contemplation, is all solitude and retirement; it is for ourselves we enjoy, and for ourselves we suffer. (*Serious Reflections*, 2–3)

Robinson's thirty years of solitude on a desert island is the metaphor of this selfishness. In fact, his story is based on the etymological metaphor "islanded"—isolated. When Robinson was in Brazil, he "used to say, I lived just like a man cast away upon some desolate island that has nobody there but himself" (VII, 39). The whole book has to do with the progressive materialization of spiritual metaphor for what is implicit in Robinson's condition from the beginning, in the same way that the book itself is a factualization of the metaphors of the whole tradition of spiritual autobiographies.[3]

Selfish, isolated, but is he really alone? Other Defoe narrators are just as solitary in the midst of society. Robinson's island isolation is after all only a metaphor for the solitary selfishness of all men. This seemingly impenetrable selfishness, however, is a Hobbesian "state of nature," transposed into a social world, atomistic, volatile, where the mere existence of another person, for Robinson even the *possibility* of the existence of another person, is a threat to the self. Even Robinson in his wilderness, through all those years of never encountering another human being, is constantly haunted by a sense of menacing otherness. He must always be on guard. He never loses the agonizing sense of being watched. Far from only being a representation of Robinson's egocentric isolation, the book is peopled by signs of the constant presence of the other—Robinson's fear, the footprint of a man, the Hand of God, the constant presence of the older Robinson in the double perspective of the narration, the presence of the spectator-reader before whom Robinson rehearses his solitude. In a sense, no Defoe character, not even Robinson, is ever alone.

The need for secrecy at the moment of narration for most of Defoe's "autobiographers" is no mystery. With the exception of Robinson and H. F., they have committed crimes for which they can be called to justice. Near the beginnings of their stories, however, they also are all bereft of family and protection and are thrown into a harsh and dangerous world of deceptive appearances, whose inhabitants are indifferent, conniving, and menacing. Some, like Robinson or H. F., orphan themselves seemingly by

choice. Others, like Colonel Jack and Bob Singleton, are virtually
cut off from their origins, and so from their true names. Roxana,
even as a young girl, long before she is deserted by her husband
and left to protect herself and her family, is removed from France
and her childhood, bringing with her nothing "but the Language."
The separation from any guardian structure is sharp. Their isolation is complete.

No wonder, then, that Defoe has been said to have discounted the importance of personal relationship in his novels.[4]
There is no richly complex conflict between wills more or less
equal in strength in his fictional world. The Defoe character has
to struggle against all the others, against a harsh necessity.[5] There
is no sense of an individualized other consciousness confronting
the protagonist as there is in the worlds of Richardson, Austen,
or George Eliot. The paradigm is Moll in a crowded London
street; her survival depends on her ability to take "the advantages
of other people's mistakes" while remaining unseen herself. The
value of her story for the reader will be in its warning "to Guard
against the like Surprizes, and to have their Eyes about them when
they have to do with Strangers of any kind, for 'tis very seldom
that some Snare or other is not in their way" (II, 92). Otherness
for a Defoe character is generic, anonymous. Individual antago-
nists like Roxana's landlord or even her Amy, Moll's various men,
Robinson's Moorish captor, or Friday can be tricked or subordinated without much apparent difficulty, but a single, anonymous
footprint in the sand seizes Crusoe's mind with uncontrollable
terror. However easily any Defoe "I" can deal with any individual
menace, the unnamed dread remains. Perhaps the most striking
example is the London of the plague. The "others" of the *Journal*
are anonymous numbers of dead and dying. Any conversation,
even the slightest human contact, carries the risk of death.

When Robinson finds himself shipwrecked, almost his first
act is to begin to build a wall around himself. He further insu-
lates himself; he creates an island within the island. His action is
obsessive. He spends almost three and a half months building the
wall—"I thought I should never be perfectly secure 'till this Wall

was finish'd" (VII, 87). Although he longs for deliverance from his solitude, he is compelled to hide his presence so "that if any People were to come on Shore there, they would not perceive any Thing like a Habitation" (VII, 87). So in the midst of a threatening and unknown space, Robinson creates for himself an ordered interior, crowded with things that can be listed and enumerated to his satisfaction. He "furnishes" himself "with many things." Like the fallen angels, Robinson sets about to build and secure his own Pandemonium, following the advice of Mammon to "seek / Our own good from ourselves, and from our own / Live to ourselves, though in this vast recess, / Free, and to none accountable" (*Paradise Lost* II, 252–55). But, of course, their self-reliance is a sham, and their Pandemonium is a parody of Heaven, founded upon denial of the divine Other, whose power they can never escape. Like the angels, Robinson's concern with things is a symptom of his fall.

Moll Flanders in disguise in the middle of a crowded London Street, H. F. in his "safe" house surrounded by the plague, Robinson in his fort—the image is a recurrent one. Earlier in Robinson's account, in Brazil he carves out a plantation "among Strangers and Savages in a Wilderness, and at such a Distance, as never to hear from any Part of the World that had the least Knowledge of me" (VII, 30). Still earlier, there is Robinson quavering in the hold of the ship that takes him from home, surrounded by a raging sea.

At the beginning of the book Robinson's father points out to him that his "was the middle State, or what might be called the upper Station of *Low Life*, . . . that this was the State of Life which all other People envied" because

the middle Station had the fewest Disasters, and was not expos'd to so many Vicissitudes as the higher or lower Part of Mankind . . . that this Way Men went silently and smoothly thro' the World, and comfortably out of it, not embarrass'd with the Labours of the Hands or of the Head, not sold to the Life of Slavery for daily Bread, or harass with perplx'd Circumstances, which rob the Soul of Peace and the Body of Rest; not enrag'd with the Passion of Envy, or secret burning Lust of Ambition for great things; but in easy Circumstances sliding gently thro' the World, and sensibly tasting the Sweets of living, without the bitter, feeling that they are happy, and learning by every Day's Experience to know it more sensibly. (VII, 2–4)

At the outset, then, Robinson already possesses the kind of security, freedom from exposure, that most other Defoe narrators and later even Robinson himself long for. What is given to Robinson is suddenly taken from other Defoe protagonists by circumstances over which they have no control. Moll Flanders and even H. F. must expose themselves to danger in order to survive. Why does Robinson give up so easily what the others have to struggle so hard to gain? In a sense, this is the question implicit in the beginning of this essay: expressing so strong a desire for concealment, why do they offer their confessions at all? This is as difficult a question as asking why Defoe wrote novels. The desire for concealment could have been easily satisfied by silence, by writing or publishing no books at all.[6] The obvious answer to so manifestly impossible a question—that Defoe wrote books to make money, that is to say, like Moll or H. F., to survive—is less satisfactory than it might at first appear. There were other ways to make money, many of which Defoe tried. Much of the other writing Defoe did involved the need for secrecy or masking.

Defoe's narrators seem obsessed with concealing themselves, but the impulse leading them toward exposure appears equally strong. Complete concealment is impossible, perhaps not even desirable. On the one hand there is the insistence on building a faceless shelter around the self, but on the other a recurring compulsion to move out into the open. This double compulsion can be expressed as a double fear. When an earthquake makes him fear the security of his cave, Robinson writes that "the fear of being swallow'd up alive, made me that I never slept in quiet, and yet the Apprehensions of lying abroad without any Fence was almost equal to it" (VII, 94). These two fears, however—fear of being swallowed up by the earth, fear of lying in the open—are the same at bottom. Why does Robinson fear sleeping without the protection of a wall? He is afraid of ravenous beasts and cannibals. If one is caught abroad with one's guard down, unconscious (sleeping), one risks loss of self. But the dangers are as great, apparently, if one never ventures out. Both fears are basically fears of engulfment: one, the fear of being lost in the recesses of one's own nature (the earth), of solipsism and anonymity; alternately, fear of being captured, "eaten" by the other. Perhaps behind both, Defoe's fear of imprisonment.[7] Fear of forms, equally strong fears of the formless. The fear of being devoured recurs throughout Robinson's narrative. At the beginning, he is afraid of being swallowed alive by the sea. Near the end, he defends himself against the devouring wolves.[8]

Besides fear or biological need, there are other reasons apparently for venturing abroad. Curiosity forces H. F. constantly to risk infection. Moll learns that the others betray moments of unconsciousness from which she can profit: "a Thief being a Creature that Watches the Advantages of other Peoples mistakes" (II, 92). Why does Robinson surrender his initial security? The reasons are intentionally vague to point to the fact that his motivation is beyond his understanding and ambiguously beyond personal choice, for the reasons are generic and at the same time subject to his accountability. His motivation or lack of justifiable motivation, involving disobedience of the father, is a restlessness of spirit which is simultaneously culpability and its own punishment. He describes the sources of his "meer wandering Inclination" as "something fatal," a "Propension of Nature," symptoms of what he shares with general man, the heritage of the fall. "Design'd" by his father "for the Law," he "would be satisfied with nothing but going to Sea," great symbol of the unformed. The opposition could not be more clear. What is most threatening is also most alluring. Throughout his life, even after his conversion, Robinson will feel the compulsion to leave behind the preformed, the already-given world of law, and face the unknown and undifferentiated, full of menace for the self and simultaneously full of promise. Unable to accept the given definition of himself, the will and legacy of his father, the world of law, Robinson experiences himself as incomplete and searches mistakenly for completion in the world outside. He does not possess himself but is scattered among a world of things. He must externalize himself in the world. He must create a self out of the formless sea of pure possibility, out of the surrounding, anonymous wilderness. The world is for him to make something of his own.

Here is the source of his egocentricity. His feeling of loneliness in Brazil at being "at such a Distance as never to hear from any Part of the World that had the least Knowledge of me" suggests that this distance is an alienation from a part of himself held in thrall by the world outside. This alienation, his longing for companionship through his years of isolation on the "Island of Despair," and his fear of the other all testify to his continuing sense of incompleteness, but also reveal the lie behind the way he has sought fulfillment.

Fear of the other, determining need for concealment; necessity, allurement of the world offering some form of completion to the self, determining the impulse to risk exposure. These oppositions suggest an explanation of the concealment and exposure, or guarded exposure, of Defoe's narrators that is revealed by the play of names. Hiding behind the disguise of Robinson and his factual-seeming narrative, Defoe is doing what Robinson does — constructing and hiding inside a "natural" fortification that cannot be perceived as a "habitation" from the outside. In a sense, this is as close as we can get to an answer to the problem formulated at the beginning. Pursuit of the mystery might, however, give a fuller sense of the implications of this strategy for the development of the novel.

III. The Necessity of Becoming Other

> I preferred to excuse myself and blame this unknown thing which was in me but was not part of me. The truth, of course, was that it was all my own self, and my own impiety had divided me against myself.
> — Augustine, *Confessions*

After fifteen years, after this material and spiritual security has seemed complete and his only confrontation has been hearing unexpectedly his own name pronounced by his parrot, Robinson experiences the incredible shock of seeing the "naked footprint of a man." The hidden self-other structure of the book is brought into the open. The footprint is the merest sign of the near presence of another human being—yet shouting significance for Robinson in the very fact of its inadequacy of signification.

It is the sheerest kind of accident, almost miraculous, as he realized, that he has seen it. Characteristically he sums up the odds: "twas Ten Thousand to one whether I should see it or not, and in the Sand too, which the first Surge of the Sea upon a high Wind would have defac'd entirely" (VII, 179). A footprint in the sand—a partial signature whose power lies in its mystery and ambiguity. A sign of transience—in both the sense that it is the mark of action and that it is temporary, contingent—it is the static trace of a human movement and a recent movement at that. But rather than being any signal to Crusoe's hopes—of company or of deliverance—in a flash the footprint destroys all his hopes and all his security.

The contradiction between Robinson's desire to externalize himself and his fear of being seen receives sharp definition:

The first Thing I propos'd to my self, was, to throw down my Enclosures, and turn all my tame Cattle wild into the Woods, that the Enemy might not find them; and then frequent the Island in Prospect of the same, or the like Booty: Then to the simple Thing of Digging up my two Corn Fields, that they might not find such a Grain there, and still be prompted to frequent the Island; then to demolish my Bower and Tent, that they might not see any Vestige of Habitation, and be prompted to look farther, in order to find out the Persons inhabiting. (VII, 184)

Seized by this terror at the possible presence of another human being, Robinson wants to remove all traces of himself from the island at the cost of destroying all that he has worked for, all that he has created of himself in things. He wants to disappear, to be invisible, to see without being seen. When he recovers his reason, he will try to accomplish this same end by more practical means. He will build a second wall, further enclosing himself; he will go out of it only rarely, when it is necessary, and then only with the greatest caution and circumspection; and he will go to great lengths to provide armed vantage points, hiding places where he can spy on intruders without himself being seen.

Before he conceives of the idea of erasing all trace of himself from the island by destroying his possessions, he imagines more reasonably such destruction by those who left the footprint:

> Then terrible Thoughts rack'd my Imagination about their having found my Boat, and that there were People here; and that if so, I should certainly have them come here again in greater Numbers, and devour me; that if it should happen so that they should not find me, yet they would find my Enclosure, destroy all my Corn, carry away all my Flock of tame Goats, and I should perish at last for meer Want. (VII, 180)

When he considers doing the same thing to himself, it is almost as if he would be acting in place of the others, doing to himself what he most fears at their hands. At this point in his narrative, in a confused way, a dialectic between self and other begins to emerge.

At first Robinson thinks the footprint must have been made by the Devil to frighten him. This idea removes the element of the contingent from the sign, gives it purpose *for* him. Curiously, his idea also mitigates the otherness of the sign. Later, when he is frightened by the dying "he-goat" in the cave, he comments "that he that was afraid to see the Devil, was not fit to live twenty Years in an Island all alone; and that I durst to believe there was nothing in the Cave that was more frightful than myself" (VII, 205). In the *Serious Reflections*, he notes the old proverb "that every solitary person must be an angel or a devil." Here the same association is implicit, for he moves from the idea that it is the Devil's footprint to the persuasion that it is a "meer Chimera of my own; and that this Foot might be the Print of my own Foot" (VII, 182). If this is true, "I might be truly said to start at my own Shadow," but he is unable to convince himself completely of this solution. He records his terrors when he leaves his shelter as if he were seen by someone else: "But to see with what Fear I went forward, how often I look'd behind me, how I was ready every now and then to lay down my Basket, and run for my Life, it would have made anyone have thought I was haunted with an evil Conscience" (VII,

183). Roxana also thinks of herself as being haunted by her own evil conscience when the daughter named after her reappears in her life.

All these speculations—the chimera, his own foot, his own shadow, and evil conscience, the curious ability to see himself as another would see him—amount to a confusion between the self and the other. The island, which is an extension of himself, has dark areas Robinson has never explored; he is constantly startled by versions of himself, the voice of the parrot, the dying goat. In the same way, the other holds a dimension of himself which Robinson has ignored, a reflection of himself that in his selfishness he has not recognized, and more, the other holds a part of himself in thrall, in an interdependence to which he has been blind. There is also an otherness *in* him. At this point, a brief comparison with an earlier autobiographer might be illuminating. The young Augustine, as he reports in the *Confessions*, was alienated from himself in his acceptance of the Manichean belief that evil was a foreign substance in the soul: "The truth, of course, was that it was all my own self, and my own impiety had divided me against myself."[9] As a result of this blindness toward the true location of himself, he had fragmented and scattered himself among the objects of the world.[10] Similarly, Robinson is unable to account for whatever it is in him that constantly leads him to his own misery and destruction, his "foolish inclination of wandering abroad" (VII, 42), which leads to his scattering of self among the objects of his desire and fear.

Recognition of the nature of this otherness and its relation to himself comes gradually as he is exposed to the other in a series of very strange stages over a number of years: first, the footprint, then human bones—"all my Apprehensions were bury'd in the Thoughts of such a Pitch of inhuman, hellish Brutality, and the Horror of the Degeneracy of Humane Nature" (VII, 191)—and then finally the sight of the cannibals themselves from a distance. He is so horrified by them that he thinks of slaughtering them, making himself God's agent of justice, but he realizes both the presumption of this notion and its dangers for himself, so he decides

to hold himself hidden and apart from them. To attack the cannibals without direct provocation to himself would not only question the design of God's providence for all creatures, but would
also mean that he would be matching their barbarity with his own.
Such an action on his part, he realizes, would be like the cruelty
shown by the Spaniards in America, "a meer Butchery, a bloody
and unatural Piece of Cruelty, unjustifiable either to God or Man;
and such, as for which the very Name of *Spaniard* is reckon'd to
be frightful and terrible to all People of Humanity, or of Christian
Compassion" (VII, 199). The irony of this identification of the
enemy as Spaniards and cannibals, both outside the pale of what is
human, should be apparent, for Crusoe's first friends on his island,
the first human subjects of his "common-wealth," are two cannibals and a Spaniard. He not only will be forced to recognize their
humanity, but also will be driven to acknowledge their barbarity
in himself, or at least in those with whom he identifies.

For the moment, Robinson's two fears of exposure and of
being devoured are now focused on this one representative of a
cannibalistic nature which is ambiguously human. When another
ship wrecks off his island and the entire crew is apparently lost,
Robinson is given a strong sense of the possibilities in his own
condition. One of his fantasies about the fate of these men is that
they might have tried to make the shore in their boat but instead
were carried out by the current "into the great Ocean, where there
was nothing but Misery and Perishing; and that perhaps they
might by this Time think of starving, and of being in a Condition to eat one another" (VII, 216). So, there are circumstances
which could turn shipwrecked sailors like Robinson into cannibals. This possibility is reinforced when he and Friday witness the
treacherous cruelty of the English mutineers—"O Master!" Friday
says, "*You see* English *Mans eat Prisoner as well as* Savage *Mans*"
(VII, 42).

On the other hand, it is the humanity of Friday and later of
the Spaniard that Crusoe comes to know. The discovery of Friday's loyalty and devotion causes Robinson to reflect that even on
savages God had bestowed

The same Powers, the same Reason, the same Affections, the same Sentiments of Kindness and Obligation, the same Passions and Resentments of Wrongs; the same Sense of Gratitude, Sincerity, Fidelity, and all the Capacities of doing Good, and receiving Good, that he has given to us; and that when he pleases to offer to them Occasions of exerting these, they are as ready, nay, more ready to apply them to the right Uses for which they were bestow'd, than we are. (VII, 243)

Robinson must come to see himself in the other and the other in himself. His "social contract," the statement of his subjects' dependence on him, is his covert admission of dependence on them, since it is he who insists on it. He also comes to a greater self-knowledge by seeing himself and his works reflected in their eyes. Earlier he had seen himself from the outside as another, totally unsympathetic and possibly hostile, might have seen him. Now he sees himself from the perspective of a friendly providence in the misery of the English seamen who are about to be beached by the mutineers: "This put me in Mind of the first Time I came on Shore, and began to look about me; How I gave my self over for lost; How wildly I look'd round me: What dreadful Apprehensions I had: And how I lodg'd in the Tree all Night for fear of being devour'd by wild Beasts" (VII, 43). This time he sees his despair in someone else, and from the point of view of their and his deliverance. He reflects that just as he did not know that first night that the storm would drive the ship close enough to land for him to receive supply for his needs, "so these three poor desolate Men knew nothing how certain of Deliverance and Supply they were, how near it was to them, and how effectually and really they were in a Condition of Safety, at the same Time that they thought themselves lost, and their Case desperate" (VIII, 43). Now, more than twenty-five years after Robinson's shipwreck, he knows that the same thing had been true of him, that he had been "in a Condition of Safety" when he had thought himself lost.

IV. The Conversion of Conversion

Crusoe's ability to stand outside himself is related here to his understanding of the providential meaning of experience. That he is able to see the other Englishmen from the standpoint of a providence of which he is now the agent results from his discovery of the plan of his own life much earlier in the book, when he was still alone on the island. This "objectivity" of the self and the corresponding vision of time's plan, transcending the experience of the isolated self, are the consequences of a conversion which in Defoe never seems a single moment, a sudden and total turning which restructures the self for all time, as it is, for example, in Augustine's *Confessions*. Crusoe does experience something like that moment—there are the misunderstood providential warnings, the despair about his isolation, the new warning in the storm, earthquake, and dream, the sickness that is symbolic of death, the discovery of the biblical message, the prayer and conviction of spiritual deliverance. But in time his certainty is dissipated as if by time itself. And each discovery of a new danger, for example, Crusoe's discovery of the footprint, at least temporarily wrecks all certainty.

Conversion is a recurrent need, a revelation followed each time by another lapse, a forgetting that is like an absence, requiring a new dialectical struggle. Crusoe must constantly be brought back to the self discovered in the initial conversion and by that movement freed from self-deception, freed in a sense from self. And this must happen again and again. He will suffer the consequences of the original fall, the restlessness, the "foolish inclination to wander abroad," as long as he lives. He must constantly refound himself in providence, placing all his reliance on his God.

It is just here that resides buried the curious message of the episode of the corn, curious because it never became completely explicit and because it holds great meaning for Crusoe's egoism. When the corn sprouts first appeared, Robinson thought them miraculous, a divine suspension of the laws of nature for his benefit. When he remembered that he had shaken out a bag of chicken feed in the place where the barley and rice were growing, "The

Wonder began to cease; and I must confess, my religious Thankfulness on God's Providence began to abate too upon the Discovering that this was nothing but what was common" (VII, 89–90). In the perspective of the narration, Robinson's judgment on the vacillations is that

> I ought to have been as thankful for so strange and unforeseen Providence, as if it had been miraculous; for it was really the Work of Providence as to me, that should order or appoint, that 10 or 12 Grains of Corn should remain unspoil'd (when the Rats had destroy'd all the rest), as if it had been dropt from Heaven; as also, that I should throw it out in that particular Place where it being in the Shade of a high Rock, it sprang up immediately; whereas, if I had thrown it anywhere else, at that Time, it had been burnt up and destroy'd. (VII, 90)

Critics who, like Robinson, attribute spiritual significance to his experience regard the episode as symbolic of the "seeds" of Grace. In this context of Robinson's egoistic blindness, against which the episode renders judgment, the implications of the passage seem to be more probing. Surely the scriptural reference is to John 12: 24–25: "Except a corn of wheat fall into the ground and die, it abideth alone: but if it die, it bringeth forth much fruit. He that loveth his life shall lose it; and he that hateth his life in his world shall keep it unto life eternal." Robinson must die to himself and place all his reliance on God.

Radical individualism in all its isolated inwardness was implicit in Christianity from its beginning, in its emphasis on the brotherhood of all men, its message explicitly cut across the limits of family, tribe, or nation. One expression of the subjectivist implications of Christianity was in the intense self-exploration of Augustine's *Confessions*, a work that informs Defoe's fictional project. The implications of this individualism were worked out in the Renaissance and in a more radical way in the Reformation, of whose Puritan strain Robinson is a well-known representative. Yet Christianity was also provided with this antidote to the narcissism that threatened it—the notion of the symbolic death of the self. Robinson's resistance to God's call manifested itself in one way in his obsessive fear of the loss or death of self involved in being "swallowed up" or devoured by his beginnings, by the unformed chaos of the sea, by the other. Robinson does undergo a sickness unto death, literally and figuratively, a symbolic death of the self from which he emerges with a clearer if temporary understanding of God's plan for him. And as the text from John suggests, and as it was for Augustine, in his sacrifice of self Robinson is given himself for the first time.

The nature of this gift is expressed more explicitly in Moll's conversion in Newgate. Her experience is at first wayward fluctuation between repentance and selfishness. When she discovers that her Lancashire husband is bound to be hanged for a highwayman, she is so overwhelmed by grief for him and by reflections on her own previous life that "in a Word, I was perfectly chang'd, and become another Body" (II, 107). But this transformation is a return to self: "The wretched Boldness of Spirit, which I had acquired, abated, and conscious Guilt began to flow in my Mind: In short, I began to think, and to think indeed is one real Advance from Hell to Heaven; all that harden'd State and Temper of Soul, which I said so much of before, is but a Deprivation of Thought; he that is restor'd to his Thinking, is restor'd to himself" (II, 107). Inasmuch as she is still concerned about her own fate, she is still selfish, and the Moll who narrates doubts the sincerity of her repentance at this point. Finally, when she receives the condemnation of this court it is "a Sentence to me like Death itself" (II, 112), and she feels "real Signs of Repentance" (II, 113). Like Augustine and Robinson, she sees the things of this life in a new way: "I now began to look back upon my past Life with abhorrence, and having a kind of View into the other Side of Time, the Things of Life, as I believe they do with every Body at such a Time, began to look with a different Aspect, and quite another Shape, than they did before" (II, 113).

In his conversion, Augustine is also given a "view into the other side of time." He also is transformed into "another body," which paradoxically is a matter of being "restored to himself." Restored to himself first in this sense, as he says: "O Lord, you were turning me around to look at myself. For I had placed myself behind my own back, refusing to see myself. You were setting me before my own eyes so that I could see how sordid I was, how deformed and squalid, how tainted with ulcers and sores" (169). But he is also restored to himself in a larger sense. Augustine's last doubts before giving himself over to God were his doubts concerning his ability to accept continence. For this, he must throw himself on God's strength, not try to rely on his own. By being made capable of continence by God, Augustine is given himself, for as he explains: "By continence we are made as one and regain that unity of self which we lost by falling apart in the search for a variety of pleasures" (233).

The similarities between Defoe's fictional memoirs, particularly Robinson's, and their ultimate model, Augustine's *Confessions*, are striking, but their differences are of signal importance. Both Augustine and Robinson have relied on themselves, on their own strength and reason, in important though differing ways. Each experienced himself initially as incomplete. The early life of each was a wandering, yet for each every erring step was guided by Providence, bringing him to the moment of salvation. To each the command of God comes by discovery of a chance word in a *Sortes Biblicae*. Each is brought by the symbolic death of conversion to an understanding of time and to a self-knowledge, the "proof" of which lies in the act of confession or narration.

For Defoe, however, the gift of self is as "symbolic" as the sacrificial death. Self will continue to reassert itself and be lost consequently in distraction. For it is Defoe's insight that the essential characteristic of a symbolic death is that it is only symbolic and must be repeated endlessly. All solutions in this life are symbolic, perhaps "figural" is a better word, and fallen man is never free of the consequences of Adam's sin until he suffers its original punishment, actual death. If he can be "justified" only by God, the promise figured by Providence can be fulfilled only in Heaven. From this point of view, providence is sight cast forward, into the not yet. Is it too commonplace to say that modern realism is born in the split between the symbolic and the actual, in the despair over the real efficacy of the symbolic?

One consequence is that there is a necessary discrepancy between the allegorical truth and the fact of the story. For example, Tom Jones calls "father" a man named Allworthy, who is squire of Paradise Hall, from which he evicts Tom for his wrongdoing. But Allworthy is not omniscient, and Tom has not done what he has been accused of. Instead he is a victim of deceit, treachery, and misunderstanding—certainly no orthodox allegory of man's fall. Moreover, in the course of the novel Tom must acquire worldly wisdom and aspires to Sophia, who is not (at least in this novel) wise. Similarly, Richardson's Clarissa disobeys an inexplicable demand of her father and is seduced from her garden by the serpent-like Lovelace. Of course, in this case, the demand of the father is not only inexplicable, it is also patently unjust, and Clarissa runs away with Lovelace to escape that injustice. The pattern is there, however, but from this point of view the realistic story, life in this world, is an incomplete, distorted shadow of its spiritual truth. Hence the traditional dissatisfaction with the "allegory" of *Robinson Crusoe*. The point is not that these writers tried and failed to write novelistic allegories, but that life could not be reduced or raised to a spiritual meaning.

The experiences of both Augustine and Robinson find their clear focus against a scriptural and sacred background. For example, the pear tree of Augustine's adolescence, the garden where his struggle with salvation takes place, and the fig tree under which he is saved are types of Adam's tree of forbidden fruit, the garden of Gethsemane, and Christ's "tree" or cross under which man is redeemed. Robinson's story is the story of Jonah and of the Prodigal Son. But it is the "real" Augustine who is offered in the *Confessions* by way of these stories, the real Augustine purged of the accidents of a purely personal life and revealed in the figural patterns of the Scriptures. On the other hand, Robinson is not a real person—the fact of his memoirs is their factitiousness. If, as Robinson insinuates in his *Serious Reflections*, his story is only allegorically true, then either it is true (as some have thought) of Defoe's own life, or its truth is offered as the general truth of everyman's life. If it is Defoe's truth, then the accidents of his own life are given in what is *essentially* true in Robinson's adventures. If it is a general truth, then another reversal has taken place, for this universal essence is offered as the *actuality* of a very eccentric individual life. Symbol and fact are united in Augustine's *Confessions*, but forever divided in Robinson's.

This split is demonstrated in a striking way when Robinson appears to the English mutineers "as another Person": "So that as we never suffered them to see me a Governour, so I now appear'd as another Person, and spoke of the Governour, the Garrison, the Castle, and the like, upon all Occasions" (VIII, 65). Here it is his metaphoric or spiritual condition (as "governor" of the island, "viceroy to the King of all the earth" [*Serious Reflections*, 179]), which is held aside, while his disguise, the *other* person he becomes, is his *actuality*, in all the fantastic garb of an eccentricity which has survived almost thirty years of isolation. His disguise is almost like the lies of Odysseus—more plausible than the fantastic adventures he has undergone in the *Odyssey*. I have said that the split is between the symbolic-essential and the accidental-actual, but here the value of these poles has been reversed and the actual has become "other" than the truth. The split in Robinson's being in this passage is also, and not incidentally, the same as the split between the bourgeois *legal person* and the unique individual.

Through his conversion Augustine gains both the true order of life and his true self—one and the same thing in confession, which is the *full* giving of self in speech whose truth is guaranteed by the presence of the Divine omniscient Other. The "real" self of Defoe's various "memoirs," however, is a fictive self. Defoe's confessions are not *his* confessions at all. The pattern of Christian truth has become the design of a lie masked as actuality, the plot of a novel. The symbolic death of the Christian pattern has become truly symbolic on another level, in as much as even actual death in fiction is still a symbolic death. And the symbolic deaths of Robinson's or Moll's conversions are the doubly symbolic deaths of surrogate selves.

The full implications of this death by proxy are revealed in the story of Roxana, where the death is carried a step more distant and conversion is either impossible or no longer necessary. Roxana makes her escape into the curious oblivion of the end of that book disguised by the clothes and sanctimonious speech of a Quaker, symbols of a conversion she cannot attain. The split in Roxana, indicated by disguise, is more complicated than Robinson's self-division. She appears as the self she would like to be (her "spiritual truth") at the same time she is confronted by her past self projected onto the form of her daughter, who bears Roxana's true name, whom she deserted as a child, and who later appeared again as her servant at the moment she became the notorious Roxana. Now, it is this poor scapegoat of a daughter, the alter ego of a fictional character, yet the only truly individualized "other" of any of Defoe's fictions, who is made to suffer a sacrificial death for which Roxana will never be forgiven.

The death is brought about in a way that is curious, in light of the dialectic between self and other in Defoe's novels. The witness to Roxana's first crime against morality was her servant Amy. Roxana felt compelled to force Amy to sleep with her seducer: "As I thought myself a Whore, I cannot say but that it was something design'd in my Thoughts, that my Maid should be a Whore too, and should not reproach me with it" (47). As witness to her crime, Amy would become the dangerous other. Seducers or seducees never seem to have enough self-consciousness to appear as threats to the self in Defoe. The witness is the dangerous other. Roxana, by watching Amy's seduction by the same man who has ruined her, has rendered Amy "safe." She has made her an accomplice, an adjunct to her own will. When, at the end of the book, Amy does away with the daughter by some means that Roxana can't bear to think about, Amy has become like an element of Roxana's personality capable of acting autonomously (somewhat like the daughter herself). That Amy is enacting Roxana's secret will is proved by Roxana's overwhelming sense of guilt. The book ends in the uncertainty of the unspeakable. It is either the most resolved or the most unresolvable of all the dialectical struggles between self and other in Defoe's fiction.

What is certain is that the symbolic death has been moved a

step farther away from the "I" who narrated all of Defoe's books. The conversion has disappeared completely, although Roxana, beyond her Quaker costume, does become another person. Near the beginning of her account of her life, but speaking from the obscurity into which she disappears at the end, Roxana says: "Being to give my own Character, I must be excus'd to give it as impartially as possible, and as if I was speaking of another body" (6). What has replaced the conversion is the act of narration itself.

And what can be said of Defoe? In the Preface to *Roxana*, he describes himself as the "Relator" who will "speak" the words of the Beautiful Lady. Unable to give a true account of the self, he is doomed to speak the words of "another-body" as if they were his own, putting on the disguise of one fictive self after another.

V. Providence and Writing: A Natural Habitation

When Robinson began to ponder the mystery of the footprint found on the beach, he discovered that he could not be certain that he had not left the print himself. Like the mystery of causality itself, the footprint is a trace of an intentional act seen from the outside: "Again, I consider'd also that I could by no Means tell for certain where I had trod, and where I had not; and that if at last this was only the Print of my own Foot, I had play'd the Part of those Fools, who strive to make stories of Spectres, and Apparitions; and then are frighted at them more than any body" (VII, 182). The enigmatic footprint is like a ghost story, a genre most interesting to Defoe, whose power is great enough to deceive even its own teller. The footprint then is similar to a myth, told by an individual who yet cannot claim authorship, like the dream separated from its source by disavowal. In short, the footprint is a figure for the book of Robinson's adventures. Did Robinson leave the footprint, or was it left by the threatening other? Are the adventures authored by Defoe who disavowed them, by the Robinson who signed them, or by the other in whose constant presence they are structured and who is their destination?

Perhaps there is already on Defoe's part a glimmer of that suspicion of the concept of the unified and identifiable "subject" with which it has been seen by later thinkers, particularly by Nietzsche and Freud and more recently by Derrida and others. For Defoe's project seems to have involved the creation of more or less autonomous voices, themselves without a center, that is to say, irredeemably eccentric voices. Or, rather, voices whose center is a felt lack of center, the absence of which could be explained by the insertion of the myth of fallen man, yet voices created without the distance or structure of a consistent irony, a fact that has troubled the criticism of Defoe's books. Voices calculating a world of facts but who are themselves fictions after all: books whose ambiguity is deep, thorough, and finally unresolvable.

The problem of Defoe criticism is well stated by the title of an early twentieth-century study, William Trent's *Daniel Defoe: How to Know Him.* My strategy has been to chip away at the hard flint of that ultimately unanswerable question in the hope that the sparks will illuminate, if only slightly, the surrounding terrain.

How can Robinson tell for certain where "I had trod and where I had not"? Time, the shifting sand on the beach, how indeed can they afford a true history or a stable identity to a subjectivity so isolated, to a subject so elusive? An heir of Adam, Robinson has lost the opportunity of "sensibly tasting the sweet of living, without the bitter" offered by his father at the beginning of the book. He can only come to knowledge dialectically, by contraries. He can only know good, his good, by experience of evil. Robinson's obsession with reason as *ratio*, measurement, his sometimes comical "accounting" point not only to his empiricism but also to the curse of fallen man. All evaluations of his condition are relative. When he considers himself ruined, he must acknowledge that there are others who are worse, just as in the beginning when his father tried to convince him he was set for life, he thought he could become better. In order to account for his condition after the shipwreck, he *has* to draw up the famous profit and loss sheet, the spiritual bookkeeping for which he (and Defoe with him) has been so often derided. The curiosity of this debit-credit sheet lies in its slipperiness. One *fact* is not registered against another. The facts are the same on both sides of the sheet; each side merely interprets the fact in a different way. There are no true alternatives present. Instead of representing Robinson's in-genuous calculation, the sheet does give a true account of the flux of moods, moods considered as facts, the dizzying back and forth of a subjectivity deprived of an external gauge of truth.

Robinson's journal itself is another form of this spiritual bookkeeping. If one cannot gauge the meaning or portent of each moment, perhaps the pattern formed over longer periods of time would reveal the truth. Such an accounting might provide a true profit and loss tally of the spirit. Crusoe's journal not only docu-ments his recall of day-to-day events as he recounts them more than thirty years later, it also represents an attempt to give the shifting moments of a subjective time something like a spatial ordering in the same way that he carves notches into a post to mark each day he is on the island. The journal is an attempt to define a situation by ordering the present as it becomes the past. Writing also means to Robinson a deliverance from the agoniz-ing and confusing impact from momentary impressions about his condition: "I now began to consider seriously my Condition, and the Circumstance I was reduc'd to, and I drew up the State of my Affairs in Writing, not so much to leave them to any that were to come after me, for I was like to have but few Heirs, as to de-liver my Thoughts from daily poring upon them, and afflicting my Mind" (VII, 74).

Robinson wants what Sartre's Roquentin, one of his heirs, desires: "I wanted the moments of my life to follow and order themselves like those of a life remembered. You might as well try and catch time by the tail."[11] Crusoe's journal, like the greater ac-count of which it is a part, is an attempt to do precisely that—catch time by the tail. The events of each day are recorded into the journal, already culled and selected, already abolished by the past tense of language and presented to us, a legacy to heirs that the Crusoe *living* each moment could not expect. We can never, however, get close to the lived moment, and neither can Robinson capture it. Even the journal shows signs of a later editing, at the time of the principal narration, from the perspective of a story already closed. Moreover, such a perspective inheres in the narrative past tense. As Roquentin observes, "You have started at the end . . . and the story goes on in the reverse: instants have stopped piling themselves in a lighthearted way one on top of the other, they are snapped up by the end of the story which draws them and each one of them in turn, draws out the preceding instant" (57–58). The whole book is caught up on a past tense suggesting an end which renders significant each sentence.

Crusoe's story, however, goes backward in more obvious senses than that meant by Roquentin and Sartre. We are given no fewer than four accounts of Robinson's first day on the island, each differing in some small detail: the main account in Robinson's narrative, *two* journal accounts, and finally when Robinson relives his plight as he watches the English mutineers and their victims. First, we have the account in the chronological course of Crusoe's narrative, written years later, long after even his return from the island to civilization.

The second version is composed at the same time. This is the journal that might have been, if he had started it when he first landed on the island, and it curiously is the one most different, although it is ostensibly contemporaneous with the narration of the book. The reason that he did not begin the journal the first days was that he was too busy then making himself secure, but also that he was "in too much discomposure of mind, and my journal would have been full of many dull things." The writing of the journal, then, is the result of the *composition* of his mind, and although it has precedence in time over the other two versions, it is still separated from the event by an extensive period of time. Robinson doesn't begin it until he is more or less settled on the island — perhaps six weeks after the shipwreck, after he finished the table and chair, probably November 12, according to the journal itself.

The differences between these accounts of his first days, mainly concerning whether he wept with joy or with terror, despair or thanksgiving, whether he slept on the ground or in a tree, are less significant than the fact that there *are* differences. What are we to make of this confusion, other than to see it as an emphasis on the elusiveness of even the facts of this narrative and an admission of an irreparable tear between the written account and the naked, lived moment? The journal—trace of the event—is vacant like the footprint. In fact, it is marked by a double absence. The writing of the account relieves Robinson from the pain and confusion of experiencing—"to deliver my thoughts from daily poring upon them, and afflicting my mind." The journal serves the same purpose. And it is also removed from the event. It objectifies and orders both Robinson's thoughts and his daily experiences.

The gap cannot be closed. Narrative language removes the contingency and absurd inconsequence of the lived moment by abstracting that moment from the field of open possibility and directing it toward a certain outcome which will define it and give it significance. As Roquentin comments,

"It was night, the street was deserted." The phrase is cast out negligently, it seems superfluous; but we do not let ourselves be caught and we put it aside: this is a piece of information whose value we shall subsequently appreciate. And we feel that the hero has lived all the details of this night like annunciations, promises, or even that he lived only those that were promises, blind and deaf to all that did not herald adventure. (58)

Annunciations, promises, and, one might add, portents and warnings—for that is precisely the way Crusoe lives, or rather re-lives in his narrative, each event of his experience. What in the already realized end guarantees the significance of each event is identical with the ordering of written narrative and the opposite of the subjective flux of the lived moment—the discovery of God's plot, His Providence. The point of view of narrative is precisely a providence. In God's plan, Robinson's end *is* in his beginning— each step along the way is either a promise or a warning, but always an annunciation of a divine structure which exists outside of time, but which operates in and through time. Sartre's argument with narrative is that the foundation of the passing moment in narrative language bestows on it a privilege, robes it with a destiny, that is altogether false to experience, but Robinson's discovery of a special providence saves the moment, placing on each moment a heavy burden of significance.

Providence not only underwrites Robinson's narrative, it is also discovered by means of the writing of the journal. The subject caught in the flow of time is blind to the providential meaning of his experience. Crusoe suffers the flickering onrush of momentary sensations and is driven by selfish appetites and fears that change as rapidly as circumstances change. "Everything revolves in our minds by innumerable circular motions, all centering in ourselves" (*Serious Reflections*, 2). "And by what secret differing Springs are the Affections hurry'd about as differing Circumstances present! To Day we love what to Morrow we hate; to Day we seek what to Morrow we shun; to Day we desire what to Morrow we fear; nay even tremble at the Apprehensions of" (*Robinson Crusoe*, VII, 180).

Though Crusoe is given many warnings, many chances for repentance, as soon as the warning danger has passed, so dissolve Robinson's resolutions and promises. The Defoe self in isolation is the self of Hobbesian sensationalism. The order revealed one moment is obliterated by the new sensations crowding in the next. It is the function of narrative, with its double perspective, to remember.

By means of his journal, Robinson discovers the startling concurrence of his "fortunate and fatal days":

as long as it [the ink] lasted, I made use of it to minute down the Days of the Month on which any remarkable Thing happened to me, and first by casting up Times past: I remember that there was a strange Concurrence of Days, in the various Providences which befel me; and which, if I had been superstitiously inclin'd to observe Days as Fatal or Fortunate, I might have had Reason to have look'd upon with a great deal of Curiosity.

First, I had observed, that the same Day that I broke away from my Father and my Friends, and ran away to *Hull*, in order to go to Sea; the same Day afterwards I was taken by the *Sallee* Man of War, and made a Slave.

The same Day of the Year that I escaped out of the Wreck of that Ship in *Yarmouth* Roads, that same Day—Years afterwards I made my escape from *Sallee* in the boat.

The same Day of the Year I was born on (*viz.*) the 30th of *September*, that same Day, I had my Life so saved 26 Years after, when I was cast on Shore in this Island, so that my wicked Life, and my solitary Life begun both on a Day. (VII, 153–54)

Later, when Robinson leaves the Island of Despair, he is "deliver'd from this second Captivity, the same Day of the Month, that I first made my Escape in the *Barco-Longo*, from among the *Moors of Sallee*" (VIII, 74). Robinson will justify our belief in such amazing coincidences by detailing examples in his essay on Providence from the long tradition of such concurrences, beginning with the Scriptures and continuing into modern political history. The scriptural example alone marks the meaning of this pattern in Robinson's life. It is in Exodus 12: 41–42 and has to do with the children of Israel leaving their exile and imprisonment in Egypt the same day of the year, 430 years after they entered into it. Robinson's isolation has also been an exile and imprisonment, but the justification has a larger meaning, as do all the scriptural parallels. Robinson's exile from himself and from the truth has been a type of the exile of the chosen people and of everyman, but as the real history of a man, as it is presented, it represents a figural truth. In the Preface to his *Serious Reflections*, when he admits the story is allegorical, Robinson does not give up the claim to its authenticity. He simply claims to have "displaced" its literal truth:

All these reflections are just history of a state of forced confinement, which in my real history is represented by a confined retreat in an island; and it is as reasonable to represent one kind of imprisonment by another, as it is to represent anything that really exists by that which exists not. The story of my fright with something on my bed was word for word a history of what happened, and indeed all those things received very little alteration, except what necessarily attends removing the scene from one place to another. (xii)

One is reminded that among the earliest meanings of *figura* was its usage in rhetoric to conceal the truth (in a figure of speech).[12] It usually had to do with suggesting without actually expressing a truth which for political or tactical reasons, or

simply for effect, could not be expressed openly. This was precisely
Defoe's purpose.

Any discussion of the question necessarily collapses into the
ambiguity Defoe left surrounding it.[13] No sooner are we satisfied
with his admission of allegorical truth in the Preface to Robinson's
Serious Reflections than we discover that among the reflections it
prefaces is "An Essay upon Honesty" and another on "the Immorality of Conversation," which contains a section about "Talk-
ing Falsely." No oversight on Defoe's part. In case we miss the
point, he at first distinguished from the lying tales he is attacking
such "historical parables" as those in the Holy Scripture, *Pilgrim's
Progress*, or, "in a word, the adventures of your fugitive friend,
'Robinson Crusoe'" (101). But then he makes the standard Puritan
attack on realistic fiction: any fiction that offers itself as historical
truth is a dangerous and damning lie. Lest we dismiss the discrepancy as mere ingenuousness on the part of Defoe, he adds the
following disclaimer: "If any man object here that the preceding
volumes of this work seem to be hereby condemned, and the history which I have therein published of myself censured, I demand
in justice such objector stay his censure till he sees the end of the
scene, when all that mystery shall discover itself, and I doubt not
but the work shall abundantly justify the design, and the design
abundantly justify the work" (103). Does that settle the issue?

Ambiguity aside, it is possible to say that, while Defoe is
impersonating Robinson Crusoe, he is also impersonating on
another level Providence itself. Just as the double vision made possible by the Christian conversion is replaced by the double vision
of narration, the structure of narration has stood in place of providence.

It is no accident, and may in fact be "the end of the scene"
Robinson alluded to earlier, that the last story he tells in his *Serious Reflections* concerns a young man who speaks to an atheist in
the voice of a mutual friend and is taken instead for the voice of a
spirit, messenger of God and medium of His Providence, by the
disbeliever who is thereby saved.

Defoe's fortress is complete, constructed according to the

laws of nature and concealing the plot of Providence. It is a natural habitation, in which, like Robinson, Defoe can live in the open but unseen and unmolested by devouring eyes. In his essay on "Solitude" Robinson countered the voluntary withdrawal into the desert wilderness of the religious hermit by the voluntary exile in the midst of society by means of something like disguise. Peaceful solitude

> would every way as well be supplied by removing from a place where a man is known to a place where he is not known, and there accustom himself to a retired life, making no new acquaintances, and only making the use of mankind which I have already spoken of, namely, for convenience and supply of necessary food; and I think of the two that such a man, or a man so retired, may have more opportunity to be an entire recluse, and may enjoy more real solitude than a man in a desert. (13–14)

Defoe's fiction has provided him with such a hermitage.

Many novelists who followed Defoe were strangers in a strange land and found means of both concealing and exposing themselves in their novels. Pseudonymity and anonymity haunt the novel throughout the eighteenth and nineteenth centuries. Perhaps these novelists, too, confronted the necessity of becoming other persons in their narrators. There was Richardson's "editorship," for example, and while Jane Austen's and George Eliot's concealment of their names was perhaps only conventional for lady writers, Stendhal's need for pseudonyms was obsessional. Scott, already a famous author, concealed himself behind the tag of "the author of *Waverley*" and became the most visible "great unknown" of his day. Defoe's discoveries about the nature of narrative and its plots made the novel an apt genre for a society of isolated and mutually suspicious individuals.

3

Tom Jones:
The "Bastard" of History

"And is a Wench having a Bastard all your News, Doctor?" cries
Western. "I thought it might have been some public Matter, something about the Nation." "I am afraid it is too common, indeed,"
answered the Parson, "but I thought the whole story all together
deserved commemorating. As to National Matters, your Worship
knows them best. My Concerns extend no farther than my own
Parish."

—*Tom Jones*

Let us be clear about this. Every effect obviously has its cause,
which can be retraced from cause to cause into the abyss of eternity;
but every cause does not have its effect to the end of time. I admit
that all events are produced by one another. If the past gives birth
to the present, the present gives birth to the future. All things have
fathers, but not all things have children. This is exactly like a genealogical tree: we know that every house goes back to Adam, but
plenty of people died without posterity.
There is a genealogical tree of this world's events.

—Voltaire, *Philosophical Dictionary*

An Hermaphrodite, may be Heir according to the Prevalency of the
Sex. Bastards, Monsters, that have not human Shape, Aliens . . . cannot be Heirs.

—Wood, *Institute of the Laws of England*

I

NO ONE SEEMS EVER TO HAVE BEEN literal-minded enough to
quibble with the most obviously fictional element of the titles
of Henry Fielding's two novels—*The History of the Adventures of
Joseph Andrews* [etc.] and *The History of Tom Jones, a Foundling.*[1]

Before addressing larger problems of the relationship of fiction to truth (however it is defined), one might note the curious fact that, even within their own respective systems of reference, the titles are superficially fictional or fictitious—that is to say, they are erroneous. What the reader learns along with the protagonists at the unraveling of the narrative riddle is, among other things, the answer to a riddle not even suspected. Joseph Andrews's name is not properly Andrews, and Tom's name should not be Jones. On the other hand, if the novels' titles gave the "true" names of their protagonists, the "story" would have been "spoiled"—another indication of the requirements of "fiction." In neither case does the narrator or Fielding call attention to those rather obvious facts. Since Bridget Allworthy, not Jenny Jones, proves to be Tom's mother, presumably he could take that name when he is restored to Allworthy. Joseph is not an Andrews but a Wilson. He had been kidnapped by the gypsies and substituted for the Andrewses' own child, Fanny. That this is so might perhaps be allegorized as part of the shifting and substitutional nature of the relationship between Fielding's text and Richardson's. In the second case, the question of the suitability of the hero's name is overshadowed by a number of other thematic recoveries at the end and by what appears to be an even larger sleight of hand on Fielding's part. Everyone—and that presumably includes the reader—is so relieved to discover that Tom will not be hanged, so shocked and then relieved that he has committed and then not committed incest, so gratified that as Allworthy's nephew he can substitute for the repugnant Blifil as Allworthy's heir and Sophia's husband, that not only is the question of the name made trivial, but a more significant problem is forgotten. Everyone is so excited by the discovery of Tom's good birth that they forget it is still a bad birth—that is, illegitimate. He remains a bastard, and there is a question whether as such, by English law, he can inherit anything.

The novel itself has anticipated that question early on, when Captain Blifil, who objects to the idea that his newborn son will be raised together with Tom, reminds Allworthy that " 'tho the

Law did not positively allow the destroying of such base-born
Children, yet it held them to be the Children of no body; that
the Church considered them as the Children of no body; and that
at the best, they ought to be brought up to the lowest and vil-
est offices of the Commonwealth'" (II, ii, 79). Martin Battestin
underlines the issue by his gloss of this passage from a contemporary law book,[2] although he does not refer again to the issue
at the point of the revelation of Tom's true parentage, when his
prospects of inheritance become presumably real: "A *Bastard* is he
that is born out of Marriage. He shall never inherit or be Heir to
any one. He cannot be of kin to any one. For in Law he is *Quasi
nullius Filius*, and no Man's issue." Blackstone's slightly later *Commentaries* extends this gloss, while at the same time testifying to
the long tradition of the prohibition before and after Fielding:

> I proceed next to the rights and incapacities which appertain to a bastard.
> The rights are very few, being only such as he can *acquire* . . . for he can
> inherit nothing, being looked upon as the son of nobody . . . and some-
> times called *filius nullius*, sometimes *filius populi*. . . . Yet he may gain a
> sir-name by reputation . . . though he has none by inheritance. . . . The
> incapacity of a bastard consists primarily in this, that he cannot be heir
> to any one, neither can he have heirs, but of his own body . . . for, being
> *nullius filius*, he is therefore of kin to nobody, and has no ancestor from
> whom any inheritable blood can be derived. . . . in all other respects, there
> is no distinction between a bastard and another man. And really any other
> distinction but that of not inheriting, which civil policy renders neces-
> sary, would, with regard to the innocent offspring of his parents' crimes,
> be odious, unjust, and cruel to the last degree: and yet the civil law, so
> boasted of for its equitable decisions, made bastards, in some cases, in-
> capable even of a gift from their parents. A bastard may, lastly, be made
> legitimate, and capable of inheriting, by the transcendent power of an act
> of parliament, and not otherwise . . . as was done in the case of John of
> Gaunt's bastard children, by a statute of Richard the Second.[3]

One might note in passing that, while Allworthy's caveat
against punishing the child for the sins of the parent is stated as a
principle in the commentary of the law, the bar, essential "to civil
policy," against the bastard's inheritance remains unaltered.

That Tom can be thought of as *filius nullius*—son of no one—

or *filius populi*—son of the people—would seem to support the now common notion of Tom as a novelized version of the allegorical Everyman. That he is at once son of no one and son of everyone also makes him an appropriate "generic" emblem for Fielding's text.

Whatever the means it is assumed that Allworthy will take to make good his legacy to Tom, beyond recourse to "the transcendent power of an act of parliament," the problem is stated here and later affirmed by the lawyer Dowing (XII, x, 659), but the solution is never specified in the novel. Later, I will try to demonstrate the thematic significance of the fact that Tom probably cannot inherit Allworthy's estate, but can only receive it by some means such as a deed in trust.[4]

My purpose in raising this issue here is simply to underline a rather basic pattern of genealogical disturbance—for Tom (at the end of his story as well as at the beginning) in the strong language of the law "cannot be heir to any one, neither can he have heirs," he is "kin of nobody, and has no ancestor from which an inheritable blood can be derived." He descends from no one.

Except the mother. A third genealogical aberration is introduced late in both *Joseph Andrews* and *Tom Jones* in the form of an "accident," without apparent narrative or thematic necessity—incest. That it can be a question apparently derives from the fact that identity is or becomes problematical in each novel. Joseph is comfortable in his own identity until he discovers that Fanny, his stay against the various temptations to which his sister Pamela has succumbed, may in fact also be his sister. The moment of potential but not actual incest marks the point at which Fielding's novel, which has begun almost as a parasite to Richardson's, a corrective parody and therefore secondary, derivative, and supplemental, disavows that relationship and discovers and asserts its own originality. The ambivalence of textual reference, however, remains in the title.

In *Tom Jones* the transgression is purportedly actual, though just as quickly disproved, but it also marks a fold in which a disorder of identity is stabilized. In both cases, transgression of the incest taboo at once marks a limit to possible narrative drift and serves as a threshold to the revelation of a proper name. It is literally the point of no recuperation. More obviously in the case of *Tom Jones*, it is the test of the limits of a thematic which I will try to make explicit in the following pages, for if Tom derives from no one, incest could never be a problem. While generically the issue underlines the distinction between tragedy and comedy in Fielding's "new species of writing,"[5] it also provides the possibility of closure and return in Tom's narrative function as literally a floating signifier. More simply, perhaps, it suggests the most obvious and ultimate genealogical aberration.

II

What are the implications of this pattern, and what is its bearing on other patterns, themes, and concerns in Fielding's novels? To try to answer this question is to begin to see one relationship of Fielding's work to problems of history and historiography suggested by his titles for these novels as "histories." The pattern of genealogical disturbance raises into question an assumption about the ordering of narrative, history, and society—an assumption of great resonance in the eighteenth century, but by no means restricted to it, and of particular relevance to the immediate historical situation of the 1745 Jacobite Rebellion as the context in which Fielding places the novel *Tom Jones*.

Biological or genetic patterns, genealogical or dynastic sequences, are still conventional metaphoric ways of thinking about causal relationships in both history and narrative, of referring any event or representation to a prior event or reality or "author," whatever is considered as standing outside and before it. The causal relationship between event and subsequent event, between event and textual representation, between text and text, or between writer and text, is understood by means of an assumed analogy with the sexual generation of offspring by parents. Also implied by the metaphor is that the produced event, text, or person will *inherit* its own derived power or "authority" to produce, however secondary, belated, or supplementary that authority. Not only, then, is it assumed that "events have events as women do babies," as Robert Nisbet has put it,[6] or that "the past gives birth to the present," in Voltaire's words.[7] Not only would history take the form of genealogy, event begetting event in a continuous, linear, and dynastically descending succession, but also the authority of a given text, law, son, or sovereign would be traceable back to an originating authority or act, a first cause, which would guarantee and regulate the continuity, legality, fittingness, and order of the entire chain and any link in it. Ultimately, the metaphor would ground itself in the metaphysical assumption of the authority (in all its senses) of the origin over what it originates. In one form or another, any theory of mimesis, but particularly the neo-classical theory, would refer to these assumptions, which also govern the notion of sequence in conventional narrative, fictional or historical.

In recent years, a good deal of contemporary criticism has begun to examine the recurrence and implications of this metaphorical pattern,[8] but any glance at eighteenth-century texts will discover a peculiarly widespread self-conscious use or questioning of genealogical patterns within a variety of areas of discourse. One thinks of Vico's history, on the one hand, and Sterne's *Tristram Shandy*, on the other. The metaphoric cluster, however, also had a very active life in English political debate and in the relationship between that debate and an emergent concern with national history that incidentally stimulated the emergence of history as a discipline. *Tom Jones* establishes itself at the intersection of these various lines. It places itself (and the meaning of this placing has always presented a problem for its interpretation, on the outskirts of the events of the 1745 Rebellion in England) and was itself, in a sense, the culmination of a variety of texts—pamphlets, newspapers—with which Fielding intervened in the political situation surrounding the Rebellion.

In 1745, the last of the Stuarts, the "Young Pretender" Charles Edward, landed in Scotland and, with mobilized Highlanders, the

uncertain support of the French, and the expectation of rousing
Jacobite sympathies in disaffected English "country" Tories and
Whigs, moved south toward London. Charles's claim to the
throne was based on his direct descent and hereditary right from
the last Stuart King, James II, unseated in the Glorious Revolution of 1688. His claim for restoration was in defiance of the Bill
of Rights and the Act of Settlement, documents which affirmed
the supremacy of Parliament over the monarch, who held his authority in trust, and the Protestant succession of a more distant
line of the Stuarts, the house of Hanover.

The 1745 Rebellion, not irrelevantly a moment in the larger
and complex series of European wars of succession, was the occasion of a resurfacing of issues surrounding the sovereignty of king
and Parliament fought out in the seventeenth century, two principal texts of which were the Royalist Robert Filmer's *Patriarcha*,
itself already enjoying a somewhat anachronistic posthumous life
in the late seventeenth century, and John Locke's answer to it in
his *Two Treatises of Civil Government*. Filmer stressed the origin of
the Stuart claim in the scriptural authority of God's gift of dominion to Adam—the claim of divine right—and in the descent of that
right to modern kings in genealogical succession—the absolute
authority of the father in natural law descending to the eldest son.
Locke's part in the destruction of both of those notions, with his
contractual origin of sovereignty based on reason, is well known.
Most of the elements of the genealogical analogy I've discussed
above enter into Filmer's and later Jacobite arguments.[9]

The same argument had been waged for more than a hundred years on another level, but still with political implications
and motives, in the battle of the lawyers, antiquarians, and party
historians concerning the nature and immemorial origins of the
constitution. It is possible to show that what started in the seventeenth century as research into the origins of common law or,
in fact, into its lack of origins—that is to say the idea that English common law and hence the constitution were immemorial,
had always been what they were then—modulated into the political argument that Parliament, and particularly Commons, was the

immemorial guardian of that law and that no one—no king—had prior authority. It was assumed that if any king had instituted the law or had called Parliament, both the law and Parliament would continue to be subject to the king. The Norman Conquest, as an historical "accident" interrupting the continuity of tradition, obviously provided a critical problem for this notion, and a good deal of effort was spent explaining it away. The development of the Royalist counter-argument eventually resulted in the discovery and examination of English feudal structure and law as Norman importations after the Conquest and the working out of the implications of that discovery. Curious by-products of this debate, then, were the development of the concept of English legal structure and the constitution and the establishment of history as a discipline.

My sketch of this material, although overextended, is slight, but what is essential to note for my present purposes is an assumption common to both sides—that what was once so must always be so. As J. G. A. Pocock has said:

the possibility that the idea of custom might give rise to the ideas of law being in continuous development was altogether suppressed . . . the notion of historical relativity—the suggestion that the law still in force might indeed have been made by a king in some high and far-off time, but in conditions so remote that neither "king" or "law" meant what they meant at the present day, and that consequently no conclusions could be drawn as to current rights and liberties—was after all still virtually unknown.[10]

The foundation of this problematic, it seems to me, serves as a paradigm for what I am suggesting in this book is the question or ruse of institution.

In a sense, the argument was genealogical in both form and content. The development of the historical notion came from the insistence of the Tory side on an origin of both the law and the Commons in the will and particular acts of monarchs whose sovereignty descended genealogically from Adam. The Whig argument was eventually forced to give up its own claim for the immemoriality of the constitution, resorting to Locke's ridicule of

Filmer's genealogical derivation of sovereignty and his assertion
of the irrelevance of any historical origin in the face of principles
of universal reason, which declared that men were free by nature
and had voluntarily assembled in society, and that sovereignty was
contractual and limited.

The historian Isaac Kramnick has demonstrated the per-
sistence of this debate in the eighteenth century. Bolingbroke,
the leader of the "country" Whig and Tory opposition to Walpole's government, "revived seventeenth-century common law
and Whig notions of an ancient constitution with immemorial free
institutions, among which was a Parliament containing a house
for commoners" (Kramnick, *Bolingbroke*, 10). English history had
been, from the country opposition point of view, a history of
betrayals and revivals of ancient popular freedoms residing in a
representative body of commoners, a tradition of freedom now
facing a new threat from the corruptions of the new economics and
the Walpolian administration. Walpole's tactic was surprisingly a
Whig revision of Tory history. There were no ancient rights, no
constitution to renew:

The birth of real freedom in England was the Glorious Revolution, pro-
claimed Walpole's press. . . . As the *Gazetteer* asked, "a renewal of what? a
renewal of a non-entity. We never before had a constitution as was settled
at the Revolution. That sure can't be renewed which never existed." (Augustan Politics," 41)

This argument was, of course, bolstered by the Lockean one that
whatever the history of English slavery, "liberty was our original
right, our right from nature or reason."

Although, as Kramnick shows, Walpole's historians went beyond Tory historians in explaining the emergence of Commons
in the decline of feudalism, they also followed closely earlier descriptions of its origins in "the competition of nobility and monarch for political allies": "To such low beginnings and such private
views," the *Daily Gazetteer* commented, "do we owe the origins
and foundations of all our liberties." The Walpole Press, according
to Kramnick, cited James Harrington's

description of the new distribution of power created by the changed balance of property brought on by Tudor legislation. It even anticipated the "hardship of the nobility" thesis of more modern scholarship with a description of a hard-pressed nobility caught in the price revolution, over-extending itself in fashionable luxury and leaving its estates to be broken up "which the Commons, grown wise and industrious by the enchanting novelty of property got into their hands." ("Augustan Politics," 43)

In other words, part of the cause of the emergence of Commons, and therefore English liberty, had to do with changing power relations, which in turn arose from changes in the nature of estate acquisition and inheritance, an argument perhaps not irrelevant to *Tom Jones*.

My own recourse to this rather crude form of intellectual political history will serve, I hope, to add resonance to the themes and structures in *Tom Jones* that I wish to explore later. Fielding's involvement in the political debate surrounding the '45 Rebellion and the involvement of that debate in his novel are well known, but perhaps also require some bare rehearsal here.[11] Walpole's ministry had fallen in 1742 to be replaced by members of the opposition Fielding considered opportunist, but these were soon replaced by a "broad-bottom" coalition of both Walpole Whigs and members of the opposition, including friends of Fielding. His loyalty apparently went to the new government, although there has always been some controversy concerning when and why he gave the government his support.[12] Soon after the invasion, Fielding published three or four pamphlets attempting to awaken concern about the threat—which few, not including George, who was in Hanover, took very seriously—and satirizing the claims and beliefs of the Jacobites. He also began a weekly newspaper, *The True Patriot*, to report news of the war, stir up interest, and counter the false stories and propaganda of the opposition. He perhaps set aside the writing of *Tom Jones* to carry forward this work. Fielding ended publication of *The True Patriot* in 1746. Again in 1747 he took up his pen in support of the ministry during an election crisis, publishing a couple of pamphlets and starting another weekly, *The Jacobite's Journal*, written for the most part in ironic Jacobite persona, apparently to keep the Jacobite issue alive and thus discredit the opposition and stabilize support for the Pelham ministry. He continued *The Journal* through most of 1748, dropping it when he was named magistrate for Westminster, perhaps finally weary of political writing. The next year he published *Tom Jones*.[13]

Most of the story of Tom Jones is placed alongside the events of the '45 Rebellion. Tom briefly joins the soldiers on the way to Scotland to put down the Rebellion and speaks for the constitution throughout (for example, with the Man of the Hill). The Jacobite Partridge mistakes Tom's intentions when he joins him on the road by assuming that he is on his way to support the Pretender. Sophia is mistaken on the road for Charles's mistress, Squire Western argues politics confusedly with his Hanoverian sister — a good many of the references to the Rebellion in the novel have to do with confusion. The narrator offers the adventure of Tom and Partridge with the gypsy king as a parable of absolutist rule and, early in the book, distinguishes his role as author-narrator from that of a divine right absolutist, allegorizing in a political way his own authority:

For as I am, in reality, the Founder of a new Province of Writing, so I am at liberty to make what Laws I please therein. And these Laws, my Readers, whom I consider as my Subjects, are bound to believe in and to obey; with which that they may readily and cheerfully comply, I do hereby assure them that I shall principally regard their Ease and Advantage in all such institutions: For I do not, like a *jure divino* Tyrant, imagine that they are my Slaves or my Commodity. I am, indeed, set over them for their own Good only, and was created for their Use, and not they for mine. Nor do I doubt, while I make their Interest the great Rule of my Writings, they will unanimously concur in supporting my Dignity, and in rendering me all the Honour I shal deserve or desire. (II, i, 77–78)[14]

Aside from these references to the historical situations, readers for a long time have felt the presence of a more basic relationship between the issues of the rebellion and the plot of the novel, although that presence has always been a problem for interpretation. Paul Hunter recently has stated the case for the parallel convincingly: "The cultural consciousness that Fielding recorded in his modern epic is that peculiar moment, 1745, when constitutional government was threatened by nostalgia for old ways and universal absolutes" (*Occasional Form*, 182). Commenting on the general significance of the novel, Hunter adds:

> In establishing Tom at last as the proprietory heir of Paradise Hall, Fielding is making a theological, philosophical, psychological, legal, and political statement. As an heir who earned his estate—a rightful heir in the sense of moral right—Tom is the new man of English society, the man who needs education, experience, prudence, wisdom, and the grace of a benevolent deity to fulfill his responsible place in the fabric of English national life. Paradise Hall, debased even at the beginning of *Tom Jones* by the loosened satanic forces and the false judgment abounding there, becomes at the end a paradigm of the possible new order, and in its redemption and in Tom's gaining of Sophia, Fielding demonstrates postlapsarian possibility and registers his hope of a new culture. (*Occasional Form*, 184–85)

One has to assent to the general cogency of this reading, though perhaps stopping piously short of granting the reduction of the novel to "statement," for all the old bugbears of intention, paraphrase, and allegorical reduction are raised, along with the still urgent theoretical question of the "exteriority" of texts. Still, Hunter's is the most promising of the new political or "circumstantial" readings of a novel that provides perhaps the most notorious site of battles between critics who insist on the fictionality of fiction and those who insist on its textual or nontextual referentiality.[15]

Hesitating to enter the fray, one is continually teased by the possibilities of reference apparently offered by the novel. Even a cursory glance at the late Stuart succession and some of the large events of English history suggests almost comic parallels with the plot of the novel. One of the crucial points was the inevitability of the openly Catholic James's succession to his brother Charles II. What prevented the passage of the Exclusion Bill, which would have substituted Charles's bastard son, the Duke of Monmouth, for James as king, was, at least in part, the fact that James had two Protestant daughters, Mary and Anne, who would succeed him. Shortly after James came to the throne in 1685, Monmouth attempted to seize the throne and failed disastrously, an episode in which Fielding's Man of the Hill participated on the side of the rebels and which is described in the novel. James II's insistence on royal prerogative, suspension of liberties, and campaign to revive Roman Catholicism in England provide targets for most of Fielding's later anti-Jacobite spleen. When James's second wife gave birth to a son who would be raised as a Catholic and would prevent the succession of Mary and Anne, there was a good deal of turmoil, and William of Orange, Mary's husband, was invited to bring a Dutch army to England to restore constitutional rights. James fled to the continent, and the myth of "the King over the Water," whom Squire Western toasts, began. Since neither Mary nor Anne, who succeeded William and Mary, had surviving children when she died, the Whig council had to search for the nearest possible Protestant heir, finding, significantly enough for Fielding's novel, a distant descendant of James I, Sophia, Electress of Hanover. Meanwhile, with a good deal of fanfare and anxious documentation, the wife of the "Old Pretender," James III, gave birth to Prince Charles, the "Young Pretender," the "Chevalier" (after whom Western names a horse) of the '45 Rebellion. Charles was bred and raised with but one goal—his restoration of the main Stuart line to the throne of England. Despite the almost comically elaborate precautions of his father, the myth persisted, or at least the Whigs, Fielding among them, made it persist, that Charles was a bastard of unknown derivation.[16] One story even had it that he or his father at birth had been sneaked surreptitiously into his mother's bed in a warming pan. Beyond the scurrility of these stories, they had the obvious intention of casting doubt on the Stuart genealogical legitimacy, although it is not to be taken that Tom was identified with Charles. The first readers of the novel even raised objections to the fact that Fielding left Tom a bastard after revealing his birth as an Allworthy, when it would have been easy to have revealed a secret marriage between Bridget and her illicit lover, who had died anyway. (Jacobite critics even suggested that an earthquake that threatened London and other cosmic disorders were God's punishment for this indecency.) Moreover, the fact that Tom can probably only hold Allworthy's estate in trust, as the constitutional acts of the Revolution specify that the monarch holds sovereignty in trust, seems too pat to ignore.

What does one do with these parallels?

III

Without claiming a solution to the theoretical problems raised above, I wish to explore another level of genealogical disturbances and interruptions—interferences in narrative movement which may be related to the above discussion in a way I can only describe as metonymic contagion, metonymy being a figure both for circumstantial association or affiliation and for the cause and effect sequence of narrative.[17] It seems to me almost as if Fielding has translated the genealogical metaphor, a paradigmatic relationship, into metonymic sequence to destroy it by extending it. An essential characteristic of metonymy is, of course, its tendency to move by accidental contiguity. To suggest any such connection between the novel and an historical situation is to suggest that the novel is allegorical.

One traditional definition of allegory is an extended metaphor or simile.[18] An obvious problem with this definition is that of marking a precise boundary between the figures. One of the difficulties with understanding the form of the novel perhaps lies in the fact that it locates itself at a point where tropological terms such as allegory, metaphor, simile, metonymy, synechdoche, analogy, exemplum, and parable cross, becoming ambiguous and indeterminate. Perhaps parabasis will prove to be the clearest descriptive term for what happens in *Tom Jones*. To think of allegory as developing from the extension of a metaphor or simile suggests a theory of the way fictional stories can be generated. In another way, it may also suggest, as I will try to show, a theory of history.

It is commonplace that the example and the extended or epic simile are constant features of Fielding's style, are part of his mock epic equipment, functioning comically in *Tom Jones*, as a mockery of pretension, including the narrator's own epic ambitions.[19] They are also part of a more general textual pattern of providing extensive comparative frames of reference, of analogies between high society and low, between court and country, between the grand and the mean in human action, between, in short, microcosm and macrocosm, as the serious extended similes in Homer, for example, are thought to function. These analogies, it should be noted, operate in a quite complicated way. For instance, they seem to mock low pretensions by using the terms of high event, while simultaneously raising the low and suggesting that the grand action is perhaps no less mean.

More to my point, by their comic digressiveness, Fielding's extended similes constantly divert the text from its proposed narrative goal and function as parabases. One of the best examples of this tendency is the extended simile which a chapter title (V, xi) describes, digressively, as "A Simile in Mr. Pope's Period of a Mile." At the end of the previous chapter, Tom has been discovered by Thwackum and Blifil in the bushes with Molly:

As in the Season of RUTTING (an uncouth Phrase, by which the Vulgar denote that gentle Dalliance, which in the well-wooded Forest* [*This an ambiguous Phrase, and may mean either a Forest well clothed with Wood, or well stript of it (Fielding's note).] of *Hampshire*, passes between lovers of the Ferine Kind) if while the lofty crested Stag meditates the amorous Sport, a Couple of Puppies, or any other Beasts of hostile Note, should wander so near the Temple of *Venus Ferina*, that the fair Hind should shrink from the Place, touched with that Somewhat, either of Fear or Frolic, of Nicety or Skittishness, with which Nature had bedecked all Females, or hath, at least, instructed them how to put it on; lest thro' the Indelicacy of Males, the *Samean* Mysteries should be pryed into by unhallowed Eyes: For at the Celebration of those Rites, the female Priestess cries out with her in *Virgil* (who was then probably hard at Work on such Celebration),
    —*Procul, O procul este, profani;*
    Proclamat Vates, totoque absistite Luco
    —Far hence be Souls prophane,
    The Sibyl cry'd, and from the Grove abstain.
                                        Dryden

If, I say, while these sacred Rites, which are common to *Genus omne Animantium*, are in Agitations between the Stag and his Mistress, any hostile Beasts should venture too near, on the first Hint given by the frightened Hind, fierce and tremendous rushes forth the Stag to the Entrance of the Thicket; there stands he Centinel over his Love, stamps the Ground with his Foot, and with his Horns brandished aloft in Air, proudly provokes the apprehended Foe to Combat.

Thus, and more terrible, when he perceived the Enemy's Approach, leap'd forth our Heroe. Many a Step advanced he forwards, in order to conceal the trembling Hind, and, if possible, to secure her Retreat. (V, xi, 259–60)

Obviously, the simile's suggestions of a law of Nature enlarges the frame of reference of the novel. The simile allegorizes the main story.

I will return later to the question of allegory. What I want to analyze now is the textual movement of the passage and what surrounds it. The simile, an interruption, is itself immediately interrupted by the parenthetical definition of the preliminary word "RUTTING." This parenthesis is in turn irrelevantly interrupted by a footnote about the ambiguity of the phrase *well-wooded*. Then, one element of the comparison, the shrinking of the female at intrusion, is extended for explanation, apparently under the influence of the metaphoric description "Temple of *Venus Ferina*," into the violation of "*Samean* mysteries." This comparison expands to a further hyperbolic and redundant analogy of the "female priestess" who cries out against the violation. This comparison is then compared with the Sibyl in a line of Virgil which then is repeated in translation by Dryden. After these paths leading away are escaped and the simile returns to its first situation, by a sort of metonymic contamination "RUTTING" and "Amorous Sport" have become "sacred Rites" (inevitably glossed as "in common to *Genus omne Animantium*," which again threatens the continuity). "A Couple of Puppies, or any other Beasts of hostile Note," earlier transformations of Thwackum and Blifil, having then taken on the suggestion of "the indelicacy of Males" before female privacy and been transformed into full-scale violators of religious mysteries, now are simple "hostile Beasts," as the animal situation is recov-

ered and the simile ends on a heroic note. The inflated language of
the whole extended comparison bleeds over into the description
of Tom and his subsequent battle.

Yet there is more. The whole wandering digressive comparison about accidental intrusions, itself repeatedly interrupted by
digressive comparison, has exfoliated from the situation in the
novel immediately preceding it. My own metaphor is inexact.
The movement is more like the spreading of a stain or of a metonymic "contagion." Jones has sought the open air to cool himself
after the brawl with Blifil, brought about by his drunken celebration, the excessiveness of which reflected his release from his
great anxiety over the predicted death of Allworthy. (The casual-
ness and accidental nature of this movement are significant.) At
this moment Tom "renewed those Meditations on his dear *Sophia*,
which the dangerous illness of his Friend and Benefactor had for
some time interrupted" (V, x, 255). Tom's meditations are affected
by the "pleasant Evening" in late June, the "most delicious Grove"
where he walks, "the gentle Breezes fanning the Leaves, together
with the sweet Trilling of a murmuring Stream, and the melodi-
ous Notes of Nightingales"—a "Scene . . . sweetly accommodated
to Love"; and undoubtedly he is also still under the influence of
the emotional release and drink. Under all these influences and
his thoughts of Sophia's physical beauty, his idealized love is diverted by more inflaming thoughts: "his wanton Fancy roved un-
bounded over all her Beauties, and his lively imagination painted
the charming Maid in various ravishing Forms, his warm Heart
melted with Tenderness" (V, x, 255–56). In this mood, Tom swears
eternal fidelity to his Sophia:

"But why do I mention another Woman? could I think my Eyes capable
of looking at any other with Tenderness, these Hands should tear them
from my Head. No, my *Sophia*, my Soul shall doat on thee alone. The
chastest Constancy will I ever preserve to thy Image. Tho' I should never
have Possession of thy charming Person, still shalt thou alone have Possession of my Thoughts, my Love, my Soul. Oh! my fond Heart is so wrapt
in that tender Bosom, that the brightest Beauties would for me have no
Charms, nor would a Hermit be colder in their Embraces." (V, x, 256)

This profusive vow is interrupted now by what the narrator calls "an Accident" (V, x, 255). Molly Seagrim appears, the undercurrent of sexual arousal takes over, and the two retire "into the thickest Part of the Grove."

Such reversals are a much repeated satiric strategy in Fielding's texts, of course. A character's exaggerated profession of constancy, veracity, disinterestedness, Christian and Stoic endurance, or whatever, is inevitably undercut by an interruption that deflates the protestations. Parson Adams's speech about the necessity of Christian resignation and complacency at the loss of a loved one in *Joseph Andrews* is interrupted by the inaccurate but convincing news that his son has drowned; Molly's vow of constancy to Tom is interrupted by the accidental falling of the curtain, revealing Square in her bedroom; or Squire Western's exaggerated love for his daughter is immediately reversed into equally exaggerated threats. More to the point is the way such "accidental interruptions" frequently govern the movement of Fielding's narratives. Interruptions such as the ones in this passage function as metonymic displacements, and one is reminded that in rhetorical theory a metonym operates by substituting what is logically an "accident"—a non-essential quality—for the proper name. This particular "accident" is metonymically motivated in several ways. Molly, who is literally contiguous, displaces the absent and apparently unattainable Sophia. This displacement is made possible by the inflammation of Tom's "wanton Fancy," his wandering sexual fantasy of Sophia's physical beauty—aroused by his associations with his immediate surroundings: warm evening, gentle breeze, song of the nightingale, murmur of the water, delicious grove. In the words of the narrator, "he was not at this Time perfect Master of that wonderful Power of Reason, which so well enables grave and wise Men to subdue their unruly Passions, and to decline any of these prohibited amusements" (V, x, 257).

It is precisely these associations, the animal spirits, the "natural" lust of Tom and Molly, that govern the terms of the extended simile produced to describe Tom's hostility and Molly's flight when they are then also interrupted by Thwackum and Blifil.

So the narration that the intrusive simile about intrusions interrupts is a narrative of accidental interruptions interrupting interruptions. The whole context in which the simile is placed is concerned with swerving, diversion, and digression. Tom's situation with Sophia is "interrupted" by Allworthy's illness, which is interrupted by news of Bridget's death (and Allworthy's unexpected recovery). Blifil's mourning intrudes upon and is intruded upon by Tom's celebration of Allworthy's recovery, which is interrupted by the fight with Blifil from which Tom escapes into his fantasies of Sophia. His meditation is then interrupted by the appearance of Molly, who provides a diversion of another kind, which is then interrupted by Thwackum and Blifil, whose intrusion brings about a fight between Tom and Thwackum into which Squire Western suddenly intervenes. The Squire is followed shortly by the rest of his dinner party and Sophia, who, "from the Sight of Blood, or from Fear for her Father, or from some other Reason" (264), swoons, causing her Aunt to presume mistakenly that she is in love with Blifil. This mistake leads everyone to false expectations and eventually to Sophia's persecution and running away, while the whole episode leads in another way to Tom's banishment. Obviously, one could go on. In those last two statements, I have telescoped a causality equal in complexity and fortuitousness to the one I have more minutely described. Moreover, the narration of this sliding, digressive movement is itself replete with digressive comparisons, commentaries, and explanations similar to the extended simile with which I began this analysis and which could in many ways serve as a paradigm for the text as a whole.

Examples and exemplification are frequently noted patterns in Fielding's writings and are often thematized in them. Obviously, examples can often be digressive and intrusive, functioning in a way similar to the extended simile, which is related to the *exemplum*.

The reader often gets the sense that Fielding's novels are constructed, on some level, as classical orations in which examples serve technically as proofs for arguments.[20] Incidents or characters often seem present in the narrative more to serve the needs of the underlying argument than for any plot necessity, although they can serve that purpose also. Construction of the text as argument or parable diverts narrative causality from the level of the plot to the level of discourse. It also tends to allegorize the story. By following an apparently straightforward movement of the narrative of *Tom Jones*, I wish to explore this tendency.

The rhetorical figures of thought *exemplum* and *narratio* form the second part of the seven-part classical oration. *Narratio* "tells how the problem at hand had come up, gives the audience, as it were, the history of the problem."[21] When the narrator introduces Tom to the narrative, he reports that "it was universal Opinion of al *Mr. Allworthy's* Family, that he was certainly born to be hanged" (III, ii, 118). The "Reason for Conjecture," he explains, is Tom's "Propensity to many Vices," particularly minor theft. After offering "three Examples of those thefts," the narrator then introduces Black George, the gamekeeper, as his only friend and, not incidentally, his "accessory after the Fact. For the whole Duck, and great Part of the Apples [Tom's spoils], were converted to the Use of the Gamekeeper and his Family" (III, ii, 119). Needless to say, rather than proving Tom's viciousness, these "examples" of conventional boyhood foibles become examples in the only slightly more submerged argument of Tom's generosity, good nature, and innocent susceptability to exploitation and misrepresentation: "Tho' as *Jones* alone was discovered, the poor Lad bore not only the whole Smart, but the whole Blame; both which fell again to his Lot, on the following Occasion" (III, ii, 119).

The examples, then, serve both to explain and undercut the "universal Opinion" or "Conjecture," itself mistaken as the examples are misinterpreted or misrepresented. "The following Occasion" then becomes a similarly misinterpreted full-scale narration or example: Tom's and George's pursuit of wounded game onto Squire Western's estate, Tom's capture and George's escape, Tom's lie to protect George, Allworthy's remark that it was merely from a mistaken "point of honour," Thwackum and Square's introduction (a narrative veer), and their debates over this question. What began as a series of examples to explain or support a generalization, becomes the main narrative line. The story continues to pursue this wandering path as it pursues the relationship, generally, of Tom and George, detouring to explain the presence of Square and Thwackum (smaller narrations) and their relationship to Bridget and attitudes toward each other and Tom and Blifil, a digression concerning their jealousy of Bridget's apparent affection for Tom adduced, according to the chapter title, to give "a better Reason still for the before-mentioned Opinion" (III, vi, 136).

The story swerves again by introducing Squire Western in order to explain his relationship with Tom and George, still exemplifying the original conjecture, now probably forgotten. When Tom seeks finally to place George with Squire Western, after he is finally dismissed by Allworthy, and desires to do so by appeal to Sophia, the narrative must take another large detour to introduce her properly. Molly Seagrim receives a further digression in order to explain why Tom is not more sensitive to Sophia's beauty and wealth. Before Molly's entry, another digression is called for to explain how Tom gains the power to petition Sophia. This excursion is the extended narration of the songbird given to Sophia by Tom.

The narrative to this point has been a series of elaborated examples to explain the original opinion that Tom was born to be hanged. The level of action narrated was motivated on the level of discourse by the needs of the generalization for specification. In this way, the narrative can be called "allegorical" or "parabolic" in relation to the "conjecture." In the process of explanative narrative, however, another logic has taken over. Each example has required its own explaining narratives, which have motivated other lines of discourse, so that the whole is "allegorical" in a much more complex way. It is elaborated for its own interest until it has completely usurped the place and function of the idea to which it had been subordinated. It has also become the "source" for new causal chains—on the level of narrative discourse, on the level of action or plot, and on the level of theme. The beginning prediction that

Tom is *fated* to be hanged will retain a kind of shadowy presence, however, throughout the novel and will reemerge near the end as an immediate possibility.

The process I have just described clarifies the functioning of the notoriously full-blown interpolated digressions, such as the stories of Wilson in *Joseph Andrews*, and the Man of the Hill and Mrs. Fitzpatrick and the episode of the gypsies in *Tom Jones*. These stories more obviously usurp the place of the main narrative for awhile (interminably for some readers) and bear only a tangential, faintly analogical, or parabolic relationship to the main plot. Apparently interruptive and autonomous, they spin off from the main narrative on a very thin pretense of explaining the strangeness of someone accidentally encountered. With them the metonymic element of accidental contiguity as "cause" is much more apparent than in the narrative movement I have just analyzed, and this element is precisely what disturbs many readers.[22]

I have brought my description of this process of allegorization to one of those important nodes in the narrative from which will lead a number of other narrative and thematic lines, a parabolic scene in itself. (There was a similar one earlier, also important though I merely glossed over it, in the debate over Tom's "lie" from a mistaken "point of honour.") I want to pause over this one, concerning Sophia's bird, because it illustrates the process I have just described, and also because of the way it shows that process thematized *within* the novel.

When the bird is purloined and freed by Blifil, Tom risks his neck to recover it, though the hapless bird is devoured by a hawk. Blifil is called upon to explain the reasons for his nasty, vindictive act. He replies:

"I had Miss Sophia's Bird in my Hand, and thinking the poor Creature languished for Liberty, I own, I could not forbear giving it what it desired: for I always thought there was something very cruel in confining any Thing. It seemed to me against the Law of Nature, by which every thing hath a Right to Liberty; nay, it is even unchristian; for it is not doing what we would be done by. . . ." (IV, iv, 160).

Blifil's self-serving and calculated reply becomes the basis for interpretation by the assembled characters (a repeated activity in the novel), who never really question its veracity as a statement of motive. Each interpretation serves more to reveal the interpreter than to explain the event, although each interpretation will serve as ground, "cause," or explanation for future acts by that character.[23] Square picks up on the "Law of Nature" and "Right to Liberty" and spins off on that, Thwackum grabs at the reference to Christian behavior and amplifies that, and then the two debate as to which of them can claim credit for Blifil's virtues and which of them is responsible for Tom's moral deficiencies. Allworthy generously forgives the inconsiderateness of the act for the goodness of the motive. Western more simply and selfishly condemns the act as a theft of his daughter's property and consults a lawyer, who happens to be present, as to whether it is not in violation of the law. The lawyer's long-winded reply is incomprehensible and inconclusive and Western, in the words of the narrator, "interrupt[s]" the "Debate," itself part of a series of narrative interruptions, with a toast to Tom for risking his neck and a vow to "love the Boy for it the longest Day I have to live" (IV, iv, 164).

In another way, *Tom Jones* is full of "instant" allegories of the sort given in this episode. Blifil's explanation of his action translates that action into allegory. Thwackum and Square take up that allegory, debate it, and by their different interpretations absorb the stories of Tom and Blifil into it, but they are also allegorized by it, as are Allworthy, Western, and the lawyer. The whole episode, by "explaining" Sophia's love for Tom and her hatred for Blifil, is both allegorical on another level and a causal "event" in the plot. But there is more. Because the bird is named "Tommy" and because Jones has been associated with the natural and the free and has a problematical relationship with convention, the episode suggests in shadowy form another level of allegory altogether.

The book as a whole is a virtual battleground of clashing allegorical interpretations. The characters constantly offer parables and parabolic interpretations of the events of the novel, and they themselves temporarily assume allegorical roles—as does even that narrator, in the intrusive prefaces which open each book and in other announced digressions. His extended comparison in the prefatory chapter to Book VII, of the "world" of his book with the "world" the theatre both represents and contains, his sermon on prudence, his disclaimer in the preface to Book III about being a *jure divino* tyrant, the interpretation he offers of the gypsies episode, and his constant use of other forms of representation—painting, law, history, and literature—for purposes of description are examples of this tendency on his part.

Moreover, these "allegories" or interpretations are not simply overlays on the action of the narrative, the events of the plot, which are conceived as neutral in themselves, nor do they intervene in the action in a simple way. Allegorization enjoys a causal force; allegories are complicated events in the novel and characters act in accordance with their rules, but never completely, never consistently. Irrelevance always retains an important place.

One of the most open invitations the book offers to associate it with Jacobite-Whig political debate is the argument between Squire Western and Sophia's "politic aunt," his sister Mrs. Western, over the "government" of his daughter. Mrs. Western's habitual frame of reference is that of Hanoverian politics—marriage is like pursuit of political "place" or investment in the funds (two principal practices in Walpole's Robinocracy). There is always, of course, a multiple reference in her use of political metaphors. Her jargon not only reflects her limited capacity of thought but is also an affectation (she likes to show her sophistication in these matters), and it is also offered as a deliberate provocation to her brother, both to his country Jacobitism and what she feels is his lack of sophistication.

I do not wish to imply that the argument between Squire Western and his sister is a simple allegory of the court-country argument over the management of the nation. The text openly plays with the possibilities of that allegory, moves in and out of it with comic glee. What, in fact, the argument demonstrates is a sort of metonymic confusion or contagion, similar to the ones I have shown above, the effect of the extended and accidental wandering of an analogy. The political argument, by implication a long-standing one, is established in the narrative, and then it is displaced onto the problem of the "government" of Sophia. It never completely loses its independent status, however, and their discussion of Sophia easily slides back into an overt argument about the nation. (Squire Western, for that matter, less politically minded than his sister, often veers into his more habitual frame of reference, the hunt.)

Mrs. Western, for example, remonstrates with her brother:

> "While I have been endeavouring to fill her Mind with Maxims of Prudence, you have been provoking her to reject them. *English* Women, Brother, I thank Heaven, are no Slaves. We are not to be locked up like *Spanish* and *Italian* Wives. We have as good a Right to Liberty as yourselves. We are to be convinced by Reason and Persuasion only, and not governed by Force. I have seen the World, Brother, and know what Arguments to make Use of. . . . It is by living at home with you that she hath learnt romantic Notions of Love and Nonsense." (VI, xiv, 320–21)

Squire Western's exasperated answer mixes terms comically, and the debate oscillates between political positions, abstract principle, the threat of Jacobite invasion and revenge, and the problem of Sophia:

> "Do you think no one hath any Understanding, unless he hath been about at Court? Pox! the World is come to a fine Pass indeed, if we are all Fools, except a Parcel of Roundheads and *Hannover* Rats. Pox! I hope the Times are a coming, that we shall make Fools of them, and every Man shall enjoy his own. I hope to *see* it, Sister, before the *Hannover* Rats have eat up all our Corn, and left us nothing but Turneps to feed upon." "I protest, Brother," cries she, "you are now got beyond my Understanding. Your jargon of Turneps and *Hannover* Rats, is to me perfectly unintelligible." "I believe," cries he, "you don't care to hear o'em; but the Country Interest may succeed one Day or other for all that." "I wish," answered the Lady, "you would think a little of your Daughter's Interest: For believe me, she is in greater Danger than the Nation." (VI, xiv, 321–22)

Management of the nation, management of the daughter—the argument is the same, and the sacrifice or the loss of Sophia (Wisdom—to appeal to another level of allegory) is its conse-

quence. The argument of the Squire and his sister, between country and court interests, is in part an argument over means. Squire
Western, convinced of the absolute authority of the father, insists on his prerogative and the legitimacy of force. Mrs. Western, whiggishly, argues for persuasion and political manipulation.
They enjoy only an unstable and wavering agreement on parental
(patriarchal) authority, as the scene above suggests. In a slightly
later scene, Mrs. Western cites the standard natural law arguments
for the obligation of child to parent and one of their most quoted
sources in Plato's *Laws*: " 'On the contrary, Niece, have I not en-
deavoured to inspire you with a true Idea of the several Relations
in which a human Creature stands in Society? Have I not taken
infinite Pains to show you, that the Law of Nature hath injoined
a Duty on Children to their Parents? Have I not told you what
Plato says on that Subject?' " (VII, iii, 336). She is, nonetheless,
just as tyrannical as her brother and participates in his persecution
of Sophia—there is a double reference in this also—and later she
conspires to subvert it.

The other characters line themselves up in the same debate
over principles of natural law as it relates to the arranged marriage of Sophia. Allworthy insists on consent of the governed (VI,
iii), Blifil takes for granted his victory because he assumes the authority of the father—Sophia is his "property" (VI, vii, 295)—and
Tom gives the argument for Sophia:

"You know my Father's Intentions."—"But I know," answered he, "your
Compliance with them cannot be compelled." "What," says she, "must be
the dreadful Consequence of my Disobedience? My own Ruin is my least
Concern. I cannot bear the thoughts of being the Cause of my Father's
Misery." "He is himself the Cause," cries *Jones*, "by exacting a Power over
you which Nature hath not given him." (VI, vii, 299)

Finally, the narrator himself establishes the context for the
discussion of the obligations between parent and child in his preface to Book VI, the book that initiates the trials of Sophia and includes the banishment of Tom for filial "ingratitude." In his prefatory discussion of the nature of love, with apparent reference to

the confusion in the previous book about the difference between
Tom's feeling for Sophia and for Molly, the narrator argues that

there is in some (I believe in many) human Breasts, a kind and benevo-
lent Disposition, which is gratified by contributing to the Happiness of
others. That in this Gratification alone, as in Friendship, *in parental and
filial affection*, as indeed in general Philanthropy, there is a great and ex-
quisite Delight. That if we will not call such Disposition Love, we have
no Name for it. (VI, i, 270; my italics)

It is out of this love that Sophia wishes to please and honor her
father, but in the face of his exercise of outrageous and unwar-
ranted absolute authority, she rebels. Or rather, in terms of political allegory, Sophia's running away is not rebellion but revolution,
in the Lockean sense and tradition of the Glorious Revolution, a
return to true principles of Nature and Reason.[24] Again, an important episode of the novel that concerns the conflicting allegorizing of the characters is itself subject on another level to various
incompletely allegorical interpretations, the bases for which are
present in the text. I have not simply extrapolated them.

Allegorization, however, also rules plot causality. The rebellion in the North exists in the book side by side with the debate
over filial obligations. Squire Western's quixotic lack of attention
to it while he swears to its principles can itself be seen as the suggestion of another level of political allegory. But the news that
"things look so well in the North," apparently in reference to the
war in northern Europe (VI, iv, 285–86; see Battestin's note),
just as quixotically makes Mrs. Western complicit in her brother's
"somewhat too hasty and violent" proceedings with Sophia and
advances the action of the plot.

There is a similar wavering interaction of mutual disturbance
between allegory and narrative in the other large allegories that
are suggested by the story and sometimes seem to govern its structure. One of them is the story of man's (Tom's) Fall and exile
from Eden (Paradise Hall).[25] (The Biblical story is not irrelevantly
the basis for some of Locke's arguments against Filmer's use of
scriptural authority for the genealogically transmitted divine right

of kings, and also the Miltonic myth of the origin and necessity of history.) The problem is a familiar one: names such as Allworthy, Blifil, and Paradise Hall at once invite and question the allegorical reference. Unless one is willing to see Allworthy's lack of omniscience and occasional tendency to hold back revelation of the whole truth as a wry theological comment on the deficiencies of the Almighty, he cannot be made to fill the role of God the Father typologically, let alone allegorically. Blifil is a petty villain, not Satan, and Paradise Hall is a decidedly worldly, not earthly, paradise. Most important, unlike Adam, Tom is not guilty of the sins or crimes of which he is accused, at least not of ingratitude nor of filial disobedience. He is misrepresented. Moreover, Tom is not the Adam of the beginning, either. He has no original dominion, no right of inheritance, no identity. He opens up a fissure in a closed world. He begins as a problem of placement. So, too, the shadowy presence of the allegory of the Fall of Man signifies by way of the ironic gap between texts, between modes. When Tom is banished, the narrator pointedly alludes to Milton: "And now, having taken a Resolution to leave the Country, he began to debate with himself whither he should go. *The World*, as *Milton* phrases it, *lay all before him*; and *Jones*, no more than *Adam*, had any Man to whom he might resort for Comfort or Assistance" (VII, ii, 331). The full sentence in *Paradise Lost*, a favorite of novelists, is "The World was all before them, where to choose / Thir place of rest, and *Providence thir guide* (XII, 646–47; my emphasis). Tom's "guide" is significantly different: "'why, let Fortune direct'" (VII, ii, 330). His journey is into a world of chance or accident and misinterpretation or misrepresentation. As in *Paradise Lost*, it is a journey into the labyrinth of history.

The story of the Fall is a myth grounding distance as estrangement, time as succession, the necessity of error or wandering, and thus of fiction and history. It makes narrative possible. So, the relationship between *Tom Jones* and the story of the Fall may be incomplete and inconsistent, constantly interrupted, but it is not irrelevant.

My examples of narrative movement have all come from

roughly the first half of the book and have provided the basis for
an analysis that could be extended if space permitted.[26] Similar
movements could be traced throughout the novel. Even when the
narrative seems to move in a more or less straightforward way (if
one disregards the prefatory essays and the narrator's other intrusions), either the action is governed by accidental juxtaposition,
metonymically, as in the crossing paths of Upton—or the narrative
structures what it narrates according to thematically complicated
juxtapositions, as with the stories of Nightingale, Lord Fellamar's
proposed rape of Sophia, and Tom's liaison with Lady Bellaston,
each of which has to do with questions of "honour."

IV

The two previous sections suggested the grounds for two different modes of interpreting *Tom Jones*. Section three concerned itself
with a tropological analysis of narrative structure. Section two
was directed toward possible associations of the text with areas
apparently extrinsic to it. These areas could be divided into two
radically different lines of reference. One would be the 1745 Rebellion and the associated political situation, an order of events,
accidental in itself, some of whose accidents can in turn be associated with events and people in *Tom Jones*. The other line would be
historical discourse—history as order—including various theories
under debate that can be associated with the text of the novel. The
novel's relationship with each of these lines would seem compel-
lingly complementary, though intermittent and incomplete. The
problem would be to specify precisely the nature of the tropological relationship of the order of the text with those other two
orders, bearing in mind the necessity of working from representations or "models" of all three lines of discourse.

If *Tom Jones* seems a privileged text for the investigation of
such a theoretical problem, it may be because the difficulty with
the genealogical metaphor, in the first place, is its assertion of
an analogical relationship between discontinuous orders. In every

way, however, the novel would seem to demonstrate that "events" (however they are defined) do not "have events the way women do babies," and that representations or stories are not "generated" the way people and plants are. Moreover, the problems of order in those two other "lines" and the problems of the text's relationship to them are *allegorized within Tom Jones*.

An appropriate emblem for the textual product of these questionable relationships between orders would obviously be the "bastard" or "monster."[26] Tom is referred to several times as a "monster," notably by Allworthy, when he decides to banish him (VI, xi, 300). Western also loves him like a son but no more suspects him as a possible object of Sophia's love than he would "an animal of a different species" (VI, ix, 300). Tom resists classification, and at the same time he is a test case of "human nature," an Everyman, a problem of allegory, an aberrant Adam. As a "foundling," he will require all the historian's art of "invention" ("the art of finding out" [IX, i, 491]) to place.

A bastard is the offspring of an unlawful coupling; a monster results from unnatural coupling. Later, Tom is thought capable, as well as culpable, of incest, a coupling that serves as the threshold between nature and law. In all these ways, Tom is the perfect figure for Fielding's "new species of writing," the improper offspring of tropological couplings between incompatible systems. The novel is a text with only a borrowed, not a proper, name.

Tom is also, himself, the "original" flaw that "generates" the rest of the narrative—the principle of disequilibrium that unsettles a stable world. He begins as a *sign* that something is wrong in Paradise, that there is something deficient or excessive, something less than all-worthy in the patriarch, something hidden. For it is not simply Tom's bastardy that causes the problem. He enters the book as a sign *doubly* displaced. In the first action of the novel, the infant is "laid at Allworthy's door," literally in his bed. This metaphoric expression is repeated by various characters throughout the book. At the beginning, it is a metaphor literalized, a deliberately misleading act of false attribution, a first misrepresentation.[27] Moreover, this false attribution of origin points to a man whose goodness has been dispersed, not to say disseminated, throughout his world, but has not resulted in direct issue. A widower, All-worthy is without a direct heir, a fact that inspires the scrambling of various characters throughout the novel.

This first metonymic metaphor, in a sense, begins all the series of displacements that make up the novel. This first *acciden-tal* misrepresentation makes possible, perhaps necessitates, all the misrepresentations that follow. For, more than any other single principle, misrepresentation and misattribution operate as narra-tive cause in *Tom Jones*. In a pattern that will be repeated through-out the book, this first act of misrepresentation brings into play or "causes" an anarchic, gossipy "chorus" of interpretations—mis-representations—which, in turn, function as *actions* with scattered, unintended—accidental—effects which themselves are misrepre-sented and, in turn, result in other actions. Hence the constantly deflected, discontinuous, zig-zag path of narrative action in *Tom Jones*, and why its swerving movement has suggested so often in this analysis the displacing movement of tropes. It *is* tropological.

Here also is an indication of the function of the important theme of "the accident" as "cause" in *Tom Jones*. A good deal of interesting criticism has been devoted to this theme, as a good deal of philosophy has been devoted to the problem since the pre-Socratics. In the criticism, if the accidents are not deplored as aesthetic inadequacies on Fielding's part, they are thematized as only "apparent," disguised signs of a Christian providential order. This interpretation has demonstrated merit, but, without deny-ing it, there could be gains from giving accident full play in the book *without* taking alternative recourse to some notion of exis-tential contingency or a myth of Fortune or Chance which pro-vides closure as easily as the Christian interpretation. The theme of accidents also functions as *allusion*, as reference to strains of dis-course too varied and too complicated to analyze in detail here. I merely want to specify two general areas of reference. First, Field-ing's society was a dizzyingly speculative one, economically as well as intellectually. This was the subject of a good deal of agoniz-ing, anxious writing, pamphleteering, and politicking.[28] *Jonathan*

Wild, the stories of Mr. Wilson and the Man of the Hill, *Amelia*, and a play like *The Lottery* are some of the more prominent indications of Fielding's concern with a problem that seemed to introduce accident and chance into what had nostalgically seemed stable social relationships. Fielding's dedication to *Amelia* begins: "The following book is sincerely designed to promote the cause of virtue, and to expose some of the most glaring evils, as well public as private, which at present infest the country." And the first sentence of the novel reads, "The various accidents which befell a very worthy couple after their uniting in the state of matrimony will be the subject of the following history."[29] A good deal of this contemporary invasion of accident seemed to involve landownership and inheritance.

The other general area of allusion for the theme of accidents is the vast philosophical literature on the subject and, more specifically, on the problems of historiography.[30] From at least Aristotle on, an accident has been regarded as an unnecessary or inessential quality, as I suggested earlier, an improper property or attribute of an entity. As an event, it is regarded as unique, individual, novel, irregular, and nonrecurrent. It is an event that could as easily have happened another way. An accident is artificial or unnatural in the sense that it is not generated by causes that are imminent within itself and essential to it in the way that, say, a plant grows or a seed generates its own development; instead an accidental effect is the result of the intervention of outside force, and irrelevant to immanent laws. Until at least the eighteenth century, the accident was considered the problem peculiar to history, not to philosophy and natural philosophy, which were concerned with the normal, the regular, the lawful, the "natural." In terms of cause and effect systems, an accident is the result of the nonrecurrent, arbitrary intersection or co-incidence of separate and unrelated, irrelevant causal chains. In terms of individual agency, an accident is an *unintended* effect, as when an act with one purpose produces several effects—"side effects"—in an unforseen manner, and one of these minor side effects is more causally determinative of future effects than the one intended. As Square says, "'very minute Circum-

stances, Sir, very minute Circumstances cause great Alteration'"
(V, v, 233). Here is Fielding's comment, as narrator, on the episode of Sophia's muff:

> Though this Incident will probably appear of little Consequence to many
> of our Readers, yet, trifling as it was, it had so violent an Effect on poor
> *Jones*, that we thought it our Duty to relate it. In reality, there are many
> little Circumstances too often omitted by injudicious Historians, from
> which Events of the utmost Importance arise. The World may indeed be
> considered as a vast Machine, in which the great Wheels are originally set
> in Motion by those which are very minute, and almost imperceptible to
> any but the strongest eyes. (V, iv, 225)

Voltaire states the same principle mockingly in the entry "Chaine
des evenments" in his *Philosophical Dictionary*, from which I have
drawn my epigraph:

> This system of necessity and fatality was invented in our times by
> Leibniz, so he claims, under the name of *sufficient reason*. It is nevertheless
> very old: it is hardly a discovery that there is no effect without a cause,
> and that the smallest cause often produces the greatest effects.
>   Lord Bolingbroke admitted that the petty quarrels of the duchess of
> Marlborough and lady Masham gave him the opportunity to make the
> special treaty between Queen Anne and Louis XIV. This treaty led to the
> peace of Utrecht. This peace of Utrecht confirmed Philip V on the throne
> of Spain. The Spanish prince who is today king of Naples clearly owes his
> kingdom to lady Masham; and he would not have had it, he would per-
> haps not even have been born, if the duchess of Marlborough had been
> more indulgent towards the queen of England. His existence in Naples
> depended on one foolishness more or less at the court of London. Exam-
> ine the situations of all the peoples of the universe. They are established in
> the same way on a succession of facts which appear to be connected with
> nothing, but which are connected with everything. All is wheels, pulleys,
> ropes, springs in this immense machine.[31]

The theory of minute causes makes possible the unintended
effect. In common parlance, the illegitimate birth of Tom Jones
is such an "accident," for he is the clearly unintended product of
an illicit "summer" (another metaphor to stumble over) romance
of Bridget Allworthy. But even more, in a certain sense, all gen-

eration is the unintended effect of sexual coupling. The break between sexual act and issue can perhaps be taken as the basic model for discontinuity in causal systems as well as in genealogical systems. In this way genealogical history can be turned against itself, as it is in *Tom Jones* and in the Voltaire passage, which pushes genealogical thought to absurd limits:

I admit that all events are produced by one another. If the past gives birth to the present, the present gives birth to the future. All things have fathers, but not all things have children. This is exactly like a genealogical tree of this world's events. It is unquestionable that the inhabitants of Gaul and Spain are descended from Gomer, and the Russians from Magog, his younger brother; this genealogy is found in so many heavy books. It is undeniable that the grand Turk, who is also descended from Magog, owes it to him that he was thoroughly defeated in 1769 by the empress of Russia, Catherine II. This adventure is clearly connected with other great adventures. But whether Magog spat to the right or to the left near Mount Caucasus, whether he made two rings in a well or three, whether he slept on his left side or his right, I do not see that this has much influenced our present affairs. (*Philosophical Dictionary*, 111)

No genealogical theory of history and certainly no theory of absolute patriarchal power based on a direct line of filial descent from Adam could withstand such a notion of the proliferation of major and unintended accidental effects discontinuously emanating from minor causes. Even more, the vision of history suggested by *The History of Tom Jones*—of events which give rise to a multiplicity of representations and misrepresentations in a constantly troping, deflected associative swerve—must necessarily frustrate the search of the genealogist for determinative origins. It also suggests a theory of fictions, the necessity of the erring path of fictional narrative, and the text's tangential relationship to its own circumstantial occasions. Full explication of that idea must await another occasion. May I say here, with Voltaire, "This adventure is clearly connected with other great adventures"?

4

Tristram to the Hebrews:
Some Notes on the Institution
of a Canonic Text

There is something fallen out, however, said *Trim*, 'an please your
Honour; but it is not a chariot, or anything like one . . . .
— *Tristram Shandy*

IN *TRISTRAM SHANDY*, THE NARRATION of the birth of Tristram,
the narrator, is constantly displaced and deferred, as everybody
knows.[1] Things fall, get in the way, have to be explained. The
pointed failure of his attempt to narrate the event of his own
birth is not an indifferent matter for an autobiographer, however,
since that moment could be described as the absolute precondition of any narration at all. Inasmuch as this is a particularly "self-
conscious," self-reflexive narrative, we are always tempted to try
to read any of these "things" which substitute for the narration of
that birth as symbolical or allegorical, as figures for the moment of
narrative self-constitution. One of the problems with this temptation, of course, is the fact that so *many* things get in the way. We
are confronted with apparently an almost endless variety of possible figurative self-representations, so many heterogeneous possible self-allegorizations that we are nonplussed about which one
to privilege. In fact, the narrative of *Tristram Shandy* seems almost
nothing more than a series of *mises en abyme*, none of which is adequate "illustration" of the novel's heterogeneity, none of which

the reader finds definitive enough to organize a "generic" notion of the series, let alone provide a genealogy of the text. Together they fail to form the unity of a canon. Yet, together, in their incompatibility, they make up what has come to be a canonic text.

With these rather abstract cautionary notes in mind, I want to look at one of these problematic "things" displacing and substituting for the narration of Tristram's birth: the much discussed episode concerning the "council" over an accidentally discovered document which turns out to be a sermon by Yorick.[2] Making up this "assembly" are "my father" Walter, "my Uncle" Toby, Toby's servant Trim, and Dr. Slop the "papist" male midwife there to "second" the female midwife who is upstairs with "my mother, at this moment." This episode is marked as significant in a number of ways, not the least in that it is what has come to be called "a scene of reading," that is, a moment in a text in which other texts are "read" in a way to suggest possibilities of reading the narrative that contains them. This particular text within the text is significant also in that the sermon turns out to be written by another absent major character—Parson Yorick—whose name Sterne chose as the nom de plume for the publication of his own sermons, including this one. Moreover, Yorick very early in the novel provides, at the very least, a proleptic figure for Tristram's own death, which like "my" birth is unrepresentable as itself, and he also perhaps, if recent academic gossip is reliable, may be Tristram's real (as well as figurative) father.[3] The episode is also marked in a number of other ways, ways in which it seems to gather and organize "important" themes from the novel into its own context. For example, the chance of accident: the "sermon" is "found" suddenly in the midst of a series of digressive conversations of comically crossed purposes and uncertain receptions, Shandean conversations of mutual misunderstanding, underscoring the eccentricities of the characters—their separateness. And suddenly this "text" of fragmentary conversations is intersected by an unexpected *alien* text which *organizes* the assembly around itself without totally mitigating that separateness. Corporal Trim has been asked to find in a volume of Stevinus an illustration of his famous sailing chariot. Is there a chariot in it? The literal mind of Trim folds back the covers and shakes the volume and not a chariot but a folded document falls out—a text obviously not belonging to this book on implements of war.

The mystery of its accidental and unexpected manifestation "connects" with the theme of accidental occurrences in the novel, a "theme" irresistible to the Shandean character, and particularly to Walter, plagued like his nominal son by accidents. Like the chestnut, Toby's wound, Tristram's accident with the window sash, and so many other chance occurrences in the novel, the sermon must be picked up and made one's own—*read*. Accidents are always full of portent for the Shandys and always generate discussion, performance, and reference to texts. Chance must be turned into necessity. Accident must be made to generate representations and meanings in the vain hope of mastering chance. In general in this book the question of the accident is precisely a question of the *event* and also a question of "circumstance" or "occasion," the context of any representation. The problem of "reading" the chance occurrence is also the problem of the accident of *Tristram Shandy* as a "novel" of 1760 and "the accident" of the origin and nature of *the* novel as "genre," "institution," or "canon." These questions always seem to be silenced by a strange sense of "fatedness." As Walter says, however:

I have ever a strong propensity, said my father, to look into things which cross my way, by such strange fatalities as these;—and as we have nothing better to do, at least till *Obadiah* gets back, I should be obliged to you, brother, if Dr. *Slop* has no objection to it, to order the Corporal to give us a page or two of it. (II, xv, 119)

One kind of "illustration" is sought and another kind of "illustration" presents itself. An illustration of what? Certainly an illustration that needs further illustration. But another question forms itself that, like the question of "illustration," connects this episode not only with "themes" in the novel but also with the context in which I wish to discuss it. Falling out of one text into another "text" is a third text that properly "belongs" to neither ("falling" itself being a privileged movement in *Tristram Shandy*). This question of "belonging" not only intersects with the character of the narrator and his possible illegitimacy, and with Yorick's own curious genealogy,[4] but also with the questions of *genre* and *canon*—that is, what *properly* belongs to a text, what category it properly belongs to, and what makes it a proper member of a group of privileged texts. The question of "belonging," in this sense, also raises the problem of what is properly *inside* or *outside* a text. The birth of the narrator is "outside" his own text, and what takes place at this moment is another kind of text by the "real author" of this narrative. Yet, inasmuch as what is displaced "outside" is the self-constitution of a fictional narrator, and what displaces it as "inside" the text is the document of an outside (and extratextual) performative *event*, the presumptive relationship of text to "non-textual" event, occasion, circumstance—context becomes highly complicated. What is it precisely that is being textually represented at this point?

Another way this "found" text is suggestive of the novel as a whole is by Tristram's supplemental little apocryphal "narrative" of its strange life *after* this performance on the day of his birth and after Yorick retrieves the lost sermon the next day:

Ill-fated sermon! Thou wast lost, after this recovery of thee, a second time, dropp'd thro' an unsuspected fissure in thy master's pocket, down into a treacherous and a tatter'd lining,—trod deep into the dirt by the left hind foot of his Rosinante, inhumanely stepping upon thee as thou falledst;—buried ten days in the mire,—raised up out of it by a beggar, sold for a halfpenny to a parish-clerk,—transferred to his parson,—lost forever to thy own, the remainder of his days—nor restored to his restless MANES till this very moment, that I tell the world the story. (II, xvii, 142)

This strange journey of Yorick's text reminds us of the equally hazardous journey of Tristram's "double," his "homunculus," which also does not return to its author until after death. Tristram frequently makes the reader aware of the two times of his narrative, the time of the narrated event and the time of the act of narration. This doubleness is especially underscored inasmuch as most of what Tristram narrates happened *before* he was born, as a pre-condition for narrating his birth, because it all somehow explains how he was doomed before he got properly started. These two times are implicit in any narrative but are constantly foregrounded in this one. What is narrated is usually presumed to lead ultimately to closing those two times—to, in a word, an identity. Here the times are connected by a narrative all right, moreover a narrative of the life of a text, as in a sense, all first-person narratives are, figuratively. But here, the text whose life is narrated is *another* text (a text of an *other*), a text which enters the novel *doubly* at this point and in place of the narration of the narrator's birth. Hence, while it offers itself as a paradigm—a figurative repetition of the text as a whole—it is a very odd paradigm indeed. Yet repetition is particularly emphasized in this apocryphal narrative of this vagrant second text's odd changes of place. Repetition again figures in a complex way in Tristram's history of the various performances and publications of the sermon immediately following this narrative of loss and restoration. As example or paradigm of both loss and repetition, this narrative of the finding of the sermon, its performance in the novel at this point, and the little narrative of its subsequent wandering not only "connects" the two times of the novel, it also obviously "connects" with the novel's themes of loss and problems with repetition. The performance of the sermon, emphatically described *as* a performance, repeats the written sermon, itself delivered elsewhere in another context and published several times outside the novel in its own proper generic and canonic context. It is repeated again, with typographical oddities and with Trim's oratorical gestures, themselves doubled by Hogarth's engraving, by Tristram as part of his narration of the circumstances of his birth.

This stress on the repetitions of an outside text, which is itself an *event* inside the text, again sets in motion a certain play of opposition between outside and inside, between event and representation. Since an "event" is precisely what cannot be repeated, this event is invaded by its repetitions and representations. In the heterogeneity of its various situations and occasions, the primacy or definitiveness of any single "context" is challenged.

This accidental discovery of a document or letter immediately provokes explicit questions of genre, origin, authorship and authority, and legitimacy. By what strange path did it get there? Can we identify it? By what sign or token? Is it a Chariot?

No. Said my father, smiling, what is it then?—I think, answered *Trim*, stooping to take it up,—'tis more like a sermon,—for it begins, with a text of scripture, and the chapter and verse;—and then goes on, not as a chariot—but like a sermon directly. (II, xv, 199)

The document then is identified by its epigraphic text of scripture as the institutional form of a sermon. Given its present occasion, it will be a kind of "Birthday Sermon," like other "institutional" occasions in the book, especially those having to do with the narrator's conception, birth, naming, christening, and "circumcision." It will also provoke a kind of canonic council and debate at this point, also reminiscent of other comic canonic assemblies. A sermon? For what church? Papist or Protestant? This is a matter of some importance to these scholars. " 'Tis wrote upon neither side, quoth *Trim*, for 'tis only upon *conscience*, 'an please your Honours" (II, xvi, 120). The ingenuous Trim has made a point, but one must remember, *conscience* was a cause of some political importance to Anglicans, Dissenters, and Catholics in eighteenth-century England, with its disputes over Text and Corporation Acts and tolerance.[5] In order to lay these questions to rest, as well as to provide a diversion, the sermon *must be read*, performed in fact, by Corporal Trim. Before that can happen, a lot of "institutional" preliminaries must be taken care of: Trim's "clerical" qualifications must be examined, his oratorical "stance" described in minute detail, this latter constituting a kind of "institute" or elementary textbook on the oratorical gesture in miniature. Trim gets not much further than a performance of the scriptural "text" and the first phrase of the sermon when the debate about interpretation between Walter and Dr. Slop begins. His performance will be constantly interrupted by the commentary of his auditors, and sometimes by his own.

This first formal phrase, however, is worth reflection. It is an

incomplete phrase from the Epistle to the Hebrews, and serves in
a perfectly conventional way as the point of departure for the sermon. It is a fragment, almost as if it has been torn away from its
context in Hebrews and diverted to the sermonist's own purposes,
and in fact the possibility that the apostle's words have been so diverted is the basis for that first heated interruption by Walter and
Dr. Slop.

Richard Macksey has quite accurately called the sermon a
"purloined letter." It is one in a number of different ways. It is
diverted both from its nominal author and from its intended destination and detained in the volume of Stevinus and Vol. II of
Tristram Shandy, as well as in all the other ways described in
Tristram's little narrative.

Moreover, the sermon itself purloins a letter. (I mean, aside
from the recurrent question of whether Sterne pilfered passages
from other writers.) It is already apparent how this sermon has
purloined the Epistle to the Hebrews by tearing its "text" away
from a sentence in the epistle, moreover, a sentence dangerously
close to the "signature" traditionally given in the final lines of
Pauline epistles. The "signature" of the Epistle to the Hebrews,
however, is actually a *lack* of proper signature. Though its title in
the King James Version attributes it to Paul, its authorship has
always been contested, as far back as its history goes (the first century). Nor is there agreement on who precisely are the Hebrews
addressed by the Epistle. These doubts, along with the even more
recent speculation that it is not properly a letter at all, that the epistolary form was added by later editors to make it appropriate for
the canon, are modern problems with the text. But even *as* epistle,
the text has been diverted from its sender and from its destination
and appropriated (to) as part of the canon of the New Testament,
a "purloining" however sanctified. And in fact, its whole history
seems to be a series of such purloinings.

The epistolary form of certain canonic New Testament texts
foregrounds their relationship to specific occasions and contexts.
Obviously, the circumstantial and particular marking of this form
emphasizes the *historical* nature of the Christian revelation and its

insistence on *event*. This insistence defines both its radical break with the Judaic scripture and the nature of its narrative ties with Jewish history. Oddly enough, according to New Testament scholars, the *accident* of that form for what were epistolary instruments of early church policy apparently then became the formal *rule* for the acceptability of texts in Christian canon formation. The Epistle to the Hebrews may be an instance of this rule. That is, Hebrews, which begins rather abruptly, as if it had literally been torn away from its context, may actually have been a midrashic homily—a sermon like Yorick's—with epistolary formalities added on to the end by a later editor to make it conform to the canonic model. So in several senses, Hebrews is itself "a purloined letter."[6]

I stress these formal aspects of the Epistle to the Hebrews and its presumed circumstances for several reasons, only one of which is my avowed topic of canonic institution. While it is possible to demonstrate that the major theme of the sermon, conscience, is also a concern of both Hebrews and, in other ways, of *Tristram Shandy*, I want to stress that it is precisely the epistolary format of Hebrews which "contextualizes" it among the canonic texts of the New Testament. It is also precisely one of those formalities that is purloined by Yorick for the canonically formal mark of his sermon—the token by which it is identified *as* a sermon—and that also causes the first divisive dispute in the Shandy "council." Moreover, an analysis of the implications of enunciative form in this token fragment, as they comprehend a variety of implications in the epistle, shows that those possibilities provide a kind of protocol for Yorick's sermon. The more or less contemporary problems that Yorick elaborates are already in a sense implicit in the purloined phrase and its pronominal address. These demonstrations require that I digress a bit further on the contextual appropriations of Hebrews, those contexts that Hebrews provides for the sermon, and, by way of it, for the novel.

For these demonstrations, I must introduce another, curious "context." Late in his life John Locke, whose thought is notoriously prominent in *Tristram Shandy* in other ways, turned to theological matters and problems of Biblical interpretation, problems in particular with St. Paul's Epistles. In *The Reasonableness of Christianity*, Locke had caused a storm within Anglican orthodoxy by arguing that the scriptures were sufficiently clear to the interested reader without the aid, let alone the obfuscations, of theological interpretation or institutional mediation to explain the only articles of belief necessary for salvation: acceptance of Christ as the messiah sent from God and commitment to live in accordance with simple Christian morality (the two main features of the exhortation in Hebrews, incidentally). Locke found the Pauline Epistles more difficult, although he thought them not really essential for salvation. At any rate, he spent the last years of his life in a painstaking examination of those Epistles. The results were published posthumously in the form of *A Paraphrase and Notes on the Epistles of Saint Paul*, in effect, a translation into ordinary language to remove the obscurities with an emphasis on the main lines of Paul's arguments. Prefacing the Paraphrase was a hermeneutical essay, whose marvelously Shandean title echoes the title of Locke's most famous work: "An Essay for the Understanding of St. Paul's Epistles by Consulting St. Paul Himself." For Locke, this personal consultation meant not only an intensely attentive reading and rereading of each Epistle, but also, in explicit appreciation of the implications of their epistolary form, an attempt to read each text within its reconstructed historical context.[7]

The uncertainties surrounding the Epistle to the Hebrews, which was not paraphrased by Locke, are only a special case of the difficulties that their formally occasional nature present for the reader of Paul's Epistles. Locke nicely states these difficulties:

The nature of epistolary writings in general disposes the writer to pass by the mentioning of many things, as well known to him to whom his letter is addressed, which are necessary to be laid open to a stranger, to make him comprehend what is said: and it not seldom falls out that a well-penned letter, which is very easy and intelligible to the receiver, is very obscure to a stranger, who hardly knows what to make of it. (*Works* 3, Yolton, 14)

It is not only this tearing of the letter from its context that makes for the obscurity, but also the fact that no letter is ever actually a *single* text, even if it is a single letter in an exchange. Because it is part of an exchange, a letter is always a response to another "text," and both a solicitation and a scenario for a responsive text (or several), as well as a reference to a number of implied or encrypted contexts. Moreover, while Locke in his "Essay" underscores the problem of a number of kinds of "distances"—circumstantial, historical, and linguistic—which "alienate" Paul's letters from the modern reader, it should also be said that the letter form itself foregrounds and marks a distance in order to intend or attempt to close it. In this way, the letter only raises to a certain intensity problems inherent in all written texts. Certainly, in this regard, it really makes no difference that authority, signature, address, place of composition, data, *circumstantial contexts* of the Epistle to the Hebrews are all so disputed and uncertain. Neither does it make any difference whether it is sermon or letter, nor whether additions have been made to it to make it conform to canonical authority. The problems implied by these questions, the distances and marks of the letter's alienation, the wounds of its purloining, are "purloined" in another sense. They are *prolonged* by Hebrews. These are distances that it distinguishes *in* its statement and that, as statement or message, it demands be closed. The text of the Epistle marks a distance and asserts authority over it by reference to and on the basis of the authority of Prophetic texts, "texts" of the Christian Revelations and of the distance or difference between them. It defines by implication a church or community of Christians who have suffered much for their beliefs, but whose orthodoxy is weakened by the length (distance) of the wait for the fulfillment of the promised New Covenant in Christ's return and because of their proximity to the (now distant) Old Law and practices. It also implies that the writer is himself closer to the authorizing truth of that revelation than the addressed community who are in danger of losing its message. Moreover, it is as if it is the community's "drift away" that causes the distance that determines the necessity of a letter. Here is the passage near the end, from which Yorick tears his "token" text (in the Anchor Bible translation): "Pray for us, for we are convinced[8] that we have a good conscience, desiring to behave properly in everything. I strongly urge you to do this, so that I may be restored to you quickly" (13: 18–19). Though admittedly the demonstrative is ambiguous in reference, the implication is that the "Hebrews" can do *something* ("Pray for us" or "behave properly in everything") to close the distance.

The Epistle to the Hebrews not only serves as an instrument of church policy, it also provides an almost legalistic exposition of the theological justifications of policies and institutional practices, and like Yorick's sermon it challenges its addressees ethically and morally. The translator-editor of the Anchor Bible Hebrews, George Wesley Buchanan, says that, although a number of New Testament books speak of the New Covenant, never is it so fully or emphatically asserted as here. The writer of Hebrews speaks of the Covenant in terms of legal documents such as contracts or wills, emphasizing the legitimate sonship of Christ and what the faithful inherit by his death—a fine text for Tristram's "birthday sermon," but highly complicated if the speculations about his illegitimacy are accurate.

To this end, Hebrews makes extended use of innumerable passages of the Old Testament to ground its case midrashically for the fulfillment of its prophecies in the New Covenant and by Christ's life and death. The emphasis, however, is not on the *repetition* of prophecy but on the cancellation of any such doubling by the single *fact* of fulfillment. The emphasis is on the unexpected uniqueness of a novel *event* of Christ's death as God-become-man. The citation of (old) scriptural instances that only prefigure or anticipate that eventuality serves to underline a lack, a need, an imperfection in the Old Covenant. All the earthly and therefore inadequate representations of the Old Covenant, particularly those of the Levitical priesthood's repetition of partial sacrifices, since they are *merely* representational and repetitious, can never reach the perfection of *what* they represent. All these repetitions are cancelled by the *event* of Christ's death and ascension and everything this event *instituted*. If the relationship of Old to New is typological, it is a relationship of *copy to model*, promise to fulfillment.

The text explicitly employs these terms. The *event* of the latter in each of these cases does not repeat the former, but transforms it essentially, reduces, even *cancels* it. The *event* not only renders the former unnecessary or meaningless, but also asserts that a drift back toward the former by way of its institutional representations would be a betrayal of the event, risking loss forever of the new life it offered. For this text, which itself necessarily "repeats" and "represents" and exhorts another kind of repetition of this New Event, ritualistic practices of "atonement" and what they signify involve the repetition of the crucifixion and Christ's sacrifice—a repetition of his suffering. This is obviously a complicated matter, and not the least in that, as those last impatient days of waiting turned into centuries, orthodoxy itself required the institution of *new* representations to preserve and maintain, to prolong the event of their own denial.

From a strictly agnostic perspective, the "event" is already marked through and through by repetition and representation (e.g., Christ, who is guiltless, represents and substitutes in His death for Man who *is* guilty), and this relation of event to repetition underscores the inherent plight of any institution that attempts to preserve and therefore repeats the institution of an "event," that which cannot and in this case *must* not be repeated. Mutatis mutandi, on a less cosmic level, it is the literary problematic of the "novel."

There are many ways the concerns of the text of Hebrews are "translated" into Yorick's sermon and with it into Tristram's narrative by way of its password or "signature." The textual relationships I am describing are almost prefigured by the Hebrews' elaboration and allegorization of the structure of the Temple of the Old Covenant: a tent within a tent within a tent, each "holier" than the one containing it, each separated from the other by a "curtain" (cf. Anchor Bible, 139–146). The worshippers make their offerings in the first, only the priests enter the Holy space of the second, and only the High Priest enters the third—the Holy of Holies— and then only on the Day of Atonement with the offerings. What he does with the offering is not seen by the offerers. The event of the sacrifice of Christ as King-Priest-Advocate, as it is *seen* and testified to by the faithful, opens all these curtains, "curtains" of "flesh" (10: 20), tears these veils. Perhaps not the last curtain, or not fully until Christ's return, which will be *visible* to all, but that final opening is also promised. In this relationship of "Holy" text enclosed within the unholy and profane text of *Tristram Shandy*, which is the text and which the context at each point—which is the outside and which the inside? Each text works to contextualize the other two, and the possibility of all these eccentric divergences is already "contained" in Hebrews.

Right now I will deal with only some of the most obvious connecting passages between these texts, and mostly only summarily. There is the pervasive "midrashic" form of each, the ethical challenge of epistle and sermon, the genealogical concerns and what at once cancels and affirms genealogy in both Hebrews and the novel; and there is not only the persistent question of event and repetition or representation repeated on many levels in *Tristram Shandy*, but also the problem of the possible translations between these repetitions.

The principal subject, however, of Yorick's sermon—conscience—is also a central concern of Hebrews. It is precisely the problem of the old sacrificial practices: they "cannot perfect the consciences of the worshipper" (9: 9, RSV). If these institutional practices had been efficacious, would the sacrifices "not have ceased to be offered? If worshippers had once been cleansed, they would no longer have any consciousness of sin" (10: 12, RSV). Yorick's sermon also attacks Roman Catholic institutional practices which attempt not only to supplement but also to substitute for the necessity of individual conscience as private judgment. In Hebrews, it is precisely these practices that are cancelled by the New Covenant defined *as* "conscience," directly quoting Jeremiah 38: 33 (Septuagint) in this way:

This is the covenant that I will make with the house of Israel after those days, says the Lord: I will put my laws into their minds and write them on their hearts. (8: 10, 10: 16, RSV) then the prophet adds:

I will remember their sins and their misdeeds no more. Where there is for-
giveness of these, there is no longer any offering for sin. (10: 17–18, RSV)

While conscience cancels and replaces the institutional practices of the old church, it also places the individual under an increasingly frightening burden. "There no longer remains a sacrifice for sins, but a fearful prospect of judgement, and a fury of fire
which will consume the adversaries" (10: 26–27, RSV). The rule
(canon) of God's law imprinted on the minds and hearts of *all* his
people institutes a human community on the one hand, but on
the other no community (or institution) can save the individual
if he strays from that internal law. George Wesley Buchanan comments: "Jeremiah seemed to think if all people *knew* the Lord,
i.e., knew his commandments and will, then there would be unity
under the covenant. In his day, people followed various religious
customs and laws. If the Lord would only fix indelibly on their
minds the same rules, then the covenant community would function as the Lord planned it" (139). It is this uneasy, wavering hope
or faith in the power of community to override hobby-horsical
"interests" of individuals that marks Shandean concerns but also
brings into relief the sermon's (as well as the novel's) intersection
with the problematic Lockean epistemology.

What is at stake in this covenant is the necessity for a *community* instituted by the unity of a text (canon) of a law or rule
(canon) "imprinted" or "written" in the minds and hearts of each
individual. Within Lockean epistemology, the *novelty* and *accident*
of the event of any individual sensation or the uniqueness of any
combination of sensations imprinted on the individual mind creates a problem for any possibility of communication or common
knowledge, uniting individuals.[9] Or for that matter, any possibility of self-identity of *any individual*. It is also precisely this argument the writer of Yorick's sermon struggles with.

So the phrase Yorick "lifts" from Hebrews is not an indifferent selection. By playing on another grammatical ambiguity, rhe-

torically, our "proof text" stages a similar problem. I will repeat the full passage: "Pray for us, for we are convinced that we have a good conscience, desiring to behave properly in everything." After the distances noted above, after the sharp, even harsh, admonitions of the preceding text, who is this "us," this "we"? Who precisely is "desiring to behave properly in everything" in the epistolary proprieties of this closing, after this long textual exhortation of an "I" for "you" to understand and act according to this new propriety of rule imprinted in all *our* hearts, the very basis and precondition of any *us*, which *I* have had to make clear to *you*?[10]

The "we" of the close of Hebrews is as subtly admonishing as anything else in the text, at the same time as it is an apparent peace offering. First of all, it is the authoritarian, imperial "we" of an individual who reduces the "you" of a manifold, a community, into an individual. As such, it signs the assertion of authority over the vagrant community of addressees. At the same time, it implies that though my words have been harsh, they have been spoken out of loving concern and community *with* you. So that even their placating tone institutes a communion of belief, transcending or cancelling all differences of place or propensity. In this way, as in so many others, the appropriateness of this text to the canon of Biblical texts is clear. Yet these words also say that, though my words have been harsh, they were justified—*my* conscience is clear; I have behaved properly towards you. See to your own conscience and behavior and this meaning implies a necessary, affirming response.

But, finally, isn't there a shadow of a doubt crossing that "conviction" of certainty, emphasized by the King James translation as "trust," implicit in its assertiveness or need for it, implicit also in the possible internal divisions of the pronoun "we," a possibility underscored by the differences that divide the "we" made up, by the you and I together? And because of that self-division, isn't trust the pre-condition of the transformation of an "I" into a "we," or of any possible "we"? What guarantee do *I* have that "our" conscience is clear *except my* conscience, *except* the mantle of the institutional "we" which I here take on, except the "canon" (not yet canonic) of texts of the Revelation, which I witness (thus belatedly)

and which authorizes me to speak so authoritatively, but which at
the same time frees (deprives) me from the internal divisions of an
"I," and which at once affirms and cancels my personal signature?

Yorick's Sermon also takes up that possible internal difference in the "I" and exposes it in a different way. By quibbling on
the word "trust" in the phrase, the writer at once divides the "we"
of parson and congregation into a collection of "I"s and then immediately goes on to open up an internal division of self-reflection
in each of those "I"s:

> Trust! trust we have a good conscience! Surely if there is anything in this
> life which a man may depend upon and to the knowledge of which he is
> capable of arriving upon the most indisputable evidence, it must be this
> very thing, whether he has a good conscience or no. (II, xvii, 125)

By playing off the question of conscience against the group
conscience of the "we," Yorick not only changes the reference
of the "we" of Hebrews, but also brings into question the possible *community* of conscience. He acknowledges this question and
the possibility of further (specular) self-division by his immediate movement into the third-person singular. The chain of "alien-
ations" suggested are now made almost explicit:

> If a man thinks at all, he cannot well be a stranger to the true state of this
> account;—he must be privy to his own thoughts and desires;—he must
> remember his past pursuits, and know certainly the true springs and mo-
> tives, which, in general, have governed the actions of his life. (125–26)

From here on, the sermonist speaks of himself only in the
first-person singular. He runs his changes upon the theme of the
self-deceiving, self-serving possibilities of a (displaced) conscience
(or self-consciousness) through a series of fictional third-person
"characters" or examples until he develops an expanded "composition of place" for the solicited imagination of a "you," not unlike
Tristram's various appeals to and scenarios for the "you" of the
readers of his text.

These themes and modes of the sermon implicitly "comment" on the various "attitudes," "hobby-horses," and "interests"

of the various characters of the novel in the immediate context of
this "scene of reading," as various critics have noted. The beginning themes of the "knowledge" which a man has as depending
on "the most indisputable evidence" of a private self-reflection—
"conscience is nothing else but the knowledge which the mind has
within herself" (126)—along with other elements in the sermon
place it in general within the Lockean problematic, but without
particularly *marking* that connection in any way. The marking,
however, is provided by its context in the novel and the novel's
explicit references to Locke. Moreover, these references, "echoed"
in the sermon although it was written earlier and in another context, seem to be *organized* and *structured* now by the sermon into
a kind of statement or commentary. Locke had argued specifically
the question of conscience in Book I (ch. ii) of his *Essay Concerning Human Understanding* disputing it as proof of the "innateness"
of ideas, and Yorick here repeats many of Locke's arguments. For
both, conscience is neither "rule" nor "law" but a kind of private
court of judgment—a means by which an individual may read and
judge his own motives and actions in terms of "what is written
in the law of God" and according to "calm reason and the un-
changeable obligations of justice and truth" (132). A properly extended reading of Locke in terms of the sermon, however, might
reveal severe problems for Lockean "certainties." For one thing,
the severe doubt and self-division opened up at the beginning by
Yorick in this context could open a "wound" in the ground of self-
certainty and self-identity on which certain knowledge depends.
My question here, however, concerns the involvement of a text
in multiple contexts, other circumstances, other times and places,
and especially in texts that are marked specifically as canonic and
institutional. This question of "repeatability" also involves questions made earlier on *genre*, of "properly belonging," of property.
The questions raised by this narrative "scene of reading" of a
"found" text, a "purloined letter," pertain to a text's possibilities
(or capacity or faculties) for different *kinds* as well as instances of
narrative insertion, for either grounding or articulating other narratives, or for *instituting* articulations with other texts or contexts.

Admittedly, *Tristram Shandy* opens these questions by proposing them in the oddest, most eccentric and idiosyncratic ways. Yet these questions would seem to point to the *pre-conditions* of any possible understanding of a canon or institution or genre. In both the largest and the most precise senses, these questions cannot finally be answered. That is, I cannot say *why* this particular text was chosen (or its own apparent self-nomination confirmed) for the canon of the novel, nor how and why fictional narratives form or were institutionally selected to form the genre of the novel in particular ways and at different times, nor finally by what institutions at those different times that institutions were instituted. I cannot answer these questions not only because of accidents and contingencies it seems to me they necessarily implicate, accidents and contingencies highlighted by *Tristram Shandy* in its oddness, but also because the necessities those "accidents" institute can always be read back somehow to cover over the accidents themselves. Moreover, the power of texts to *appropriate* (in all its senses) any possible context, as the trajectory of these particular texts and their "institutions" demonstrates, does not leave untouched any "outside" sufficient to *define* genre, let alone institutings of genre, literary canons, or practices (institutions) of reading.

These translations of texts into different contexts were described earlier as a "purloining," a kind of misappropriation of a text, the tearing away of a text or a part of a text from its own appropriate contexts and its insertion in another (or *other*) context. In reading this particular scene in *Tristram Shandy*, a reading that cannot by nature be completed, I have concentrated on (and this was only a *selection* of richer possibilities) the narrative's (self-defined) misappropriation of a sermon by Yorick (or Sterne), and that sermon's misappropriation (again so questioned within the narrative) of a phrase from the Epistle to the Hebrews, a part or fragment of the Holy Canon of the Bible. In turn, I pursued the question of the possibilities of "misappropriation" involved in the translation of the Epistle from its own particular circumstances as a letter into that canon. What this analysis seems to suggest, however, is not only that these "translations" translated more into the new (con-) text than was expected, but that the "stolen" text seems to have the power to order structure, to institutionalize the new context according to its own rule (canon)—that is, to "authorize" its own appropriation. The process of appropriation would then seem to be a complicated "two-way" proposition.

Since no text is really inherently or "naturally" canonic, there will always seem to be something arbitrary or accidental in its selection. It is precisely the nature of institutions to rationalize, order, structure the accidental, the arbitrary, the novel event—a birth, a death—a text. On the other hand, the accidental text seems to have the power to structure, to define or delimit the field of possibilities indicated by other forms of fictional narrative (whether written earlier or later) in order for it to be appropriated for the canon of the English novel, but at the same time its own oddness and singularity had to have been maintained. The canon of the novel is a canon without a single model, a canon without a rule.

This process does not, however, stop with *Tristram Shandy*. This novel also "authorizes" and institutes, as well as institutionalizes, its own readings—that is, certain *practices* of reading, including my own. It "appropriates" certain questions it proposes as a (particular) kind of commentary. In a sense, it almost "dictates" its reading as by a kind of prosopopoeia, which is *Tristram Shandy*'s own rhetorical manner. Earlier I characterized the form of Hebrews as a kind of midrashic interpretation. Yorick's sermon, this episode of the novel, and my essay on it are also midrashic. This term has recently gained some new currency, and Buchanan has useful things to say about it. Noting that "the midrashic method of biblical exegesis, employed by the author of Hebrews, was basic to the Samaritan, Jewish, and Christian understanding of the role of scripture in religious life" (xix), he explains that the word "midrash" comes from a Hebrew root, meaning to "examine," "question," or "search": "a person preparing a midrash was one who searched the scripture to find its true meaning, which he then expounded, so the word came to mean to 'expound' or 'interpret'" (xx). According to Buchanan, there are two major types of midrash—"running commentaries" and "expositions" on special

texts. He notes that Hebrews is a homiletical midrash or exposition on Psalm 110. Yorick's sermon would also follow this form,
while the episode of *Tristram Shandy* in which it is inserted becomes "a running commentary." Moreover, the special conditions
of the midrash, its rule, would seem to be followed by the writer
of Hebrews, by Sterne, and by most commentators on the novel.
Scholars who prepared midrashim, as Buchanan points out, were
not simply "objective, dispassionate interpreters whose only purpose was to present the text." Always, it was a problem of articulating a canonic text in and to their own (institutional or circumstantial) contexts. Buchanan adds in a way most appropriate to
our circumstances:

> The reason such a method was necessary was that the official interpreter
> had to relate an ancient text that was considered sacred to the needs of
> a worshipping community in a different period of time and under situa-
> tions that differed from those that prompted the writing of the scripture
> on which they depended. Authors of midrashim were not free to ignore
> the text and present their ideas on the basis of contemporary need and
> normal logic. The scripture gave them their authority to speak. (xxi)

Yorick's sermon, my essay, and in a funny way, the conversation of
Walter, Toby, Trim, and Slop all are spoken under the "authority"
of an institutional "occasion" and a canonic text.

The possibility of freedom from text which Buchanan might
imply is not really relevant, and perhaps is utopian, but it could
be posed in another way, as a question of the institutions of the
text and the limits set by the text and its institutions on our own
discourse. And it is not only a question(ing) of the authority of
the text over, as well as for, our discourse. Even more than in
Buchanan's description, the text is not *simply* a matter of conve-
nience. But the hidden question, implicit in his apt description, is
then *what else* authorizes us to speak, *at this moment*, a question of
the institution of the canonic literary text?

In closing this investigation, for the moment, I want to return to Tristram's little apocryphal parable of the strange (future/
past) errancy of the text of Yorick's sermon from its scene of read-

ing in the hour of Tristram's birth to its even odder return to Tristram and to Yorick's spirit in the hour of Tristram's narration.

Time and occasion prevent the extended analysis this little narrative requires. But perhaps a few brief remarks can suggest its provocations. It would seem at first to suggest an allegory of the *lack* of control a text has over its possible contexts, but actually the stress would seem to be on the exchanges and recognitions the text occasions—despite how muddied it is by its accidental worldly contacts. Actually, the moral seems to have something to do with the value it generates as it passes. It serves as a kind of currency. It is good for a bit of change. It *connects* at the same time it promotes—literally—a certain economy.

Another text, however, appropriated by this little liturgical narrative, even if only in apparent contrast, suggests another kind of currency. I can best illustrate the text suggested in this passage by the juxtaposition of a couple of phrases: "buried ten days in the mire,—raised up out of it by a beggar" / "suffered under Pontius Pilate, was crucified, dead and buried, descended into hell, on the third day rose again from the dead." The text is the one that came to be known as the Apostle's Creed—the short summary of the belief, of the doctrine of the faithful, used in the catechism and at certain other ritual moments.[11] The reaches of its history are uncertain, but apparently it has been around since early Apostolic days. It was probably used originally in the form of three questions and answers in early baptismal ceremonies (appropriate in a number of ways to its textual moment in *Tristram Shandy*). It was called *Symbolum* by the early church fathers—nobody knows exactly why. The Latin word *symbolum* meant, among other things, license, warrant, contract, documentary authority, token. Speculation has it that the creed got this name by being used as a password for the identification of Christians to each other or by isolated communities during the persecutions. Or it might have received this name by its use as a form of contract in the baptismal ceremony. Either way, it marks and facilitates a rite of passage, a translation.

Yorick's sermon has complained of the vagaries of the text of individual conscience and has directed that it be submitted to the law of another text for interpretation and judgment, and has in turn provided a rule for a reading of the vagrant minds of the characters of the novel. The sermon has even "presided over" the moment of birth of its narrator and, in that sense, has character-ized the self-constitution of its own narration. In this little fable it has become itself vagrant but has been "returned" to the text of the novel and is available for future exchanges and transactions. The text of itself orders if not all at least enough of its contexts. The text of the sermon falls and not only survives its accidents, its worldly occasions, but by another "accident" or miracle is picked up for a half-penny by a parish clerk and transferred to his parson who can only "speak" by the authority of a text and an institu-tional occasion. The sermon provides that authority, and perhaps that is why the question of Sterne's plagiarism has always seemed so nonsensical. Whether he wrote it or not, he is not the author nor can he be. It is not his nor can it ever be, and this too is the nature of the instituting "event" that is always past and absent. Nor is the text returned to that authority except in public memo-rial—"nor restored to his restless MANES till this very moment, that I tell the world the story."

5

Sir Walter Scott and the Institution of History: The Jacobite Novels in the Relation of Fathers

> The structure of this event is such that one is compelled neither to believe nor disbelieve it. Like the question of belief, that of the reality of its historical referent is, if not annulled, at least irremediably fissured. Demanding and denying the story, this quasi-event bears the mark of fictive narrativity (fiction *of* narration as well as fiction as narration: fictive narration as the simulacrum of the origin of literature at the same time as the origin of law—like the dead father, a story told, a spreading rumor, without author or end, but an ineluctable and unforgettable story. Whether or not it is fantastic, whether or not it has arisen from the imagination, and whether it states or silences the origin of fantasy, this in no way diminishes the imperious necessity of what it tells, its law.
>
> —Jacques Derrida, "Before the Law."

> Once the state has been founded, there can no longer be any heroes.
>
> —Hegel, *Philosophy of Right*.

I. History as Anachronism

THE REFERENCE TO THE 1745 Jacobite Rebellion in Sir Walter Scott's subtitle to *Waverley—or 'Tis Sixty Years Since*[1] is so well known and seemingly commonsensical as to deflect the equally strong reference to Fielding's *The History of Tom Jones, a Foundling*, also set during the '45 Rebellion and published just four years after its bloody conclusion. Scott named Fielding "the first of British Novelists," a category to which Scott's *Waverley* was itself to be a major, innovative contribution.[2] Scott's story of a young Englishman on the road to discover and prove himself, at the very same time Tom's journey to identity crossed paths with this rebellion, could not have been written, or for that matter read, without reflection on Fielding and his novel; indeed *Waverley* is replete with references to Fielding, as are Scott's other novels. As I argued earlier, the 1745, based as it was on conflicts in presumptions about the order of history and the socio-political order history legitimates, served Fielding analogically as a figure for a basic change in the order of the private family, confirming a dynastic change in English political order to reveal a new way of imagining the history of the individual. For Fielding, it seemed to go without saying that these changes were exclusively English; by implication, they had already happened and are but revealed by Fielding's "history" of the contemporary English subject. For Fielding, the events of 1745 were a contingency of the near present, hardly concluded at the time Fielding started writing *Tom Jones*, a "framing" present, geographically distant from the setting of its story, whose historical consequences and significance could not at that juncture even be imagined.

On the other hand, it would seem a needless truism to point out that for Scott the 1745 was precisely history, as were Fielding and his "experiment in British literature" (*Lives*, 67). For Scott, Fielding's *Tom Jones* and the rest of his works offered the history of his times, as did the narratives of Defoe, Richardson, Smollett, and many others. They belonged as much to the past, in fact, as the 1745, or for that matter, as earlier Romances.[3] If the extravagantly fictional medieval romances of chivalry gave real insight into the history of the culture that produced and which they in turn had helped to produce, it was because these fictions, no matter how much the events they narrated defied belief, showed significant "truths" about culture's institutions, its manners, values, desires, beliefs, and ways of life. It would follow then that the fictions of the early eighteenth century were similarly historical, revealing the contours of a pastness that never was exactly present except as past. That is to say, they could never again be read in the way they would have been read in the 1740s, namely as images of an ambient world, but only from a constantly recontextualized historical or historicist attitude, however vague or subliminal—that is to say, as anachronism.

The event of 1745, which no doubt for both Scott and Fielding confirmed the basic constitutional changes effected by the 1688–89 Revolution and Settlement, then doubly demonstrated the anachronism of Jacobite dreams of restoration. That desperate attempt at present restoration was merely incidental and contemporary both to the "events" of Fielding's "History" and to its first readers, and however thematically analogous the issues of the rebellion and its claims might be to Fielding's story, their anachronism was for him a matter for satire and ridicule because they defied the continuity of development of the English state after the 1688–89 Revolution. From Scott's standpoint *in* Scotland sixty years later, and in a narrative that fully participates in the dream or "romance" as well as the "plot" of the Rebellion, anachronicity is essential to a Scot's sense of history, to a present experience of the past's irrecuperable pastness. For Scott, who was oblivious to neither the comic nor the serious effects of anachronism, the 1745 brought about a major rupture in history, creating an uncrossable gulf between Scotland's ancient past and any foreseeable present world. For Scott, the 1745 was not only an English problem but also a *British* tragedy, forever rendering irrecuperable a major portion of Scottish culture and, at the same time, compromising Scotland's position in relationship to England in the unequal Union and burgeoning commercial empire.

It is worth pausing a moment on this Jacobite dream of Restoration which figures so significantly in what is thought of as Scott's invention, or institution, of the historical novel. This dream of restoration, a desperate attempt to recover some past state of things, implicates the ambition of the historian as well. Anachronism not only haunts any such project, it also belongs to the very structure of the "historical." It is only by the experience of anachronism, of an impossible and improper trace of pastness in the present, that the past can be known at all. Nor, on the other hand, can we know the present as such except in relation to that anachronistic trace of the past. If the name of Scott is always associated with the narrative recovery of a romantic past, with the institution of history as such, his mode of operation can be compared with that of his eponymous character "Old Mortality," who goes about the countryside to repair the tombstones of the martyred Covenanters persecuted in the time of Charles II — "cleaning the moss from the grey stones, renewing with his chisel the half defaced inscriptions, repairing the emblems of death" so that all memory of their stories will not be lost (*Old Mortality*, 30). The traces of the past in the present are the signs of its loss. The renewal of the marks of that loss is the task of the Scottian historian.

Another variation on anachronism might take the form of the co-presence of two or more even slightly conflicting histories of the same past events, which, paradoxically, confirm the reality of the events and their pastness. A third move involving anachronism could also be derived from *Old Mortality* and is a version of what Derrida calls *contretemps* or "counter-time."[4] This instance would involve the confusing perceptions of a subject who experiences in a strong way shocking discrepancies of two different times in the same place. Such a discord is particularly apparent when *Old Mortality*'s protagonist, Henry Morton, returns to Scotland after enduring a ten-year exile for his participation in a bloody rebellion of the outlawed Covenanters. The conflict had culminated in the rebels' defeat at Bothwell Bridge in 1679 by an English army led by Charles II's illegitimate son, the Duke of Monmouth, along with the hated Stuart persecutor of the Covenanters, John Graham of Claverhouse. Morton returns in 1689, the year after the British Revolution, after Monmouth himself has been executed for leading a rebellion against the accession of his uncle, James II, who has now been forced off the throne. With the reestablishment of the Presbyterian Church, those moderate Covenanters who accept the Church are now legal. History has doubled back on itself to produce one paradox inside another, as each side, as it were, rebels against itself. The fanatic fringe of Covenanters, now doubly anachronistic, are still in rebellion, even though their Stuart persecutors have been outlawed and exiled. Indeed, Claverhouse is now in the Highlands trying to foment a rebellion that will restore James to the throne, and to accomplish this end, he has fallen in with his own arch enemy—Burley of Balfour, the assassin of Archbishop Sharp. In general, many of those who had made policy and employed official state violence now are either subject to the same violence they handed out or are themselves perpetrating violence against the state—precisely the offense they were so zealous in punishing while in power. Morton, who had many divided loyalties but joined the rebel Covenanters earlier out of a sense of justice, is now confronted by a world ironically turned upside down. Morton's and the reader's sense of the dislocation of warring pasts within the present is all but overwhelming, as the legitimate are delegitimated.

The problem this situation raises is, on the one hand, that of the arbitrariness of legitimate violence as such, a radical question raised more often in Scott's novels than their reputation for conservatism would suggest. On the other hand, what *is* legitimated with legitimation of select acts of violence is the state as an impersonal institution no longer identified with a particular ruler or even a ruling family or dynasty. Since legitimation can be regarded as a major motive for history and perhaps accounts for the beginnings of modern historiography,[5] this question is not insignificant. Certainly, the problem of legitimation and delegitimation shapes both *Tom Jones* and *Waverley*, on several different levels. Among them is Fielding's attempt to legitimate his "new species of writing." Has Scott set out to delegitimate it? By rewriting Fielding, has Scott tried to broaden what he considered its too provincial and "untranslatable" Englishness by his own "experiment in British literature"?

The disjunction of historical times, and the problem of legitimation can be considered not only the most common gesture of Scott's novels, but also the principle in forming their structures in the common form we receive them. That is to say the original narrative in their first editions, already in many cases framed by multiple narrators or fictional editors and punctuated by supplementary notes, becomes in later editions sandwiched by additional introductions signed by Scott, now explicitly admitting their authorship. These new additions provide fuller narratives of the novels' composition, the historical originals of characters, of places, and of the stories themselves and interlace the text with notes and references and contrary versions of what "really" happened in actual history, frequently in more or less direct conflict with the original narratives. These moments of achronicity or heterotemporality might be characterized as historiographic, in that the present of the story becomes traversed by doubts, by the possibility of alternative chronicles and, most perplexing of all, by later "present" moments of the author, that contextualize the text's composition, its multiple publications, and the contemporary reading process. Scott's verse romances, have similar features and later additions, with the contextualizing reference to the present moment their composition in terms of the author and/or nation.[6] Questions of origins become very complicated indeed.

In this regard, it is revealing to return to Scott's fable of "the same common origin" of "Romance and real history" in the story told by the "father of an isolated family, destined one day to rise into a tribe, and in farther progress of time to rise into a nation" ("Romance," 134–35) discussed in my Introduction. As I suggested then, Scott's "some common origin" isn't really an origin but a deviation from an earlier origin, itself a deviation. Even so, Scott's stories, whether they take the form of novels or of the verse romances, never return to those moments of national origin or even to times appropriate for romance. What seems to interest him most, even to the point of fascination, are instances of passage into some version of modernity. More precisely, these moments for the most part involve the emergence of the modern nation-state from the ruins of feudalism, which he identified with the institutions of chivalry and romance. Even in *Ivanhoe* the demise of chivalry is already clearly on the horizon, as the novel moves toward a centralized government, joining together select Saxons and Normans. The key moments in these narratives can also be characterized as times riven by conflicting stories, warring histories of origin.[7] Such times are usually accompanied by more or less present-day references, most often to the French Revolution and its Napoleonic aftermath, crucial events in the development and theorization of the modern nation-state. This reference is perhaps most conspicuous in the Introduction to *Quentin Durward* (1823). This novel's machiavellian Louis XI is faced with a disunified kingdom, with a growing, increasingly powerful, and necessary burgher merchant class on the one hand, and warring, chivalric feudal Barons who care mainly about their own honor, power, and fiefs on the other. Louis uses every strategem, every lie and dirty trick, to centralize the government and create an administratively unified modern state. He does it in a way, however, that leads inevitably to the later French Revolution and Napoleon. Young Quentin, idealistic believer in the values of chivalry, is chosen by Louis as his special agent and forced to become almost as wily a politician as his master. The protégé, in contrast with his master, acquires the guile necessary not only to make Louis appear honorable but also to ensure just results. This transformation of what is shown to be anachronistic—chivalric values—into an effective practice of modern nationalism surfaces frequently in Scott's novels as it did in earlier verse romances. *The Lady of the Lake* is set against the background of the Scottish monarch James V's attempt to unite warring feudal clan chiefs into a state system capable of resisting English encroachment. This James uses several of the tactics Scott later associates with Louis XI.

Waverley also has a field of resonance in the present time of its composition. The points of Scott's beginning, his returns to the manuscript after two periods of neglect, coincide with important junctures in the rise of Napoleon and Britain's attempt to stop him. Scott takes up the writing of *Waverley* in late 1805, telling us in chapter one that he fixes the date of his story as "Sixty Years before this present Ist November, 1805" (*Waverley*, 4). (Ironically, given our point of departure, if one dated this novel from its publication date, then sixty years before the earliest date it could be opened by a reader would be 1754, the year of Henry Fielding's death.) At any rate, Napoleon had himself crowned Emperor in December 1804, and, as Richard Humphrey points out, Scott begins the novel just weeks after the British victory at Trafalgar.[8]

He sets the manuscript aside, and according to Claire Lamont's dating, takes it up again "about 1810" (*Waverley*, viii). During Britain's involvement in the Peninsular War, he puts it aside once again not to return to work on the manuscript until the Autumn of 1813, on the eve of the Battle of Nations. He completes and publishes this novel during the pre-Waterloo time when "the British nation was officially—if prematurely—celebrating peace in Europe" (Humphrey, 5). (Humphrey also points out that Scott and Napoleon shared the same birthday, Scott being the younger by only two years.)

I want to examine the development of these themes in the three novels Scott wrote about the Jacobite rebellions of the eighteenth century. In many ways, these particular novels bear most directly on Scotland's passage into the modern world; Since the Jacobite rebellions began with and in a sense tested the validity of the 1688–89 revolution, its subsequent settlements, and the Union between Scotland and England, they also chart the modern formation of the British State. Given his focus on an event so recent and crucial to Scottish interests, a gamble the outcome of which is already well known, we can think Scott meant this history at once to achieve closure of a certain past and to open onto the future. At any rate, it is at this conjuncture that Scott chooses to situate his first novel in the achronological production of a series that begins in 1814 with *Waverley*, a novel about the 1745 Rebellion regresses with *Rob Roy* in 1817 to the earlier Jacobite rising of 1715, and loops around in 1824 with *Redgauntlet* to the rumored final return of the Stuart Prince Charles to Scotland in the mid-1760s.[9] This last novel in the series is perhaps the oddest of all Scott's novels. It concerns a conspiracy that never comes to any historical consequence, because the government refuses to recognize its existence, making it an historical novel about an event that never happened—in short, a "pure" fiction. *Redgauntlet* serves Scott as an opportunity to look back at the Jacobite Risings that—whatever they meant for England (or Fielding)—were Scotland's last hope of restoring a *Scottish* king, thus of extricating herself from the asymmetrical Union with England and, perhaps, achieving in-

dependence. *Redgauntlet* also seems to afford Scott a retrospective
on the last century's principal prose fictions.

In both cases, what is involved is history. In terms of Scotland's future, this entails a cultural loss of a certain past and
the nation's ambiguous profit by that loss as the result of the
'45. In 1824, when *Redgauntlet* was written and published, Scott
also came to the reluctant decision to conclude his series *Ballantyne's Novelist's Library*, to date the most inclusive gathering of
the variety of prose fiction published in English during the eighteenth century. I will have more to say about this project in Chapter 6, but it should suffice for now to emphasize that the *Novelist's
Library* was not only historical in itself but also served to institute a genre as both historical and heterogeneous. In terms of the
genre and its past, as with Scotland's lost past, what is at question
is the historicity of institutions, the complex economy of loss and
conservation involved in both the practice and the very idea of
institution. It could be argued that *Redgauntlet* provides the postscript to this historical project as well as to the Jacobite dream. If
Waverley involves the introduction of a young, sensitive, and sympathetic Englishman to both Lowland and Highland Scotland
and to Scottish problems, and *Rob Roy* brings a comparably unsympathetic and prejudiced young Englishman to Scotland. Com-
pleting the international symmetry, then, *Redgauntlet* features the
journey of two young Scotsmen south to England to witness the
death of the English Jacobite dream, casting this problem as that
of both nations, rather than the issue that divides them. Just as
the '45 serves as the opening to Scott's whole series of novels, the
series itself will acquire the corporate name of the first in the series
chronologically—*The Waverley Novels*. To focus on three novels
that are thus scattered across the first decade of Scott's novel production is to set oneself at an historical conjuncture that determines what larger social, historical and national problematic will
animate the major part of Scott's work.

Since I have already suggested that restoration is one of the
basic motives of the historian, I must remind my readers that the
historical plot in these novels—the attempt to restore the Stuart

monarchy—is itself a thrust *against* history. Certainly, then, the word "plot," at least in relation to the Jacobite novels, has more than a single meaning. I have suggested this notion's implication in the historian's occupational ambition, but I must also insist on Scott's ambivalence about the Jacobite plots. On the one hand, there are the Scottish interests in the Restoration—Scott's reported remark that if he had been a young man in 1745 he would probably "gone out" with the rebels, his sense of all that Scotland suffered and lost in its aftermath, and his nostalgia for that lost past. On the other hand, we have his progressivist philosophy and hopes, his suspicions that the Stewarts were selfish, cynical about Scotland's prospects, and were less than firm in their loyalty to the nation, and above all his sense that their attempt at restoration went *against* history. These ambivalences pervade his representations of the Jacobite cause and find expression in the final chapter of *Waverley*.

II. Purloined Individuals and Letters

But there are other plots as well. Besides the historical plot to restore the Stewarts (Scott seems to prefer the Scottish spelling to the English normalized "Stuart") to the British throne, there is the account of the young man's adventures, an initiation plot. In addition, some of the Jacobite conspirators plot in some way to get the hero involved in the larger intrigue. Finally, the latter minor conspiracy is part of the novelist's plot—on the surface (but there is more to it) to get both hero *and* reader involved in the historical conspiracy before either knows what is taking place.

Aside from the thematic parallels between these related intrigues, what strikes me as particularly important is the similar way in which these last two conspiracies are carried out. The young hero always functions as a sign to be shown or a text to be read in ways unimaginable to himself and to the reader as well. Waverley is such an unwitting sign from the outset, as he serves as the open-minded Englishman and sympathetic point of view whereby Scott can introduce Scotland to the readers of her sister kingdom. Even before that he is made a sign or token, as when his Tory uncle asks his Whig father's permission to send him on a tour of the continent. His father's superior, the Cabinet Minister, whom the toady Richard has consulted in turn, worries that the appearance in suspicious Continental venues of the son of a government official from a family already known to have ancient Jacobite loyalties (which also accounts for Richard's success since he too functions as a sign or prize for the government) might be compromising to the Minister himself. As soon as Waverley crosses the border into Scotland as an English military officer, he becomes a prize to be sought out and seen with by the major conspirators. As a scion of an important *English* Jacobite family, his visits with those known to be leading Jacobite conspirators signifies the readiness of rich and important English gentry and perhaps even ranking military to support Prince Charles. Even the Prince himself acquires symbolic capital by being seen by his other followers in what appears to be serious consultation with Waverley.

The protagonists of the other two novels similarly operate as signs in an historical game of competing nationalisms. Moreover, they, like Waverley, are initially involved in this game by means of intercepted or purloined letters or papers. For lack of these letters or papers, the hero misconstrues the nature of his situation and unwittingly takes up a part in the intrigue. The use to which the letters are put by others for whom they were not intended feeds rumor or gossip and provides evidence for misrepresentations that make the hero's involvement other and more culpable than it actually is. The fact that the letters (and other news) from Waverley's commander warning him about his situation and ordering him back to his command are stolen and kept from reaching him perpetuates the romantic, narcissistic stupor that blinds him to his actual historical situation. His failure to respond to those letters, the use of his letters and seal as proof of his authority to provoke mutiny among his men, and the misleading nature of the documents he himself is carrying in his portmanteau, all provide documentation to Major Melville in support of the charges against Waverley's treasonable activities. By recontextualizing these details from the narrative past, Scott puts their meaning through a sequence of changes resembling that undergone by Yorick's sermon or Tom Jones's adventures. Moreover, the offering of these new readings of him and the texts in his portmanteau at this later stage of the narrative reveals the possibility of understanding Edward's intentions and the details of his journey in an entirely new way, redoubling the narrative we have been reading up until now. That narrative reveals itself to be a war of interpretation that amounts to two different narratives or histories. (There is a similar effect in Darcy's letter about midway in *Pride and Prejudice* explaining his actions and motives, a letter that requires anguished repeated readings by Elizabeth as well as a review from this unexpected perspective of a number of previous events.) Such instances of stories doubling back on themselves in this way suggest the history we think we have been reading may not be the only way such a history can be told.

In *Rob Roy*, Frank Osbaldistone's teasing insinuations about himself to a paranoid fellow traveler provide the basis for a misrepresentation that results in Frank's arrest as a Jacobite conspirator/highwayman, after the traveler is robbed of government money and secret papers. But these are only momentary difficulties in this novel. The real trouble begins when Frank's letters to his father, warning him that his cousin Rashleigh is not to be trusted, fail to reach their destination. Rashleigh is consequently put in a position of trust and power where he can interrupt the circulation of paper credit and abscond with important papers that could ruin Frank's father. Rashleigh uses those papers to pressure Highland lairds into joining the 1715 insurgents. Since this turn of events is the result of Frank's impetuous refusal of his father's wish that the two go into business partnership in favor of his own desire to become an itinerant poet, Frank is overcome with guilt. As he explains to Die Vernon, "I grieve not for the loss, but for the effect which I know it will produce on the spirits and health of my father, to whom mercantile credit is as honour" (*Rob Roy*, 159). This transference of the language of chivalry to modern commerce becomes a pattern in this novel. Later, Frank's friend and accomplice in the attempt to rescue these papers, the Glasgow merchant the Bailie Jarvie Nicol, redefines this tranference as a supercession: "But I maun hear naething about honour—we ken naething here but about credit. Honour is a homicide and a bloodspiller, that gangs about making frays in the street; but Credit is a decent honest man, that sits at home and makes the pat play" (231). Similarly, the language of chivalric adventure and heroism is systematically transferred to his father's dedication to commerce, as in the noble description Frank delivers in the first chapter:

> Love of his profession was the motive which he chose should be the most ostensible, when he urged me to tread the same path; but he had others with which I only became acquainted at a later period. Impetuous in his schemes, as well as skilful and daring, each new adventure, when successful, became at once the incentive, and furnished the means for farther speculation. It seemed to be necessary to him, as to an ambitious conqueror, to push on from achievement to achievement, without stopping to secure, far less to enjoy, the acquisitions which he made. Accustomed to see his whole fortune trembling in the scales of chance, and dextrous at adopting expedients for casting the balance in his favour, his health and spirits and activity seemed ever to increase with the animating hazards on which he staked his wealth; and he resembled a sailor, accustomed to brave the billows and the foe, whose confidence rises on the eve of tempest or of battle. (10–11)

When it comes to the purloining of significant papers, *Redgauntlet* provides a special variation on the theme. The novel starts off as an epistolary relationship between two friends—the romantically inclined and errant Darsie Latimer and what appears to be his more prosaic companion Alan Fairford. The beginning of the two heroes' troubles and, according to critics, those of the novelist as well is marked by the breakdown of that correspondence with the abduction of Darsie and the beginning of authorial narration. The correspondence which has earlier been intercepted and read by Redgauntlet not only helps him to identify Darsie as his long-sought nephew but also misleads him as to Darsie's character, thus prompting his abduction.

Gossip and rumour also come into play in *Redgauntlet*. A notable example—paradigmatic in a way for the ambivalence of these Scott novels—is the fact that Redgauntlet has been out around the countryside telling men "stories" about their fathers' exploits in the '45. This is his way of scaring up recruits for his own belated plot for rebellion. If readers from his time to ours have misread Scott as the author of romances rather than anti-romances, such misreading is both enabled by the obvious ambivalences of his novels and also thematized there. It is perhaps worth noting that it is with letters from mistaken sources that Frank is able to penetrate the Highlands in search of his father's papers in *Rob Roy* and that Alan Fairford of *Redgauntlet* is able to penetrate the circle of conspirators by means of a series of sealed letters.

I have argued in my first chapter that the displaced or pur-loined letter and gossip, as well as the relationship between them, are more than ubiquitous plot devices in novels: this is one way that novels emblematize their own nature as fictional texts.[10] In many novels, letters are linked to origins and either contain or are thought to contain the secret that will solve a puzzle created by the novel's plot. The displacement, withholding, or postponement of that truth makes possible the plot as a series of errors, most often figured by gossip, rumor, or misrepresentation. To be sure, letters and gossip certainly serve this purpose for Scott, but another kind of reading or misreading, possibly related to the misreading of the letters, is also prominent.

If the young heroes are led, for their initiation into manhood, into a land of "romance and fiction," as in *Waverley*, it is their reading or misreading of the literature of romance that has drawn them there, that has motivated their own pursuit of poetry, their quixotic and anachronistic dream of realizing romantic adventure in a return to a more heroic past, their attraction to the mysteri-ous and "wrong" woman in a place that insistently is irredeemably *past* by definition and is a simulacrum of origins. (This dream also motivates such villains as *Heart of Midlothian*'s George Staunton.)

III. Family Romance and the Deformation of Gender

Like that of the historical conspirators, the heroes' quest for ad-venture involves rebellion—rebellion against the present, against established or de facto authority, against the immediate father, as in Frank's case, or in some other way, that suggests a rejection of the father. Waverley is, in effect, rebelling against the present in the form of his absent and indifferent, opportunistically Whiggish father. His adventures take him through a series of surrogate fathers or uncles. He is raised by his Jacobite uncle and aunt who promote his romantic inclinations, and later the Baron Bradwardine acts in loco parentis. Then follows a succession of father figures. There is his military commander, Colonel Gardiner, and more importantly, a series of older brothers, always acting in the name of the father, figures such as Fergus, who becomes temporarily a model for Waverley. There is Colonel Talbot, who comes to search for him out of filial respect for Waverley's uncle and who replaces Fergus as model. Finally, there is the patronymic Prince Charles himself, who doubles for the shadowy Jacobite Father whose attempted restoration temporarily engages him.

The fact that the rebellion against the authority of the father or the present always ambivalently represents a search for a father or origins is underlined by this series of surrogate fathers. But this paradox is perhaps most apparent in Darsie's rebellion against both the authority of present commercial values and the career at law that his father's friend and substitute has imposed on his own son, Alan. For Darsie is in fact searching for the truth about his own origins and about the father he has never known. It would appear doubly odd, then, that his rebellion almost is made to serve a claim for direct descent and hereditary right, as well as for the monarch's *absolute* authority based on the natural authority of the father. But the real irony of Darsie's situation lies in the fact that this claim can as easily justify the presently constituted and established authority of the Hanoverian dynasty. Wavering between personal affront, attraction to Fergus and Flora, and "inexpressible repugnance at the idea of being accessory to the plague of civil war," Edward Waverley reasons in the following way:

Whatever were the original rights of the Stuarts, calm reflection told him, that, omitting the question how far James the Second could forfeit those of his posterity, he had, according to the united voice of the whole nation, justly forfeited his own. Since that period, four monarchs had reigned in peace and glory over Britain, sustaining and exalting the character of the nation abroad, and its liberties at home. Reason asked, was it worthwhile to disturb a government so long settled and established and to plunge a kingdom into all the miseries of civil war, for the purpose of replacing upon the throne the descendants of a monarch by whom it had been willfully forfeited? (XXVIII, 140–41)

The present government has now become sanctified by a new line of descent and a new representation of the nation-state. Each of the heroes of these novels will, at one time or another, confront this argument. While such a Humean judgment is later argued by Talbot and seems virtually the same as that of Scott and even the novel itself, Waverley will fall away from this position once his bruised feelings begin to recover from Flora's rejection and when he is captured by a Whig mob and subjected to a stern interrogation by Melville.

"Under which king?" Scott will ask, quoting lines from *Henry IV, Part II* as the epigraph to *Waverley.* The novels involve not only the struggle between generations, between past and present, a problem of sequentiality, but also a problem of authority within generations, a problem of simultaneous claims of authority and legitimacy—civil war, brother against brother, cousin against cousin, a conflict between sibling Kingdoms. And the novels involve not simply a question of fathers, but of uncles as well; that is to say, the brothers of a previous generation.

These questions involve the Stuarts and their Hanoverian cousins—that is to say, the historical struggle, as well as the personal problems of the fictional protagonists of the novels. It is impossible to overstate the thematic coincidence of the two plots—the historical struggle represented by the novels and the adventures of the individual heroes, despite the scruples of various critics about their lack of coherence in this respect. The two plots are mirror images of each other, and that image is refracted in all the parental, avuncular, and fraternal relationships that are multiplied throughout the novels. Beyond the familial relationships of the heroes, most of the other characters are explicitly involved as well in problematic familial relationships or surrogates for them: Jarvie Nicol's piety toward his father and the fact that he is always identified by means of him; Die Vernon's pious loyalty toward her father who disguises himself as a "Father" or priest; Rob Roy's concern for and mistaken pride in his own sons; Alan Fairford's obedience to and then temporary rebellion against his tyrannical but loving father and the career at law that "has come to him in a hereditary way." Frank Osbaldistone's father threatens to disinherit him in favor of his treacherous cousin Rashleigh, but Frank's father had been himself, as elder brother, disinherited by *his* father in favor of his foxhunting Jacobite younger brother. Later in *Rob Roy*, that action is again repeated when Sir Hildabrand disinherits his remaining living son, Rashleigh, as a traitor to the Jacobite cause, in favor of Frank, who is actually the legitimate heir by his own father's primogeniture. That Frank mistakenly thinks Rashleigh's machinations will render that inheritance "a dead letter" is not irrelevant to the theme I noted above. In addition to the larger and numerous clan loyalties and ancestral claims that are set in motion in the novels, there is the fact that Bonnie Prince Charles, the young Pretender, returns, disguised as a priest-"Father" in *Redgauntlet*. Charles not only adventures for the Stuart claim of legitimacy, he acts in the *name* of his still living father, James III (the Old Pretender). As for civil war, besides the conflict between brothers and cousins suggested above, there is the hopeless case of the comic Peter Peebles—a long-standing claim against a dissolved partnership (which began in 1745), complete with its own genealogy of failed representations, a claim no more foolish and unreasonable than that of Prince Charles.

The problem of parents touches every aspect of these novels, I am suggesting, including their relationship to their author. Scott states in the 1829 "General Introduction" that disclosure of his name as author of the series "restored to him a sort of parental control over these works" (*Waverley*, 347), which he performs by revision, the addition of supplementary introductions explaining the genesis of each novel, and footnotes documenting the actual origin of events and characters. Using a metaphor that is as old as writing and as ubiquitous as the novel, he claims to have engendered these texts which are also his children, as if in appearing now in his own name, like a long-lost monarch, means that authority has been restored to him. In other words, he restores on the level of authorship and as fiction what cannot be restored *in* the story or through history. But the problem is more complex than this conclusion suggests. While the attempted restoration of the Stewarts fails in the novels and in history, the ancestral romance of the Jacobites is restored *as* text *by* the novels and in them, in a curious way, the authority of the father *is* reinscribed, if in name only.

Although each of the heroes begins by rebelling against his father, or at least against the order of the "ordinary" contemporary world, each reverses himself at the turning point of the novel and sets out to "save" his father. Indeed, Waverley sets out twice to recover his name and honor and, in effect, save his uncle and/or father. The novel ends as he participates in the restoration of the forfeited estate and treasured family cup to the Baron Bradwardine, earlier his surrogate father and now his father-in-law. Frank, when he learns of his father's financial dangers, repents of his romantic folly and familial neglegence, and sets out into the Highlands to recover his father's "papers" and save his business and his good name. Once again, *Redgauntlet* is a special case. Darsie has no father—that is, he does not know who his father is or was. The turning point of the novel comes when he discovers that he *is* the father in question in the novel. His importance to Redgauntlet (who turns out to be his uncle) stems exclusively from the fact that Darsie is the legitimate head of the clan—as son of his uncle's older brother, slain in the '45—and the uncle cannot lead his clan in the new rebellion without the authority of the rightful chief. It is himself Darsie must save. At the same point, Darsie understands the mysterious young lady "Greenmantle," who has been strangely interested in his welfare and of whom he has romantic fantasies, is actually his sister, which discovery brings me to another point.

There are innumerable fathers and uncles in these novels, but almost *no* mothers, no major ones anyway. This lack perhaps reflects the single-minded patriarchialism that is at issue in these novels, but the displacement of matrilineality suggests other darker possibilities that *Redgauntlet* approaches most directly. First, let us recall the notable exceptions Janet Gallatley, Darsie's unnamed mother, and Rob Roy's wife Helen MacGregor. One should also mention that Edward acquires much of his "romantic" education from an aunt who is the depository of ancestral traditions. He is nursed back to health by old Janet, once accused of being a witch, who is the mother of a dead poet, and mad Davie, whose memory preserves his dead brother's poetry, a trio associated with the past and with the death of poetry. Edward receives help here and elsewhere from (usually) mysterious and romantic women. Darsie's mother, dead by the time the novel begins, has the only major role of any of the heroes' mothers who have conveniently disappeared long before their respective novels begin. After the death of his father, Darsie's mother has tried to "save" Darsie from the penalties of the Jacobite participants in the '45 rebellion and from the legal guardianship and machinations of his uncle by changing his name and keeping him out of England. She is also trying to save him from the ancient curse on the Redgauntlets, originating in the primordial murder by a father of his son for political reasons. So there is something powerful, often angry, masculine, and uncanny about these women.

The third prominent mother is the most frightening of all—not the mother of the protagonist, but the wife of the titular character and the mother of his sons, Helen MacGregor of *Rob Roy*. She both saves and threatens Frank Osbaldistone at a crucial moment when, as Scott puts it, with the "specks of blood on her brow," the "flushed countenance, and the disordered state of the raven locks which escaped from under the red bonnet and plume that formed her head-dress, seemed all to intimate that she had taken an immediate share in the in the conflict. Her keen black eyes and features expressed an imagination inflamed by the pride of gratified revenge, and the triumph of victory" (290). This image, which seems to Frank to "approach nearly to the ideas of those wonderful artists, who gave to the eye the heroines of Scripture history," seems more obviously, if anachronistically, to evoke the well-known image of the French Revolutionary. Helen is relentless in her resentment, her need for revenge, and her clannish isolation. Her ferocity dooms her sons. She seems the paradigmatic case for Scott of the deformation of gender as a result of political injustice. Her single-minded devotion to a disinherited family is related to the equally single-minded devotion of the more prominent and idealistic heroines, Flora MacIvor and Die Vernon, to the Stewart cause, except that even in this extreme case Flora blames herself and her own fanaticism for her brother's downfall.

If it is peculiar to Scott that each of the heroes must come into contact with this kind of mother-figure, then the love choices he makes for these heroes are even more curious. Each of them pursues someone who treats him in a sisterly fashion. Only in *Redgauntlet* does the sibling relationship become explicit eroticism and therefore forbidden. Edward falls in love first with a woman so married to the cause that she can only regard him as a friend and sister, and then with a woman whom *he* has formerly regarded as a sister and who *is* indeed daughter to the man he regards as father. Die Vernon considers Frank her brother until the deaths of the Stewart cause and of her father.

It is perhaps significant that Darsie is forced to dress as a woman during one episode of his kidnapping. This ordeal serves as his re-education, as it forces him to repeat a number of the moves Prince Charles made in escaping from Scotland after the failure of the '45, cross-dressing being but one of them. The femininization of the Waverley hero is a critical commonplace.[11] Other transgressions in the novels range from the symbolic penetration of a magical and forbidden territory associated with one's origins, to the more literal transgressions of treason, rebellion, and disobedience to the father. The shadowy presence of incest in these novels suggests not only the brush with ultimate transgression, but also the ultimate implications of the self-enclosure of the Stewarts' strict dynasticism, the isolation and self-enclosure of the Highland clan system, the *self*ishness of the adherents of both, and the lack of ordered communication and commerce between realms. Finally, "incest" both suggests the self-reflexive nature of these novels and repeats a significant motif of Scott's major precursor, Fielding. At any rate, in a number of ways—literal and figural—the hero in each of the novels is at some point put in the place of the woman as a necessary step on the way to becoming a man. It is tempting, given the emphasis on Scott's masculinization of the novel-romance in contemporary critical notices of these novels, to see this marking of the place of the woman as something on the order of a tribute to the very women's fiction about which these critics had complained but which, in our time, seems much more the condition of possibility for Scott's novels than for the work of Fielding and Defoe.[12]

It could perhaps be argued that the authority of the father is restored in another, simpler, but more obvious way. Readers have long been troubled by the perfunctorily "happy" endings of these novels. Scott's notorious carelessness with endings only thinly masks the abortive nature of his heroes' initiations into manhood and even their questionable romantic disenchantment. Not only does established authority recover from threat (because perhaps its establishment is seen as not susceptible to individual intervention), but on a more personal level the *father wins*. Waverley's future is apparent tranquility with his placid bride and inheritance of both Tully-Veolan and Waverley-Honour, where he will be free to pursue his antiquarian inclinations (the prophetic "curse" of both Flora and Fergus on him), and of course he has his memories. Frank wins his precious Die and becomes Heir and Lord of Osbaldistone Hall, far in the North away from the more modern adventure of his father's business, which he has finally validated and now wistfully desires. The business will now be inherited by his father's partner's son, his friend Will Treshham, to whom Frank's narration of the novel is addressed and which concludes with Frank's confession that "I have no more of romantic adventure to tell" (382). But even more to the point, Frank's adventure to retrieve his father's "papers," though successful, turns out to have been unnecessary; the father's name is so good, his "credit" so powerful, that it was never endangered by Rashleigh's machinations but only by the father's *absence*.

On the issue of commerce, *Rob Roy* introduces a new and significant motif. The very ability for the Jacobites even to begin an uprising depends on financing. Rashleigh hopes to extort involvement of significant clan leaders by threatening to call in their debts. In fact the major portion of Jacobite hopes is based on making a financial attack on the English government. When Frank and his father are reunited, they hurry off to London, where they "immediately associated with those bankers and eminent merchants who agreed to support the credit of government, and to meet that run upon the funds, on which the conspirators had greatly founded their hopes of furthering their undertaking, by rendering the government, as it were, bankrupt" (354). Frank's father is "chosen one of the members of this formidable body of the monied interest, as all had the greatest confidence in his zeal, skill, and activity" (354–55). He is even made "the organ by which they communicated with government" and "contrived, from funds belonging to his own house, or over which he had command, to find purchasers for a quantity of national stock, which was suddenly flung into the market at a depreciated price when the rebellion broke out" (355). Meanwhile, Frank himself "was not idle" but "obtained a commission, and levied, at my father's expense, about two hundred men, with whom I joined General Carpenter's army" (355). That Frank has no campaigns to report suggests that the uprising falls short of being a "romantic adventure." It is defeated not by heroic acts and sacrifice but by commercial institutions already in place and in close "communication" with the administrative structure of State. *Rob Roy* makes the actual conflict seem nearly as comic as tragic, since it allows Scott to kill off comically the male cousins who stand between Frank and his inheritance of his uncle's estate, not to mention the uncle himself, who dies of no ascertainable "formed complaint, bearing a name in the science of medicine" (357).

In each novel, the hope of Jacobite Restoration is not only doomed from the beginning by its own anachronistic denial (or unawareness) of irreversible historical change in the form of the already present structure of what John Brewer has called "the fiscal-military state."[13] As with *Waverley*, *Redgauntlet* ends with the apparent "hero" Darsie having become "Sir Arthur Darsie Redgauntlet . . . presented to his late Majesty," George III, "in the drawingroom" (400) and apparently retired to life without incident. On the other hand, his friend, who in this case goes out on his own adventure trying to rescue Darsie and hence is a rival "hero," becomes "Alan Fairford, Esq. Advocate, of Clinkdollar," which of course identifies him with the professional legal/commercial state structure. As such, he wins and marries the heroine, who is of course Darsie's sister. The future, obviously, is with Fairford. With the emergence of the modern nation-state, not only, as Hegel said, can "there no longer be any heroes,"[14] there can no longer be any adventures, except perhaps commercial ones. Not only are the heroes of these novels made passive or wavering, impotent in relation to the historic event, but their *future* lives are also made *irrelevant* to history. Each of them retires to what is in effect an anonymous domestic life. The authority of the father is restored as I explained earlier. At this point, however, I must stress the fact that such authority is in name only, just as the civil war was fought by sons or brothers in the name of the fathers. The rule of the new state and its impersonally ordered authority and ubiquitous bureaucratic structure could best be described as "the Regime of the Brothers," to borrow a phrase from Juliet MacCannell.[15]

IV. The Rise of the Historian:
When Was Community?

If the claim of the Stuarts and the Jacobites of their historical legitimacy, of the right and law of history, was actually a powerful thrust *against* history, as I believe it to have been, then Scott successfully masks this contradiction. The rebellions and, indeed, his very narratives are made possible by his translation of temporality into topography. The idea that the struggle pits past against present is an illusion sustained by a second illusion, that on the borders of a modern civilized country there exists a society at an *earlier* stage of development. Such a conception of the state was fostered by the Scottish Enlightenment "stadialist" theory of cultural development.[16] Borrowing a structural motif as old as Western fictional narrative itself, Scott can thus have at least two of his heroes "journey" from the present into the romantic past simply by crossing from England the border into Scotland.

Moreover, borrowing a metaphor from Fielding, he can make his readers "fellow travellers" with him in a stagecoach on a similar journey from their present into this double "past" of the novel. "Mine is a humble post-chaise," he explains in *Waverley*. "Those who are contented to remain with me will be occasionally exposed to the dullness inseparable from heavy roads, steep hills, sloughs, and other terrestrial retardations; but, with tolerable horses and a civil driver (as the advertisements have it), I engage to get as soon as possible into a more picturesque and romantic country, if my passengers incline to have some patience with me during my first stages" (Ch. V, 24; see also the beginning of Ch. LXXII). Compare such a passage, for example, with this statement by Fielding's *Tom Jones*: "We are now, Reader, arrived at the last stage of our long journey. As we have therefore travelled together through so many Pages, let us behave to one another like Fellow-Travellers in a Stage-Coach" (Book XVIII, Ch. I). Scott develops this journey metaphor in *Heart of Midlothian* (e.g., Ch. I, 13; Ch. 28, 270), in a different way as a contrast between past and present modes of communication between the two kingdoms and as a foreshadowing of the difficulties confronting his new kind of heroine. This contrast between past and present sets his own work apart from earlier fiction as well. But the implications of the efficiency and speed of the modern system of travel and communication suggest again the irrevocable connection.

This anachronistic presence of the past and in opposition with the present, of fathers in juxtaposition with sons, of conflicting claims and the very possibility of *civil war* deludes both the Jacobites *and* the sons into thinking that they can turn back or reject history. On the one hand, there is Scott's basic presupposition of the "progress" of society, and, on the other the sons' illusion, that they can escape either referral to the father or their own secondariness and belatedness. Literal Jacobitism is defeated in these novels, but its larger implications remain untouched. There is another, related contradiction in the project of the rebels, a contradiction between a theory of society as family or clan under the divinely granted dominion of the father/king of direct descent and the actual adventuristic *selfishness*, the pursuit of *self-interest* of the rebel chiefs and even of the Pretender himself. This conflict between the claims of community and self-aggrandizement was earlier suggested by the father's initial narrative in Scott's fable of the beginning of romance and society which I quoted above. Fergus MacIvor, for example, is out for self-aggrandizement: "Fergus had a further object than merely being the great man of his neighborhood, and ruling despotically over a small clan. . . . [He] had persuaded himself, not only that their ["the exiled family"'s] restoration to the crown of Great Britain would be speedy, but that those who assisted them would be raised to honour and rank" (*Waverley*, 93). He covets the coronet, the earldom he is promised when the Stewarts are restored. When his plans to acquire the Bradwardine estate by marriage to Rose seem thwarted and his earl's patent is delayed by the Pretender, however, his loyalty cools. Edward himself is drawn to ally himself with the Jacobites in an act of personal petulance, when he is falsely accused by government forces:

A sentiment of bitterness rose in his mind against the government, which he considered as the cause of his embarrassment and peril and he cursed internally his scrupulous rejection of MacIvor's invitation to accompany him to the field. "Why did not I," he said to himself, "like other men of honour, take the earliest opportunity to welcome to Britain the descendant of her ancient kings, and lineal heir of her throne?" (*Waverley*, 166)

In a timely fashion, the Chevalier flatters Edward's ego with his attentions. Similarly, Rashleigh first pursues and then betrays the 1715 rebellion for personal or selfish reasons.

Prince Charles Edward, the Pretender, as the figurehead of the Rebellion, also embodies its contradictions. In his 1832 "Introduction" to *Redgauntlet*, Scott noted that the bitterness of the struggle had been dissipated in a kind of romantic nostalgia. "Those who thought they discerned in his [Charles's] subsequent conduct an insensibility to the distresses of his followers, coupled with that egotistical attention to his own interests, which has often been attributed to the Stewart Family, and which is the natural effect of the principles of divine right in which they were brought up, were now generally considered as dissatisfied and splenetic persons" (3–4). But the largest number of those ruined in a falling cause "suffered with the most dignified patience, and were either too proud to take notice of ill treatment on the part of their Prince, or so prudent as to be aware their complaints would meet with little sympathy from the world" (4). Scott goes on to supply an anecdote demonstrating that "the principal fault of Charles Edward's temper is sufficiently obvious. It was a high sense of his own importance, and an obstinate adherence to what he had once determined on—qualities of which, if he had succeeded in his bold attempt, gave the nation little room to hope that he could have been found free from the love of prerogative and desire of arbitrary power, which characterized his unhappy grandfather" (8). Later in the novel, Scott observes that the Prince's lack of generosity toward his followers

may be too probably denominated peculiar to his family, educated in all the high notions of passive obedience and non-resistance. If the un-happy Prince gave implicit faith to the professions of statesmen holding such notions, which is implied by his whole conduct, it must have led to the natural, though ungracious inference, that the services of a subject could not, to whatever degree of ruin they might bring the individual, create a debt against his sovereign. . . . To a certain extent the Jacobite principles led to this cold and egotistical mode of reasoning on the part of the sovereign. (9)

Throughout the novel, he is called "the Adventurer." The pretense of community finally breaks down in a paradigmatic scene in which Fergus, Charles and Edward are all at odds after one of Fergus's clansmen makes an attempt on Waverley's life, and with the lack of English or Gaelic on the part of Charles's French officers and the Highlanders' lack of either French or English, communication becomes impossible.

In short, the claim of sovereignty based on the notion of corporate and patriarchal responsibility has become mere egotism—"possessive individualism." If society *has* progressed, then the leaders of this "ancien régime" must have themselves progressed along with civilization in ways they have withheld from their subjects. The "romance" of the Stewart past is undercut by the fact that its adherents have all the afflictions of the present. This trace of the modern in the ancient, of the present in the past, is, of course *the* illusion, since the novels of Scott, like those of Defoe and Fielding, have themselves become the history of that pursuit. But within his texts as well, as the story of Edward's father suggests, selfish adventurism has already become the defining trait of civil society and a new state corporate system that works by tensions of competition between ambitious men who share its rule, a harassed caste of middle-managers who live in a more sophisticated, more or less organized version of the Hobbesian ancient state of nature.

If the '45 had an air of unreality about it from the beginning, even as it testified to the strength of institutions already long in force, its aftermath was the shockingly real destruction of Highland culture and society, first by the English and then by its own lairds. The English proscribed the wearing of Highland tartans, forbade Clan names and identifications, replaced Gaelic with English, destroyed the hereditary jurisdictions, confiscated the rebel lairds' "estates" and sold them to lowlanders, and burned and pillaged Highland villages. What the English started, modern economics and the Highland chiefs finished, a process already begun and reflected in Scott's Jacobite novels. This process, "the Highland Clearances" in its most general sense, was still going on as Scott was writing his novels and somehow seems a necessary prerequisite to them. As the people and their traditions disappeared from the land in actuality, one might say quite accurately, they became "literature."

V. The Death of Poetry and the Institution of the Novel

Scott's own description of the Clearances in 1816 acknowledges this transformation: among the Highlanders of his youth, "and fostered by the tales of the grey-headed veterans, who looked back with regret," he explains, "the spirit of clanship subsisted no longer indeed as a law of violence, but still as a law of love.[17] Although it continued, he contends, this voluntary, anachronistic attachment to the chief "was, like the ruins of his feudal castle, more interesting than when clanship subsisted in its entire vigour" (92). Indeed, this distinction between Highland and Lowland societies could have lasted for some time, "had it been fostered by those who, we think, were most interested in maintaining it. The dawn of civilization would have risen slowly on the system of Highland society; and as the darker and harsher shades were already dispelled, the romantic contrast and variety reflected upon ancient and patriarchal usages, by the general diffusion of knowledge, would, like the brilliant colors of the morning clouds, have survived for some time," before being "blended with the general mass of ordinary manners" (92–93). There were "laudable" instances of Highland landowners working very hard with "humane precaution to render the change introduced by a new mode of cultivation gentle and gradual, and to provide, as far as possible, employment and protection for those families who were thereby dispossessed of their ancient habitations." But in too many other cases, "the glens of the Highlands have been drained, not of their superfluity of population, but of the whole mass of the inhabitants" who were "dispossessed by an unrelenting avarice, which will be one day found to have been as shortsighted as it is unjust and selfish."

Based on these observations, Scott concludes:

Meanwhile, the Highlands may become the fairy ground for romance and poetry, or subject of experiment for the professors of speculation, political and economical. — But if the hour of need should come — and it may not, perhaps, be far distant — the pribroch may sound through the deserted region, but the summons will remain unanswered. The children who have left her will re-echo from a distant shore the sounds with which they took leave of their own — *Ha til, ha til, ha til, mi tulidh!* — "We return — we return — we return — no more!"[18]

It is the destruction of a culture so resistant to assimilation that makes it available for poetry or for speculative "political and economical" knowledge — that is to say, for literature and therefore for cultural fable. What is romantic about the Highlands, or what could have been but for modern "unrelenting avarice and selfishness," would have been the long twilight passing of that culture in a lingering contrast with modernity. What is romantic for Scott is not simply an unrecuperable past, but the present trace of what is unrecuperably past, dead, or absent—what had been terrible in the battlements of the feudal castle had become ruins "mouldered into beauty" by time, or, finally, the empty hills and the continued presence of the cry—"We will return no more." The word "romantic" often meant "the past" for the Romantics, including those who never called themselves by that name, but not the past in the sense of its repeatability as the term "Augustan" meant for much of the eighteenth century.

While he makes it seem that the Highlands must be vacated and the Highlanders die or emigrate before that entire culture can pass into literature, Scott also has another way—a generational way—of describing this necessary passage. In his introduction to *Redgauntlet*, he speculates that those who remember old Highland veterans of Jacobite struggles as "the heroes of a tale which had been told" would probably agree "that the progress of time, which has withdrawn all of them from the field, has removed at the same time, a peculiar and striking feature of ancient manners." He defines this "feature," paradoxically as "their love of past times," and contends that "their tales of bloody battles fought against romantic odds, were all dear to the imagination." We would do well to remember that the Scott who notes that "their little idolatry of locks of hair, pictures, rings, ribbons, and other memorials of the time in which they seemed to live, was an interesting enthusiasm" was himself an antiquarian collector of such relics. If the enthusiasms and often narrated memories enabling these old veterans to dwell in the past well might have suggested "political principles" considered "dangerous to the existing dynasty" if they had been voiced by younger men, then no narrator could be supposed safer or "better qualified to sustain the capacity of innocuous and respectable grandsires" than those old men (10–11). Scott himself appears later as the grandfather narrator of his history of Scotland, *Tales of a Grandfather*. What is aggressive in "the relation of fathers" becomes "innocuous" in the recollection of grandfathers —that is to say, as a retold tale.

Another passing—that of Romantic poetry into the prose of ordinary life—is also remarked in this "Introduction" to *Red gauntlet* written in the last year of his life. Scott notes that "The Highlanders, who formed the principal strength of Charles Edward's army, were an ancient and high-spirited race, peculiar in their habits of war and of peace, brave to romance, and exhibiting a character turning upon points more adapted to poetry than to the prose of real life" (3). Why then should Scott himself record this passage in novels instead of poetry? It is only commonplace to say that Scott gave up his Romantic narrative poems to write the Waverley Novels. While the novels preserve romance on another level or in another form, what they represent is its death—which in fact is the essential quality of what might be called its romanticness.[19] Indeed, each of the heroes of the Jacobite novels goes through something like Edward Waverley's realization: "These reveries he was permitted to enjoy, undisturbed by queries or interruption; and it was in many a winter walk by the shores of Ullswater, that he acquired a more complete mastery of a spirit tamed by adversity than his former experience had given him; and that he felt himself entitled to say firmly, though perhaps with a sigh, that the romance of his life was ended, and that its real history had now commenced" (LIX, 283). In this context, the facts that all possibility of adventure is canceled out in each novel and each hero ends in a kind of bourgeois domesticity suggest that Scott's novels end where the Victorian novel begins.

In such a setting, imagination, or at least too much of it, is as dangerous as it is in *Don Quixote* or the novels of Jane Austen, a theme which becomes almost generic in the later nineteenth-century novel. Consequently, poetry can seem no longer possible. Already in Scott it is translated, dangerous, associated with madness, and/or presented in notes or as *exergue*. Above all, it is anachronistic and misused. Many of the Waverley heroes have aspirations to be heroic in poetic tropes and epic cantos, but the results are pitiful, parodic, or merely translated. Edward Waverley's efforts in this direction, particularly those represented by the poetry he is carrying in his surprisingly mobile portmanteau, are what get him accused of seditious Jacobitism before he rejoins Fergus. Even Fergus and the Jacobites turn the old poetry to their own private political purposes. The most spectacular instances of this performative use of poetry are the medieval feast Fergus sets up to welcome Waverley, complete with a very rousing song sung by his bhairdh in Gaelic, the only word of which Waverley understands being the mention of his name, and the highly artificial scene Flora stages, complete with waterfall, harp, romantic chasm, and "sylvan amphitheatre," as the proper setting in which to present Edward her translation of that song. That the "real poets" are just as anachronistic or belated, in that they are mad, dead, or dying, is demonstrated by *Waverley*'s mad David Gallatly, who dresses as a court fool to sing fragments written by his dead brother. Wandering Willie in *Redgauntlet* and *Heart of Midlothian*'s Madge Wildfire are similarly afflicted. Banished from the living culture, poetry is preserved as quotation or epigraph. The poetic only achieves an afterlife as prose, a much more negative view of modern literary history than the belief of the Schlegel circle that the novel permits poetry to fulfill itself as prose.[20]

The belatedness of his novels is underlined in another way by Scott's other ventures. He was not only a man of letters but also an *editor*, a restorer of texts both poetic and antiquarian. His editions of Swift and particularly of Dryden were only superseded quite recently, and his edition what is known as the Somers Tracts (*A Collection of Scarce and Valuable Tracts*) is still an important historical resource. But more to our purposes, his edition of eighteenth-century British fiction with critical and biographical introductions for *Ballantyne's Novelist's Library* played an important part in the early recognition of the novel as *institution*. That is to say, what had been innovative but generically and socially problematical writing in the eighteenth century became, with Scott, a recognized genre that could be defined, edited, and collected *in a set*, and then described, imitated, and developed. What had been "dangerous" or literarily and morally suspect "in the relation of fathers" was now respectable as literature.

His own novels were almost self-consciously part of the institutionalization of a genre that at once breaks down and preserves all genres. I have noticed in passing some echoes in Scott's novels of Fielding's *Tom Jones* to suggest Scott's troping of his major precursor on another level of the father-son struggle, the generational/generic conflict that he thematizes in the novels. *Redgauntlet* in particular, whose pastiche of narrative forms—epistolary, journal, omniscient narration—has so often troubled critics, seems particularly haunted by Scott's precursors. Replete with references to Fielding, Richardson—the part of the novel written as a secret journal while Darsie is kidnapped seems a special, if inverted, reference to *Pamela* and *Clarissa*—Cervantes, and others, *Redgauntlet*, like *Ballantyne's Novelist's Library*, seems almost to *anthologize* the novel—its modes, material, its themes, as well as its time. It is perhaps significant that in his "Advertisement" to the First Collected Edition of *Ballantyne's Library*, Scott apologized that "the Critical Opinions are such as have occurred without much or profound study to one, too much of whose time has been spent in that 'delightful lande of faerie,' the seducing mazes of fictitious narrative" (Ioan Williams, *Scott on Novelists*, 18)—the same "fairy ground of romance and poetry" for which he reserved the Highlands in the passage from his review of *The Culloden Papers* quoted earlier.

One of the problems of Scott criticism has always been to account for the misreading, from Hazlitt and Twain to the moderns, of his novels as "mere historical romances." I have tried to suggest some complex reasons for this "misreading" in the tensions of those novels. It is important to remember that Scott was also his own editor—that the novels have come to most readers since the 1830s complete with his introductions and footnotes, identifying historical sources for places and events he had fictionalized, in many cases noting anachronisms in the narrative. In an extreme example, in the "Introduction" to *Rob Roy*, he offers a biography of the "real" Rob Roy that paints him as an almost totally different and much less admirable person than the one he depicted in the novel. But while these *supplements* may seem to testify to the authenticity of his narrative, they ultimately promote a kind of harmless antiquarianism. Their effect is to divide again the border between fact and fiction, to undercut "the reality" of the novels, and to fictionalize them. These supplements seem almost a final assertion of his own "Jacobitism"—a deference to source or origin that precedes and validates the present but which, like "the King over the Water," is irredeemably yet repeatedly lost.

6

The Institution of the English Novel

IN THIS CHAPTER, MY STUDY OF THE novel's institutions reveals itself to be circular, a seemingly constant strategy inherent in the very nature of institutions and their self-histories. I plan here to explore Scott's very material contribution to the institution of the English novel, but in order to do so, I find it useful to return to Scott, Watt, and my earliest "novelist," Daniel Defoe. Scott's fascination with Defoe itself resulted in a significant impact on the revival and reassessment of this originary figure, but it is also the very indeterminancy of the canon and its generic specificity, not to mention the question of whether Defoe actually wrote all of what is attributed to him that spotlights the peculiarly non- or anti-generic determinations of this "genre."

I

The *earliest*—does that mean first? Watt, by having the novel invented in the English eighteenth century, necessarily invokes the question of firstness, even though he tries to deflect it by the vaguer notion of the *Rise*. Everyone seems to want to avoid dealing with this question, which is already implied by the very notion of the novelty of the novel. Consider Scott's confused or at least confusing genealogy of the novel. He said that the novel was "the legitimate child of the romance" (Scott, *"Emma,"* 227) and called

Fielding "the first of British novelists, for such he may surely be termed" (Scott, *Lives*, 48), and "father of the English Novel" (*Lives*, 70) and designated *Tom Jones* as "the first English novel" (*Lives*, 63).[1] Yet he also referred to the earlier fictional productions of Defoe and Richardson and even Swift's *Gulliver's Travels* as novels and/or romances. Even in these descriptions of Fielding's "firstness," which all come from the same essay, notice the slippage of meaning along the opposition between "first" as rank and "first" in chronology. While Defoe's *Robinson Crusoe* sets the novelistic paradigm for both Scott and Ian Watt, as well as for a number of others, no one seems comfortable giving it clear priority. Throughout the history of the institutionalization of the novel, from his time to ours, Defoe's works have occupied a curiously ambiguous but pivotal place, at once there and not there.

I begin with a logical if seemingly silly conundrum. If not one, then how many novelists does it take to make a novel? For Ian Watt, taking as his point of departure the common assumption—that is to say, the received premises of a prevailing institutional history—it took three: Defoe, Richardson, and Fielding.[2] Even here, the argument of *The Rise* implies that this making becomes apparent only retrospectively, when Richardson's and Fielding's opposing "realisms" of "presentation" and of "assessment" are first combined in *Tristram Shandy* and then "harmoniously reconciled" by Jane Austen. According to Watt, with Austen's novels this conflict reveals itself to be not an opposition between two irreconcilably different kinds of novel, "but merely rather clearly contrasted solutions of problems which pervade the whole tradition of the novel and whos apparent divergencies can in fact be harmoniously reconciled" (Watt, 290–92, 296). Notice, the anachronism implied here with the solution of the problem coming historically *before* "the whole tradition of the novel" shows it to be pervasive and continuing.

A glance at some earlier moments of this institutional history might be instructive. At the end of the nineteenth century, Sir Walter Raleigh, after four chapters on the "long durée" of the development of the romance and the novel from the time of the late

Greeks, points also to three major founders of modern English prose fiction—but not the same three as Watt's choices.³ Instead, according to Raleigh, the "modern novel" is born with the publication of John Lyly's *Euphues*, Sir Philip Sidney's *Arcadia*, and Thomas Nash's *The Unfortunate Traveller*, and receives only its *second* birth with Defoe, accompanied here with Swift as was traditional, and then Richardson and Fielding, followed by the usual later writers of the century. Watt's radical reduction of history is of course predicated by his disciplined, and disciplinary, project of demonstrating what is essentially new and different in the fiction of the eighteenth-century English trio, but it is a violent shrinkage nonetheless, and one with lamentable institutional consequences that Watt possibly did not intend. The radically nationalist reduction of the relevant field to the *English* novel also effectively closed down further investigation of the relevance of the flood of contemporary translations of French and Spanish "novels," not to mention those of other countries, novels in Ireland and Scotland, and the rare fictions in English of the early British colonies. Another regrettable occlusion had to do with the neglect of the heterogeneous kinds of non-literary discourses which fed these developing fictions.

One hundred years earlier, in 1859, David Masson's *British Novelists and Their Styles; Being a Critical Sketch of the History of British Prose Fiction*⁴ declares that the "Novel as a Form of Literature" has its beginnings in the epic and classical romances as well as medieval, early Italian, French, and Spanish prose fictions and early British romances. These ancient beginnings are again developed in the eighteenth century by Defoe-Swift, Richardson, Fielding, and so forth. Clearly, these longer genealogies leading from an immemorial past have less difficulty refusing a "first" novel determination. There are other characteristics shared by these earlier institutional histories of the novel. Certainly they share an avoidance of essentialist notions of genre and a refusal to shut out other than English forms of prose fiction. Both Raleigh and Masson use Scott and the Romantic period as a crucial telos in the development of the modern novel. Raleigh's subtitle is exemplary in this regard: *A Short Sketch of Its History from the Earliest Times to the Appearance of "Waverley"*. Yet in all these histories, if less so in the earlier ones, Defoe is a problem. He is also certainly necessary. Watt derives most of the characteristics of his idea of the novel as "formal realism" from Defoe, but at the same time Defoe, unlike Fielding or Richardson, shows no pride nor even any self-awareness of origination in writing something new or, for that matter, anything even fictional. As I will discuss later, the absolute lack of any statement of intention, besides the mysterious contradictory one of the preface to *Robinson* III, coupled with the uncertainty of status of many of the writings attributed to him—whether they are his, whether they are fact or fiction, or even whether any other narratives by contemporary writers, now taken as factual, might also be fictional—seems a permanent block to the designation of Defoe as author, let alone inventor of the novel. By the same token he also provides certainly one of the most crucial tests of the construction of the author function as such. So Defoe, always there and not there—or, more precisely, there but never fully readable, is therefore always *about to be* present to and for the institution of the novel, for which he is virtually a mysterious footprint in the sand.

Raleigh's and Masson's histories as well as Charles Eaton Burch's useful later survey of the ups and downs of Defoe's reputation in the eighteenth and nineteenth centuries show continuing discussion of his fiction, often with great praise, but with little, if any, relationship remarked of his work to that of Fielding or Richardson. He seems not only sui generis, but also to suffer constant generic slippage. It is clear, for example, that by the beginning of the nineteenth century *Robinson* is read as "romantic" or as romance, usually without any denial of its realism. Burch quotes one critic in 1886 who describes Defoe as "the connecting link between the ideal romance and the novel of real life" (Burch, 423). While *Robinson* generally was granted "classic" status, it was most frequently referred to as a classic of children's literature. Raleigh: "It is a testimony to the practical nature of childhood that the book is so widely regarded as the best boy's book in the world" (Raleigh, 133–34). This relegation begins, of course, as early as Rousseau's *Emilius* in 1762, and one can handily track its most important later permutations in the "Opinions" section of Michael Shinagel's Norton Critical edition of the novel.[6] An essayist on Defoe as a novelist in *The National Review* of 1856, in a piece which Burch describes as "the most comprehensive and careful study which had thus far been undertaken; and which in some respects . . . still remains one of the most illuminating" (193), regarded *Robinson Crusoe* "as a work of genius—but of a low order of genius." "The universal admiration it has obtained," he explained, "may be the admiration of men, but it is founded on the liking of boys" (194). The case of Defoe is thus an exemplary litmus test for the mercurial changes in the way novels have been historically conceptualized over a long period of time and as such is paradigmatic of institutional histories of the novel.

Even the most intelligent modern readers betray the effects of the institution. Many critics have complained or conceded that Defoe didn't sufficiently transform his prose narratives into genuine novels. Astute and careful readers, even acknowledging that what we call the novel didn't then exist, proceed as if Defoe were seized by the dynamics of the genre he unselfconsciously employed. Indeed, arguably none of us has been free of the (natural or supernatural) power of a platonic ideality of form in our reading of Defoe, and it is this insistent force of genre that has given us the picture of the bumbling, artless, near illiterate political journalist/hack, chronic liar, who stumbled into the invention of the novel somewhat on the model of the man who invents the telephone and immediately tries to wash his hands with it. In fact, our retrospective sense of genre and our knowledge or frustrating lack of certainty about much of Defoe's life have always worked together to generate readings of his works.

According to Defoe's contemporaries and critics during most of the eighteenth century, Defoe didn't invent anything, or conversely he invented everything. That is, he had a powerful reputation of lying, for want of a better word, as Sir Leslie Stephen said.[7] Increasingly, he was credited with somehow producing a single mythic character whose story was sometimes thought, particularly in the nineteenth century, more fit for children or social theorists than for general adult readers. At any rate, he was seldom thought of as the inventor of the novel.

How does one writer invent a genre? How does a new way of telling a story become a genre? How is the legitimacy of its name established and accepted? It would not seem irrelevant that this last question points to one of the predominant plot patterns and themes in what we now call the classic novel. And the question seems peculiarly apt given the fact that so many eighteenth-century fictions have as their title a proper name and at that, a name that turns out in the story to be false or inaccurate or misleading. Take for example, not only Defoe's own novels, but also *Joseph Andrews* and *Tom Jones*.

We also know that the canonic three founders, Defoe, Richardson, and Fielding, took great pains to distinguish what they wrote from what were then called novels. Defoe said very little about genre. He was too busy claiming factual truth or at least authenticity for his narratives. Given the more explicit assertions of "a new species of writing" by Richardson and Fielding, and given the greater discussion of the problem of genre, particularly by Fielding, it is a lot easier to see in their works the invention of a new or transformed genre than it was for contemporaries to discover such novelty in Defoe. At any rate, what Fielding and Richardson wrote came to be called "novels" rather late in the eighteenth century, and Defoe was often not included in those discussions or was paired with Jonathan Swift when he was. The discussions themselves gave only vague definitions at best to the concept of the novel or the problem of genre.

We do know that Defoe was virtually ignored for most of the eighteenth century. If he was remembered, moreover, it was as a political writer, for he had a reputation both as a patriot/statesman and as a historian that grew during the nineteenth century. If he did invent the novel in 1719, his invention had been ignored and lay dormant for more than twenty years when it was taken up by Richardson and Fielding, whose novels resemble his not at all and who rarely, if ever, mention him, and never as a precursor. There may be some vague resemblances between the themes and plots (but not the form) of Defoe's conduct books, particularly *Religious Courtship*, and Richardson's novels, which as Nancy Armstrong points out, Richardson regarded more as conduct books than novels. What is clear is that the linear history of the novel as having an "origin" and "rise," the history we have been brought up on, with its genealogies, lines of descent and influence, family resemblances, is itself a fictional narrative—a kind of novel about the novel. Moreover, such a story represses the irreducible heterogenity of the discourses and forms that contribute to the institution of the English novel in a way that seems analogous to the usual English suppression of the heterogeneous sources of British culture and identity.[8]

The fact is, as one of Defoe's principal twentieth-century biographers and bibliographers John Robert Moore pointed out in 1941, that while there were collected editions of Richardson, Fielding, and Smollett in the eighteenth century, there was no collected edition of Defoe "as a standard writer of fiction" until Scott's edition in the nineteenth century.[9] What is more,

until near the end of the eighteenth century there was no considerable biography or critical study of Defoe. No book lover is known to have assembled a collection of his writings. For nearly a century most of his work had been reissued (if at all) with no indication of his authorship. The less known writings had been almost totally, and the better known ones (like *Robinson Crusoe*) had become almost independent of his name. The anonymity which was a matter of choice or of professional necessity in his lifetime was apparently becoming permanent. (710)

Moore also believed that "Defoe has been to a large extent the victim of a literary clique which determined more than two centuries ago (as Professor William T. Laprade once pointed out to me) that no writer of the Age of Anne should be known to fame except themselves and their friends" (734). One might add that this was the very clique who was busy producing the modern sense of what *literature* is. Defoe's chosen and sometimes necessary anonymity was apparently taken up and reinforced by the official Augustans. The remark of his erstwhile fellow agent to Robert Harley, Jonathan Swift, in his *Letter Concerning the Sacramental Test* seems aptly characteristic of this intention: "One of these authors (the Fellow that was *pilloryed*, I have forgot his name) is indeed so grave, sententious, dogmatical a Rogue, that there is no enduring him." [10]

In addition to the efforts of the Scriblerians to make of Defoe a non-person and the difficulty of attribution of authorship to a confusing mass of anonymous and pseudonymous texts there was yet another problem that remains with us—the problem of classifying these texts. Aside from the very small group of novels now accepted as Defoe's—including *Robinson Crusoe, Moll Flanders, Colonel Jack, Captain Singleton, Memoirs of a Cavalier*—there were innumerable other autobiographies and memoirs cutting across uncertain lines between fact and fiction, editorship and authorship. Moreover, Defoe wrote in every conceivable category of discourse. As Moore points out,

> there is in Defoe no clear line of demarcation of literary methods or forms; history, fiction, moral tract, and economic treatise often run into the same mold. When Professor Sutherland wishes to illustrate Defoe's unparalleled fondness for dramatizing the incidents of everyday life, he chooses his example from *An Essay upon Projects*. Some of Defoe's most characteristic prose fiction occurs in such unlikely places as *Due Preparations for the Plague* or *A System of Magic* or *Religious Courtship* or *The Family Instructor*, in *A General History of the Pirates* or *The History and Reality of Apparations*, or *The Political History of the Devil* or *Memoirs of the Church of Scotland*. Like his immemorial memorial to the house of Commons, Defoe's fictional writings remind us, "Our name is Legion, and We are Many." (711)

I will return to this question of unity by taxonomy and the identity of a proper name later on in this chapter, not only because it characterizes the efforts of scholarly research, criticism, and literary theory to describe a national literature but also because the quest for an impossible unity serves as a paradigm for the institutional formation of the novel.

II

In fact, an important originating moment for both processes occurs in the same years. In 1809–10, Sir Walter Scott, the man who later called Henry Fielding "the first of British Novelists" and *Tom Jones* "the first novel" (*Lives*, 48, 63), put together the first edition of what he called *The Novels of Daniel Defoe*. It is extremely difficult to find out about this edition, published by John Ballantyne in Edinburgh, and even more so to examine it. No biographer does more than mention it, and it is often confused with the larger collection of *Novels and Miscellaneous Works* in twenty volumes with prefaces attributed to Sir Walter Scott (Oxford 1840–43), or with the Bohn edition (1854–67). Moore complained about this situation in 1941, and it is difficult to see that it has changed since then.

Scott's edition contained *Robinson Crusoe* (2 parts), *Memoirs of a Cavalier*, *Colonel Jack*, *Captain Singleton*, *The True-Born Englishman*, *A New Voyage Around the World*, and the *History of the Plague in London*. As Moore points out, "the few titles accepted for the Scott edition have remained (with *Moll Flanders* and *Roxanne*) the nucleus of all collections of Defoe; hence it is that a mediocre (and genuine) work called *A New Voyage Around the World* is to be found in every such collection, whereas a fascinating (and genuine) work called *Robert Drury's Journal* is virtually inaccessible except in Oliver's inexact reprint of 1890" (711–12). Moore points to several interesting, tangled problems of authorial, oeuvre, and genre formation in this statement. The future vicissitudes of *Moll Flanders* and *The Fortunate Mistress* themselves make an interesting chapter in the changing ideas of what a novel is. The authorship and fictionality of *Robert Drury's Journal* are still being debated and there is still no recent edition of it. While most subsequent scholars, critics, and even the editors who included it might agree with Moore's assessment of a *A New Voyage*, many involved in the present moment of critical discourse would find it an interesting and significant work.

What strikes me as particularly significant in the pattern created by this edition is its preference for male adventure romances and historical fiction, obviously favored by Scott, who anticipated later nineteenth-century critics in calling Defoe the inventor of the historical romance. These categories of fiction almost disappeared from the canon in the later nineteenth and twentieth centuries as they were relegated to children's or popular escape literature. The first volume contains the biographical essay attributed to John Ballantyne but in which Scott had some hand. There are no notes of consequence, according to Moore, and only two critical introductions, and the last volume contains a list of a hundred works assigned to Defoe. According to Moore, "the long critical essay which Scott added to the life and which he continued to expand—in 1825 . . . and in 1827 for the collected edition of his own works—was one of the most influential commentaries on Defoe's art which have ever been written" (711).

In the same year, 1810, *The British Novelists, with an Essay, and Prefaces Biographical and Critical* by Mrs. Barbauld appeared in fifty volumes.[11] Barbauld's introductory essay, "On the Origin and Progress of Novel-Writing" and her individual prefaces constituted a very significant critical review of the genre. Her collection contained, in the following order, *Clarissa*, *The History of Sir Charles Grandison*, *Robinson Crusoe*, *Joseph Andrews*, and *Tom Jones*. This selection carries us through volume 21 and begins to resemble the modern canon. The following volumes are a bit spottier in that regard, but contain a good selection of the gothic and sentimental: *The Old English Baron* (Reeve) and *The Castle of Otranto* (Walpole), *Pompey the Little* and *The Vicar of Wakefield* (Goldsmith), *The Female Quixote* (Mrs. Lennox), *Rasselas* (Johnson), *Almoran and Hamet* (Hawksworth), *History of Lady Julia Mandeville* (Mrs. Brooke), *Nature and Art* and *A Simple Story* (Inchbald), *The Man of Feeling* and *Julia DeRoubigne* (Mackenzie), *Humphrey* (sic) *Clinker* (Smollett), *The Spiritual Quixote* (Graves), *Zeluco* (Dr. Moore), *The Old Manor House* (Charlotte Smith), *Evelina* and *Cecilia* (Burney), *The Romance of the Forest* and *The Mysteries of Udolpho* (Radcliffe), *Man as He is Not or Hermsprong* (Bage), and finally *Belinda* and *The Modern Griselda* (Edgeworth). The whole set sold for twelve guineas.

The battles of gender and class were immediately joined by the appearance of Medford's *British Novelists*, issued first in shilling parts (1810–17) and then in five volumes, and containing *Peregrine Pickle* and *Humphry Clinker*; *Roderick Random, Ferdinand Count Fathom* and *Sir Lancelot Greaves*; *Tristram Shandy, Sentimental Journey, Gulliver's Travels*, and the *Vicar of Wakefield*; *Tom Jones* and *Jonathan Wild the Great*; *Amelia, Joseph Andrews, A Journey from this World to the Next*. Michael Sadleir comments: "The whole affair is jerry-built"; it was issued by "catch-penny publishers" and "there is little doubt that their venture into 'British Novelists' was in parsimonious imitation of *Harrison's Novelist's Magazine* and provoked by the success of Mrs. Barbauld's collection" (141). What is interesting to me, however, is the way it more nearly approximates the strict modern canon, supplementing many of Mrs. Barbauld's omissions—and in editions to be afforded by almost anyone.

Next, and arguably the most influential collection given the great success of the Scott industry, was *Ballantyne's Novelist's Library* in 1821–24,[12] edited by Sir Walter Scott, with biographical and critical introductions, in ten volumes: I, The Novels of Henry Fielding, Esq. (*Joseph Andrews, Tom Jones, Amelia, Jonathan Wild*); II and III, The Novels of Tobias Smollett, M.D. (*Roderick Random, Peregrine Pickle, Humphry Clinker*, Smollett's Translation of Cervantses' *Don Quixote* preceded by his *Life of Cervantes, Ferdinand Count Fathom, Sir Lancelot Greaves*); IV, The Novels of LeSage and Charles Johnstone (*Gil Blas, The Devil upon Two Sticks, Vanillo Gonzales, Chrysal or the Adventures of Guinea*); V, The Novels of Sterne, Goldsmith, Dr. Johnson, Mackenzie, Horace Walpole and Clara Reeve (*Tristram Shandy, Sentimental Journey, Vicar of Wakefield, Rasselas, The Man of Feeling, The Man of the World, Julia de Roubigne, The Castle of Otranto, The Old English Baron*); VI–VIII, The Novels of Samuel Richardson, Esq. In Three Volumes (*Pamela, Clarissa Harlowe, Sir Charles Grandison*); IX, (1824) The Novels of Swift, Bage and Cumberland (*Gulliver's Travels, Mount Henneth, Barham Downs, James Wallace, Henry*); X, (1824) The Novels of Mrs. Ann Radcliffe (*A Sicilian*

Romance, *The Romance of the Forest*, *The Mysteries of Udolpho*, *The Italian*, *The Castles of Athlin and Dunbayne*).

One notices immediately the curious absence of *Pamela* in Mrs. Barbauld's collection and the total absence of Defoe's works in the Scott-Ballantyne, although Swift's *Gulliver* was included. Actually Scott proposed an eleventh volume for Defoe, apparently as an afterthought, and revised and expanded his earlier prefatory essay for it, but it wasn't published. Sadleir says this about *Ballantyne's Novelist's Library*:

> It seems almost certain that Scott deliberately supplemented Mrs. Barbauld's Collection when choosing titles . . . of the thirty-four novels he reprinted, only twelve had also been printed by Mrs. Barbauld; of his remaining twenty-two, many seem to have been chosen in order to amplify her selection from certain authors, while others (notably the novels of Sterne and some by Smollett) could appear without offence under masculine editorship, whereas Mrs. Barbauld, a stickler for feminine decorum and an editor with an eye to family reading, might well have hesitated to include them. (88–90)

In this process of constant and competitive supplementation are issues of gender, comprehensiveness, variety and range, fitness for family consumption, respectability, and affordability appearing perhaps chiefly as market considerations. Right in the middle of this period of "expansion," in the year Scott's *Waverley* was published, 1814, John Colin Dunlop's *The History of Fiction; being a critical account of the most celebrated prose works of Fiction, from the earliest Greek Romances to the Novels of the Present Day* appeared in three volumes. It was reprinted throughout the nineteenth century. Both Scott's and Dunlop's accomplishments here underscore the validation of the historical nature of the collections, and, with the extensive reviews of all these ventures, the apparent economic stability of a public desiring what amounted to a new form of cultural capital underwritten by the authority of well-known editors, all mark a congruence of production and consumption that indicate the viability of the institution of the novel. And this institution is accomplished in spite of, or perhaps because of the somewhat frantic competition fired by the relatively new problem of obtaining rights to titles, as with Scott's *Ballantyne's Novelist's Library*, when the Ballantynes' firm dissolved.

Now none of this can be reduced to the trivia of antiquarian bibliomania, as it might have been a few years ago. It should clearly be seen a mistake to discount the significance or effects of these collections. All these different texts, written under various circumstances and in various contexts and with various labels, have now taken on a lasting solidity in these magnificent sets. The English novel had been established. You could see it there on the shelves and you could continue to see it on the shelves of private, public, and school libraries in this country as well as in Britain on into this century. Many of us got our first introduction to the eighteenth-century novel either in Mrs. Barbauld's or in *Ballantyne's Novelist's Library*. I think, also, that the significance for this "moment" of institution of the success of Sir Walter Scott's own novels is not to be discounted either. Influenced or not by Scott's novels, subsequent novelists now had an established, solid body of tradition, a genre, and a genealogy.

Thus it can with some accuracy be said that the eighteenth-century novel was invented at the beginning of the nineteenth century. Here we can identify something like the canon of the novel as it is accepted today, although too many of these books are still not available in inexpensive editions. If we were to start looking for editions of Defoe outside the five or six titles made available in paperback by one publisher, one might come to the conclusion that Defoe was an arcane, esoteric interest, rather than a major author. Ironically, the same could be said of Scott. In fact, the more economical or restricted canon is a product of modernism, F. R. Leavis, and the New Criticism. Defoe, as marginal and eccentric, seemed to have suffered more than any author other than Scott and the women novelists at the hands of the modernists, although he won the praise, sometimes ironic, of Woolf and Joyce as well as some postmodern novelists. But he also won a different kind of canonization. In the late eighteenth century, Defoe's and/or Robinson's ghost haunted novels such as Charlotte Smith's *The Old Manor House* and Godwin's *Caleb Williams*.

In both cases, the island of solitude is Britain itself. In the first, Smith's hero, after fighting in the American revolution and being captured first by Indians and then by the French, is shipwrecked off the coast of England near his home, but is shunned and isolated because of his tattered Crusoe-like appearance. Again, Godwin admitted reading Defoe as he wrote the part of *Caleb Williams*, in which first London and then all of England is in effect transformed into an inescapable desert island by Caleb's persecutor and his agents, who poison his identity, thus his possibility of making a living, and place a price on his head, making him afraid to have anything to do with anyone. In the nineteenth century, putting aside the proliferation of *Robinsonades* throughout the century and novels such as Cooper's *The Crater*, we find the reviews of each of Melville's novels drawing comparisons to Defoe, much to Melville's irritation. There is a running memorial to Robinson in another noteworthy series. A mysterious Crusoe figure or at least vestiges of one appears in each of these "boy's" adventure novels: *The Coral Island*, *Treasure Island*, and *Peter Pan in Kensington Gardens*. I am sure that there are other similar memorials in many other stories as well. If the received history of the novel reads something like the Whig interpretation of history as a linear, progressive development, then an institutional history of the novel would be something like the Whig historians' creation of the ancient constitution during the eighteenth century in order to support the constitutional settlements following the 1688–89 Glorious Revolution. Or, as Hume put it, the legitimacy of a sovereign is often established retrospectively: "Princes often *seem* to acquire a right from their successors, as well as from their ancestors," adding the comment, "Nothing is more usual, tho' nothing may, at first sight, appear more unreasonable, than this way of thinking."[13] This account also serves as a perfect allegory of the contemporary establishment of the legitimacy of the novel, that usurper into the domain of genre.

If, as I am claiming, the principal dimensions of our present history of the novel were established in the early nineteenth century, then its future could not have been any more continuous and developmental than the past it had successfully smoothed over. There would be new knots and detours in which what was left out or left over, Defoe, for example, would have a curious role to play. For the moment, the tradition of the eighteenth-century novel was now complete. It was also in a sense closed off. Or better, along with those magnificent sets of books, for all intents and purposes it was shelved. If the novel was invented at this point, it was also at the same time reinvented, and reinvented as distinguished from its eighteenth-century precursors—except in one curious way. And here the chameleon-like nature of Defoe was especially important.

III

First, the reinvention. In his long review article of Jane Austen in 1815–16, Scott developed an argument to the effect that her novels represented a totally "new species of writing," a new kind of novel. Austen's novels, he said, "belong to a class of fictions which has arisen almost in our own time, and which draws the characters and incidents more immediately from the current of ordinary life than was permitted by the former rules of the novel" (Williams, *Scott on Novelists and Fiction*, 227). Scott argues that "in its first appearance," that is, in the eighteenth century, "the novel was the legitimate child of the romance . . . and the manners and general turn of the composition were altered so as to suit modern times." Yet it still "remained fettered by many peculiarities derived from the original style of romantic fiction." Although the magical or supernatural effects "vanish'd into smoke, still the reader expected to pursue a course of adventures of a nature more interesting than those which occur in his own life, or that of his next-door neighbors. The hero no longer defeated armies by his single sword, clove giants to the chine, or gained kingdoms. But he was expected to go through perils by sea and land, to be steeped in poverty, to be tried by temptation, to be exposed to the alternate vicissitudes of adversity and prosperity, and his life was a troubled scene of suffering and achievement." Scott makes sure we know to whose novels he is referring here when he names Tom Jones and Peregrine Pickle as the heroes in question. These, he says, are "the essential circumstances" in which these "earlier novels differed from those now in fashion, and were more nearly assimilated to the old romances" (229). The old novel appealed to the reader's curiosity "by the studied involution or extrication of the story, by the combination of incidents new, striking and wonderful beyond the course of ordinary life." The reader was thus made to feel that "his wonder and interest ought at once to be excited. But gradually he became familiar with the land of fiction, the adventures of which he assimilated not with those of real life, but with each other" (228). Hence repetition led to certainty and boredom: the motive force of the intricate plot no longer generated suspense or "curiosity." The dominance of story over that of character or depth of character was reversed. Excitement was exhausted by habit and the old "materials" became "stale and familiar" (230).

Accordingly, "a style of novel has arisen, within the last fifteen or twenty years, differing from the former in the points upon which interest hinges; neither alarming our credulity nor amusing our imagination by wild variety of incident, or by those pictures of romantic affection and sensibility, which were formerly as certain attributes of fictitious characters as they are of rare occurrence among those who actually live or die." Substituted for those now faded "excitements" is "the art of copying from nature as she really exists in the common walks of life, and presenting to the reader, instead of splendid scenes of an imaginary world, a correct and striking representation of that which is daily taking place around him." The difficulties and the dangers for the new style stem from the very features that generate new pleasures since "he who paints a scene of common occurrence, places his composition within that extensive range of criticism which general experience offers to every reader":

We, therefore, bestow no mean compliment upon the author of *Emma*, when we say that, keeping close to common incidents, and to such characters as occupy the ordinary walks of life, she has produced sketches of such spirit and originality, that we never miss the excitation which depends upon a narrative of uncommon events, arising from the consideration of minds, manners, sentiments, greatly above our own. In this class she stands almost alone. (231)

Here then is Scott's "Rise of the Novel," "a class of fictions which has arisen almost in our own times," "a style of novel . . . arisen . . . within the last fifteen or twenty years," that is, between 1795 and 1800.

The distinction Scott makes between Austen and her predecessors is the same distinction he makes between romance and novel in the opening of his "Essay on Romance" and attributes to Dr. Johnson, although he continues to use both terms alternately, often without distinction, often about the same texts. Here the distinction is not only historical but generational. The novel is a deviant but legitimate offspring of the romance and therefore is another version of his story about the circumstances of the origin of romance. The distinction is more than one between the fantastic and the actual or ordinary, for the new fiction lacks story: "*Emma* has even less story than either of the preceding novels," *Sense and Sensibility* and *Pride and Prejudice* (232). The novelist "paints sketches" of ordinary people and ordinary life. The Romancer weaves a complex plot which eventually reaches improbable but perfect closure: "That combined plot, (the object of every skilful novelist,) in which all the more interesting individuals of the dramatis personae have their appropriate share in the action and in bringing about the catastrophe" (228). Or, as he adds later, "a regular drama, in which every person introduced plays an appropriate part, and every point of the action tends to one common catastrophe" (229). "Here," he announces, "even more than in its various and violent changes of fortune, rests the improbability of the novel" (228). This fall into story is, of course, what places such earlier eighteenth-century novels as Fielding's too close to their parent, or "more nearly assimilated to the old romances," as indeed Watt complains.

For Scott, what makes Defoe realistic is his lack of coherent "story." Defoe will introduce such characters as Robinson's second brother and never mentions him again or set lines of action that lead nowhere and to no effect. Again, a notion similar to Watt's argument: Defoe's novels have little plot or "story," which is good; Fielding's novels have too much form or plot, which is bad. It is as if the distinction between romance and novel could be measured by shades of degree between motivated action and form and lack of it, in which case the romance form could never be completely avoided. The story of the disenchantment of romance for a protagonist such as Edward Waverley is still a romance.

In summary of his praise of Austen, Scott uses a curiously durable and iterable analogy:

> The author's knowledge of the world, and the peculiar tact with which she presents characters that the reader cannot fail to recognize reminds us something of the merits of the Flemish school of painting. The subjects are not often elegant, and certainly never grand; but they are finished up to nature and with a precision which delights the reader. (235)

You will, of course, recognize in this model the very same one which George Eliot uses in *Adam Bede* to describe her own realism (implicitly attacking the romantic fictions of Dickens). Scott also used it to praise Defoe. No two novelists probably seem less alike than Defoe and Austen to modern readers, yet Scott was not the only reader to associate them with each other.

The question that remains is not whether the newly constituted eighteenth-century novel influenced, overtly or covertly, the development of the English novel as a genre in the nineteenth century, but how and by what constantly changing rules of inclusion and exclusion the formation of its institution took place and is still taking place and legitimacy was given to individual texts of this species. Since the word *canon* means rod of measurement, what is the canon of this canon?

As I shall try to show, Scott has already provided some clues to the principle on the basis of which canonization takes place. I will also suggest the role played by the continually marginal Defoe.

IV

First, the problematic proper name Defoe. From at least the moment in the 1690s when Daniel Foe renamed himself DeFoe, no other proper name serving as indicator of an authorial function, not even that of Shakespeare, has suffered such an adventurous odyssey through such great perils, elevations, occlusions, charges and indictments, representations and misrepresentations, attributions and defrockings, and other miscellaneous transformations in the popular as well as in the "learned" mind. What Frank Kermode pointed out somewhere in another connection, about a controversial Renaissance romance, could be said about Defoe as text, "the people who had difficulty with Ariosto's *Orlando Furioso* were the learned who quarreled about its being epic or romance. What it called for, and got from the lay reader, was a new kind of attention related to several existing genres." The "novels" of Fielding and Richardson, on the other hand, were received with more ease, and the debate over the novel by the learned in the late eighteenth century was much milder than that over the earlier vernacular romances. Defoe was first mostly ignored by the learned and embraced by the lay reader with varying degrees of and sudden shifts between suspicion or approval. A new kind of attention has been called for by his attributed texts not only to several existing genres, but to a dizzying variety of them. The problem of Defoe, from the beginning, has not been whether he wrote novels or romances, but whether what he wrote was fact or fiction—and even his writing at all. Since he signed very few of his currently estimated nearly six hundred books and pamphlets, the figure and individual titles are still a matter of debate. As Moore and Pat Rogers have noted, Defoe's name was not regularly attached even to editions of *Robinson Crusoe* until the nineteenth century (Rogers, *Robinson*, 131). By rough count, Defoe is thought to have written around thirty-five fictional or semi-fictional pseudonymous biographies or autobiographies. All of them were published and most were read as authentic into the nineteenth century, some even into the twentieth.[14]

Most of these books were written or at least published after *Robinson Crusoe*, when Defoe was fifty-nine. It is estimated that in the last twelve years of his life, Defoe wrote or published one hundred forty-nine books and pamphlets including most of his novels or semi-novels, before dying at seventy-one of what someone called "a lethargy." Since at least the time of Scott, the critical-scholarly effort has been to establish the oeuvre of Defoe. Scott, in addition to being Defoe's first editor, was also one of his first collectors. Professor Moore reported that "Scott's library at Abbotsford contained no fewer than seventy-one items of the Defoe canon, many of them in several different editions" (712). But Scott also owned many other works which he did not know were written by Defoe but are now thought to be so. "As editor of the 'Somers Tracts,' he assembled so many of the rarer anonymous tracts by Defoe that the total number of Defoe's writings in his possession must have been nearer to ninety. Some of the prefatory notes remain even now important contributions to the subject" (710). Scott even edited *The Memoirs of Captain Carleton* with an introduction, not knowing that it had been written by Defoe. The "Somers Tracts," as well as *The Memoirs of Captain Carleton* and a number of other Defoe "fictions," were considered real research resources by more than a few nineteenth-century historians. Both Captain Carleton and Major Alexander Ramkins, now thought to be creations of Defoe's, were even included in the august *Dictionary of National Biography*. I don't mean to imply that the "Somers Tracts" were fictional, only the attributed authorship of some of the pamphlets included. In any case, here the opposition between fiction and history would seem particularly problematic, if not trivial.

In addition to the problem of Defoe's authorship, the facts of his life had also to be established. As Pat Rogers has pointed out,

between 1785 and 1925 there were eight full-length studies of Defoe, that is, general assessments rather than specialized monographs. Almost all of these were predominantly biographical, not critical. Each devoted considerable space to Crusoe, and indeed *RC 1* furnished a hidden key to its author for some of these biographers. When Crusoe is not required in any other mythical role, he can be made without much trouble to play the part of an abstracted and idealized Defoe. (133)

Rogers argues that these biographies played the most important role in creating or sustaining the role in eighteenth-century letters assigned to Defoe. With each biography the number of works attributed to Defoe climbed from the 1753 sketch attributed to Colley Cibber listing thirteen items (one spurious), with *Crusoe* and *Colonel Jack* the only novels mentioned, through the list of a hundred works attributed to Defoe in Scott's 1810 edition, to John Robert Moore's checklist and supplements of some 560 books, pamphlets, and journals. Many of these attributions have been based on "internal evidence." Of course, the most enormous work of detective scholarship has been done in this century by men like Moore, Arthur Secord, and Max Novak.

If one pauses to think about it, it seems a most extraordinary story. What other major modern authors in the English canon, let alone the imputed father of so important a modern genre, have had to be so totally constructed out of supposition, speculation, close reading, and lengthy argument? The question of the accuracy of these attributions aside, is there any other *major* modern author, the bulk of whose writings are still not in print or not even easily available to students?

Meanwhile, many myths about Defoe and his works have been or are being dispelled. It was once thought that Defoe wrote everything he wrote in a single, recognizable voice. This notion, like so many others offered by Scott, runs throughout Defoe criticism. Scott mentions how completely some authors could assume the character through whom they narrate their stories. Narrative personae such as Goldsmith's Vicar, Gaunt's Country Provost or Reverend Annalist of the parish, Wordsworth's Sea Captain in "The Thorn" should be, he says, distinguished in this class:

These are, however, all characters of masquerade. We believe that of Defoe was entirely natural to him. The high-born Cavalier, for instance, speaks nearly the same species of language, and shows scarce a greater knowledge of society than Robinson Crusoe; only he has a cast of the grenadier about him, as the other has the trim of a seaman. It is greatly to be doubted whether Defoe could have changed his colloquial, circuitous, and periphrastic style for any other, whether more coarse or more elegant. We have little doubt it was connected with his nature, and the particular turn of his thoughts and ordinary expressions, and that he did not succeed so much by writing in an assumed manner, as by giving full scope to his own. (Ioan Williams, *Scott on Novelists and Fiction*, 174–75)

A paradoxical claim of stylistic uniformity, one would think, for an author so much of whose works have been attributed to others, including even to Harley and Walpole! We can now argue safely, I think, if even most of the attributions are accepted, and even though most of them have been attributed to Defoe on sometimes minute issues of style, that Defoe was capable of writing in many voices, many levels of style, an argument that would undercut, of course, the very rationale, the internal evidence, for the attributions.

Similarly, many of Defoe's virtues have been chalked up to accident, ingenuousness, shallow sincerity, or lack of imagination, an argument that would seem contradicted, by his considerable reputation in his own time and, in the nineteenth century, as a diabolically effective liar. While the myth of the simple semi-illiterate tradesman and hack writer has been dispelled by investigation of Defoe's education and the sale catalogue of his personal library. Adding to the confusion is the fact that Defoe's library shares a catalogue with that of a now unremembered gentleman clergyman named Philips Farewell.[15] Nevertheless, it appears likely that Defoe had as large a library as many of his supposedly more erudite contemporaries.

The more we know or think we know about Defoe, the more mysterious he becomes. Peter Earle, the economist, who waded through most of the Defoe attributions for his admirable *The World of Defoe*, admits that "even when I finished writing this book I found that I did not know him as a person too well . . . I feel that I know far more about the world in which he lived, even if I still know too little about the man himself."[16] Confronted with the prodigious corpus of work now attributed to Defoe, and without casting doubt on the scholarship, one has to feel confronted not by a man, but an industry, a school of Defoe, a sort of eighteenth-century Homerides, or by the age itself. Defoe signed one piece as "the Age's Humble Servant." Indeed, the amount of effort required to make that library cohere as the work of a single author is the same required to bring coherence to his age.

The story of the scholarship is an exemplary one. First there are the biographies, each followed by a new list of attributions—the reconstruction of an *author*—an authority as ground to unite a diverse group of texts. Each new biography, with its new details and interpretations, incorporates a larger and more diverse set of texts. Critical interpretation then has the task of creating a totality, a motivated *concordia discors* out of that diversity, reading through, under, behind the anonymous, the pseudonymous writings, the ironic rhetorical strategies, reconstructing the variety of circumstantial occasions, changing political contexts and necessities or expediencies in order to account for apparent inconsistencies and to detect patters of regularities, deeper consistencies of concerns and motivations, similarities of voice and timber—in short, a complex intertextual structure guaranteed by the singularity of a single personality, motivated by a rational intention, stabilized by a single, unique origin in a proper though hidden name, and de-stabilized by a problematic lack of signature. This very great scholarly problem, at once unique and exemplary, overlaps with the problem of the institution of the novel. For this prodigious disseminator of a corpus of texts that refuses to close, of texts that cannot be guaranteed to return to any father, is also the putative father of a genre that itself denies closure, evades return, or places into question the return to any origin. All this is part of the reason that makes the case of Defoe so useful and so necessary for the study of canon, genre, and institution formation.

As it is, the present official canon of Defoe's novels is quite small: *Robinson Crusoe, Moll Flanders, Colonel Jacques, Captain Singleton, Roxana, Memoirs of a Cavalier,* and *Journal of the Plague Year* (still somewhat inconsistently or uncertainly accepted as a novel). This list is striking for its remarkable similarity to

Scott's 1810 collection. Simply drop *The New Voyage* and add *Moll Flanders* and *Roxana*, which was, incidentally, no easy addition — it took pretty much the whole of the nineteenth century. But setting aside, for the moment, the fact that it was a long time before Defoe was widely granted a major role in the foundation of the English novel, the canon of his novels was virtually complete with Scott. Now, we know (or think we know) about all these *other* "novels" that are still excluded from the genre or institution of the novel. What distinguishes them from the accepted "novels"? By what generic or discursive law are they excluded? In whose jurisdiction does the judgment lie? How is it to be determined whether or not they are to be considered "literature"?

Obviously, there are no easy answers to these questions. We can, however, begin to explore the implications of the fact that such questions exist. The central questions would seem to be whether determinations can be reached in terms of intrinsic textual evidence or only by institutional judgment. But if we are to understand the novel as a genre and a socio-literary institution, and its formation as a historical process, the questions are very important indeed. Important issues are at stake, and there are also a uniquely pertinent body of texts as a basis of investigation: a group of texts which were published before the novel was acknowledged as a genre but which are now almost universally known as the "first" (English) novels, within a larger group of similar texts by the same writer, texts not obviously different formally, but which still are not considered novels.

What is at stake is not simply an issue in the history of taste. To progress beyond this tautology, I believe we must first understand its historical logic: how and when were Defoe's major novels, the ones accepted now as canonical, accepted into the category of the English novel, and what might such a study of that acceptance reveal about the nature of the genre and its institution? We would next have to consider on what grounds those fictional writings were excluded which are still not widely considered novels — not only those presumed to be Defoe's fabrication but also similar narratives not so easily authorized by a recognized

name. Do either or both of these indistinct groupings constitute
a permanent reserve, a new margin from which new novels could
appear as the result of scholarly efforts, widespread university
teaching, and adventurous publishers to make them easily available? Is there yet to be another new margin, as Robinson, Moll,
and the others were once considered marginal to the novel, eventually to be appropriated? On the one hand, will the uncanoni-
cal fictions remain a permanent limit—an outside *within* the total
range of Defoe's *quasi*-novelistic fictional or non-fictional practices? And if so, on what basis? Or, on the other hand, as limit,
how do such texts define the structure of the "genre" or institution, revealing at the same time what will forever and necessarily
be missing or excluded from it? To begin to sketch out the implications of these issues might require something like a rigorous
Foucauldian analysis of the formation of what could be called
"novelistic discourse," which would include in its field both novels
and discourse about novels. A decisive first step in this direction
was taken by Lennard Davis's too much neglected (but recently
reprinted) *Factual Fictions*.[17] It would be wise, of course, to keep
in mind Pierre Bourdieu's caveat about Foucault's analyses remaining within the limits of a given discourse.[18] For no doubt
the influence on a discursive formation of what is outside and different from it needs to be reckoned in its institution, especially
since it has always been a claim of institutions that they are im-
manently self-generated and autonomous. It could be argued that
any such cultural formation or construction is defined by its margin, limit, other.

A short, flippant, pragmatic but tautological answer to these
questions would be that the first were accepted and the others will
be accepted when critics (we) learned (learn) to read them (explicate them) in a *literary* or novelistic way.[19] That answer has its
force, as I shall try to show, but it opens up a whole new pano-
ply of questions about what is meant by "explicating in a literary
way" that have to remain in the shadows of the interrogation I
make here.

To answer these questions we would have to examine the

curiously numerous but incomplete histories of Defoe's and the
novel's reception in certain ways. We would want to know not
only how Defoe's novels were thought of or characterized at any
given moment in the nineteenth-century debate about the nature
of the novel, but in each case how the Defoe novel (usually *Robinson I*) was characterized in the context of what was assumed about
novels in general and against the background of what other novels
were being either praised or damned. We might even need to examine the extraliterary as well as the literary contexts of the debate. Finally, one would need to analyze the tacit assumptions of
the critical or historical texts studied about what is novelistic.

In consulting in the most precursory manner two of the standard histories of critical discussion of the novel in the nineteenth
century, certain salient features emerge. I am thinking of Richard
Stang's *The Theory of the Novel in England 1850–1870* (1959) and
Kenneth Graham's *English Criticism of the Novel 1865–1900* (1965) —
the first written toward the telos of the Jamesian novel, and the
second a slightly modified version of the same.[20] These histories
reveal two things immediately germane to my argument. One is
the extent to which *Robinson Crusoe* was used almost always for
polemical purposes — as an example by which to damn Thackeray
or Dickens or to praise Austen or Eliot. The other is that whether
the critics were friends or enemies of Defoe, they characterized
his work in approximately the same way. And most of the themes
they sounded in doing so were originally set in motion by Sir Walter Scott, who was by this time generally condemned along with
Defoe and for many of the same reasons.

Defoe's novels were described as novels of incident not of
character, adventures for their own sake, not for any light they
throw on the suppositious narrator (Stang 1856, quoting, *National
Review*, 1851, 52). While Defoe was granted an "amazing power of
describing facts" at the expense of a "want of power in describing
emotions" (Stang, quoting Leslie Stephens, 183), he demonstrated
no power of analysis, particularly analysis of the psychological
kind. While some critics found his narratives emotionally flat and
lacking in sensitivity, others used praise of his emotional restraint

and first person reticence as a bludgeon on Dickens's emotionalism. Generally, Defoe was praised *or* criticized for the "plotlessness" of his novels, which are frequently described as a succession of adventures lacking any fixed direction.

The modernist novelist might try to represent what is most suggestive of a particular state of mind. Even a late eighteenth- or early nineteenth-century novelist might try to represent the psychological development and inner motivation of a protagonist. Defoe seems to have focused on what his central character-narrator would actually do under certain, usually extreme, social or even physical circumstances in a way that, as Alan Bewell once suggested to me, anticipated what the Scottish Enlightenment would call "conjectural history."[21] The former would register psychological motive as a major causal agency of the action of the story. In contrast, Defoe uses the extreme limitation of possible choices as the factor motivating action. Such a reduction might seem arbitrary to later readers, but this is a socially motivated arbitrariness. It should be recognized that psychological motivation and the whole system of internal development that it presupposes are just as arbitrary a social/cultural construction as the earlier one. Moreover, it would be difficult to argue that the later one requires any more imagination than Defoe's procedure, the projection of actions rather than the display of character.

Defoe became a major novelist when professional readers were able to read him in a way that moved him from one pole to the other, that is to say, when they were able to read him as a novelist of character rather than of incident, or more precisely, as a novelist who used incident to reveal character. But there is yet another chapter in the stories told by Stang and Graham. The novel of psychological analysis fell out of favor, to be replaced by the well-made novel, with its new emphasis on story, plot, meaningful incident—the organically structured novel. Here again Defoe's plotlessness and lack of a structured rising sequence and clear resolution damned him. This criticism sometimes took the form of an opposition between "historical method" (by which was meant chronological narration) and dramatic presentation.

Finally, there is the opposition marked in every Defoe preface: on the one hand, the imperative of explicit moral didactism, not integrated as ethical choice, on the other pleasure, but not an aesthetic pleasure in the artifice of the well-made plot. Here most eighteenth-century novels either were considered deficient or had to be tortured, as in the case of Fielding, to unite the pleasure of the well-made plot with the improving sequence of ethical choices. The case of Defoe was even more complicated, colored as it was by later nineteenth-century revelations about the author's supposed political and economic immorality, his opportunist political ambitions, his writing for both opposing party newspapers at the same time, his espionage activities, and so forth. This view of Defoe's life provided the background for attacks on the hypocritical didacticisms so easily contradicted by their narrators' smug pleasures in immoral activities and the values exposed by their quest for money and position. While these accusations can be traced back in Defoe criticism to the eighteenth century, they have been periodically revived with different nuances, most of them by critics in the nineteenth and twentieth centuries. Argument about Defoe's use or lack of irony centers around this question.

This criticism, although it touches importantly on *Robinson*, has had the greatest impact on the fortunes and misfortunes of Defoe's rogues, particularly his female rogues Moll and Roxana, condemned throughout the nineteenth century, from Scott's snobbish dismissal on. After commending Defoe's power of conception as like that of the picaresque or the gypsy boys of the Spanish painter Murillo and admitting that these books "contain strong marks of genius" which "are particularly predominant," in *Roxana*, he proceeds to demur:

But from the coarseness of the narrative, and the vice and vulgarity of the actors, the reader feels as a well-principled young man may do, when seduced by some entertaining and dissolute libertine into scenes of debauchery, that though he may be amused, he must be not a little ashamed of that which furnished the entertainment, so that, though we could select from these *picaresque* romances a good deal that is not a little amusing, we let them pass by, as we would persons, howsoever otherwise interesting, who may not be in character and manners entirely fit for good society. (Williams, *Sir Walter Scott on Novelists and Fiction*, 167)

This form of condemnation persisted throughout the nineteenth century, making recuperation of Moll and Roxana all but impossible until early in the twentieth. The problem of Defoe's female rogues was further complicated by the fact that his biographies habitually read *Robinson* as an allegory of the author. Were Moll and Roxana enacting his economic and political ambitions, as well as his moral judgments? The judgment on *Moll Flanders* began to undergo a reversal near the beginning of the twentieth century. According to the critics, this was at least in part a reaction to Victorian standards of morality, but it was specifically writers like E. M. Forster and Virginia Woolf who prompted the change in status of the two novels by praising them for this psychological accuracy of character. The principal issue became, and continues to be to a certain extent, the question of irony, conscious irony intended by Defoe. Moll's recuperation has reached the point where some critics claim the book as the first English novel, demoting Robinson, I suppose, to some sort of accident of nature or genius. To give an adequate account of how Defoe's novels have become so central to "the rise of the novel" in modern times would obviously require another essay. A careful analysis of Watt's argument and that of that most severe canonist, F. R. Leavis, would be necessary, among other things. What I am interested in suggesting here is only the general pattern of what actually was a process of making the heretofore marginal fictionalist retrospectively the origin and source, and often in opposition to what Defoe's practice was believed to have been.

Ian Watt, contemporaneously with Stang, placed the formal characteristics of Defoe's fiction in the context of eighteenth-century epistemology and related socioeconomic assumptions about the individual. He provided a motive for Defoe's apparent plotlessness by seeing it as an attack against previous literary conventions. Later critics such as Maximillian Novak refined this intellectual context and argued that Defoe's plots were derived from eighteenth-century speculations about the nature of man, society, and natural law. Paul Hunter and George Starr supplied another plot structure derived from the tradition of spiritual auto-biography.[22] More recently, criticism has preferred to psychologize Defoe's narrators showing how they construct a stable self in a world of unstable values and against the existential limits of extreme situations. The most recent turn of Defoe criticism has been toward studying his fiction's participation in the economic imperialism and colonialism of his time, an obvious but nevertheless neglected dimension of his adventure narratives.

The point of all this is the concerted project to make Defoe's texts meaningful within some recognizably generic notions of *the* novel, even to allegorize, metaphorize, or otherwise motivate all those "circumstantial details" to the point of recuperating the "notations" to which Roland Barthes ascribes an "effet de réal":

notations which no function (not even the most indirect) can justify: such notations are scandalous (from the point of view of structure), or, what is even more disturbing, they seem to correspond to a kind of narrative *luxury*, lavish to the point of offering many 'futile' details and thereby increasing the cost of narrative information.[23]

This is a description strangely echoing nineteenth-century complaints in regard to Defoe. But then, of course, Barthes goes on to motivate those details in a new way: "Flaubert's barometer, Michelet's little door finally say nothing but this: *we are the real*; it is the category of 'the real', (and not its various contents) which is then signified; in other words, the very absence of the signified, to the advantage of the referent alone, becomes the very signifier of realism" (148).

It is this very compulsion to motivate, to make signify, with nothing left over, that we must reflect on—it is perhaps the last rule of genre—without losing track of the fact that this quest for transparency is a redoubled compulsion in Defoe's novels. Each of Defoe's narrators seems to enact the same paranoiac compulsion—the necessity to make significant every lone footprint, every glance in the street, even the names and sequences of streets—to incorporate, in short, what may be intrinsically meaningless into a system of significance, a plot or story. But there will always be something left over, something excessive, marginal, or eccentric. Indeed, inasmuch as Defoe's novels themselves have occupied that role, it may be that what is left over is precisely the outside, the limit that defines the generic system and creates the possibility of change, without which there could hardly be an institutional history of a genre of which the "essence" is its lack of essence, its reach for what is not proper to it, or what does not "belong."

I have tried to follow the wandering adventures of the Defoe text, more complicated but not unlike the wanderings of Yorick's sermon in *Tristram Shandy*. I think it is safe to assume that these restless wanderings, not unlike those of Robinson, have not yet returned home and perhaps never can. Such a story might suggest that the Defoe text has always been at the mercy of changing protocols of reading, each of which from its own perspective has tried and failed to fathom the source of its peculiar power—power it would be erroneous to regard as purely or even mostly literary. Just as those lives that Defoe detailed take place on the margins of society their narratives lie on the margins or outside the limits of the now institutional Defoe novels, those that come to mind as the ones that set an agenda for a genre. As for these other narratives, the question remains whether they are merely "not yet" novels. We must also conclude that the problem of their generic or institutional status is only intensified by the fact that they only *may have been* written by Defoe, and so their *generic* status cannot be determined by any mere discovery of an author's name. This is a question about the very nature of what we call the literary. The institution of the novel takes place about the same time as the institution of what is always called literature, in the modern sense of the term. Thus it might be fair to imagine both of them finding neither shelter, nor closure, nor anything more than partial autonomy within the grounds or walls of their institutions. And if the novel must constantly renew its search for novelty, its very novelness, in what is by definition outside or beyond it, in its other, so would literature, driven by a similar cultural logic, have to follow in that pursuit.

Notes

Preface

1. Ian Watt, *The Rise of the Novel* (Berkeley: University of California Press, 1957), 301.

2. Watt cites this moment, singling out Austen as the instance of full generic manifestation (296–301), but ignoring Scott.

3. Gerald Graff, *Professing Literature: An Institutional History* (Chicago: University of Chicago Press, 1987), 155.

4. For Watt, "art" only defensively and apologetically—dooming critics and often students to spend the next two decades having to demonstrate conscious art on the part of Defoe and Richardson. But they had to do this as well for later "popular" writers such as Dickens. (I remember one critic who said that Dickens "could take point of view or leave it alone.")

5. I will mention only a cluster in 1957, in addition to Watt: Richard Chase's *The American Novel and Its Tradition*, Northrop Frye's *Anatomy of Criticism*, the English translation of Erich Auerbach's *Mimesis* in paperback, and outside the academy the "symposium" volume *The Living Novel*, edited by Granville Hicks, who, "alarmed by critical pronouncements that the novel is dead" (according to the dust jacket) "invited ten contemporary novelists to discuss the problems of their craft today." The group included Saul Bellow, Paul Darcy Boles, Ralph Ellison, Wright Morris, and Flannery O'Connor, who were enlisted to discuss a contemporary critical concern.

6. Michael McKeon has made this claim powerfully most recently in his *The Origins of the English Novel, 1600–1740* (Baltimore: The Johns Hopkins University Press, 1987). References to this book are given parenthetically in the text. I have discussed this book at length in my essay "Of the Title to Things Real: Conflicting Stories," *ELH: A Journal of English Literary History* 55 (1988): 917–54.

7. To be sure, this claim is much more tentative and ambiguous in Watt's book than it is in Michael McKeon's *Origins*.

8. J. Paul Hunter, *Before the Novel* (New York: W.W. Norton, 1990).

9. Pierre Bourdieu, "Rites of Institution," in *Language and Symbolic Power*, ed. John B. Thompson, trans. Gina Raymond and Matthew Adamson (Cambridge, Mass.: Harvard University Press, 1991).

10. For the novel's incorporation of romance, see José Ortega y Gasset, *Meditations on Quixote* (New York: W.W. Norton, 1961) and Edgar Dryden, *The Form of American Romance* (Baltimore: The Johns Hopkins University Press, 1988).

11. For a good account of the variety of that "experimentation," see Gary Kelly, *English Fiction of the Romantic Period, 1789–1830* (London and New York: Longman, 1989).

12. For a provocative account of Scotland and America, as well as the Scottish Enlightenment, see Robert Crawford, *Devolving English Literature* (Oxford: Clarendon Press, 1992).

Introduction

1. Giambattista Vico, *The New Science of Giambattista Vico*, trans. from the third edition by Thomas Goddard Bergin and Max Harold Fisch (Ithaca, N.Y.: Cornell University Press, 1970), li. See Edward Said on Vico and also the question of origins in his *Beginnings* (New York: Basic Books, 1975).

2. Pierre Bourdieu, "Rites of Institution," in *Language and Symbolic Power*, ed. John B. Thompson, trans. Gino Raymond and Matthew Adamson (Cambridge, Mass.: Harvard University Press, 1991), 117.

3. Notably in René Wellek and Austin Warren, *Theory of Literature* (New York: Harcourt, Brace and World, 1956), 226 and Harry Levin, *The Gates of Horn* (New York: Oxford University Press, 1963).

4. *Keywords*, rev. ed. (New York: Oxford University Press, 1983), 168.

5. Mary Douglas, *How Institutions Think* (Syracuse, N.Y.: Syracuse University Press, 1986); for Bourdieu, see note 2 above. Jacques Derrida has had a major effect on the way I think about *institution*. I will only mention a few fairly recent pieces, in their English translations: "Psyche: Inventions of the Other," trans. Catherine Porter, in *Reading de Man Reading*, ed. Wlad Godzich and Lindsay Waters (Minneapolis: University of Minnesota Press, 1989); "Mochlos: or, The Conflict of the Faculties," trans. Richard Rand and Amy Wygant, in *Logomachia: The Conflict of the Faculties*, ed. Richard Rand (Lincoln: University of Nebraska Press, 1992); "'This Strange Institution Called Literature': An Interview with Jacques Derrida" in *Acts of Literature*, ed. Derek Attridge (New York: Routledge, 1992).

6. See Franco Moretti's Darwinistic play on the eighteenth-century rise of the novel in his essay "On Literary Evolution," in *Signs Taken for Wonders: Essays in the Sociology of Literary Forms*, rev. ed., trans. Susan Fischer, David Forgacs, and David Miller (London: Verso, 1988).

7. *Blackwood's Edinburgh Magazine* 15 (1824): 408.

8. David Hume, *A Treatise of Human Nature*, ed. L. A. Selby-Bigge, 2nd ed. with text revised and notes by P. H. Nidditch (Oxford: Clarendon Press, 1980), 566.

9. The classic text for this is probably F. R. Leavis, *The Great Tradition* (Garden City, N.Y.: Doubleday Anchor, 1954), first published in 1948.

10. Sir Walter Scott, "Essay on Romance," *Essays on Chivalry, Romance, and the Drama* (Freeport, N.Y.: Books for Libraries Press, Essay Index Reprint Series, 1972) a reprint of v 6 of Sir Walter Scott's Prose Works (Edinburgh, 1834), 134–35.

11. For an excellent account of these complaints against the novel at the beginning of the nineteenth century, see the fine book by Ina Ferris, *The Achievement of Literary Authority: Gender, History, and the Waverley Novels* (Ithaca, N.Y.: Cornell University Press, 1991).

12. Sir Walter Scott, Review of *"Emma*: A Novel," *Quarterly Review* 14 (1815–16): 188–201; reprinted in *Sir Walter Scott on Novelists and Fiction*, ed. Ioan Williams (London: Routledge & Kegan Paul, 1968); also in *Jane Austen: The Critical Heritage*, B. C. Southam (London: Routledge & Kegan Paul, 1968).

13. For a curious but telling example of this complaint, see Fanny Burney's Preface to *Evelina* (1778), where, after paying tribute to Marivaux, Rousseau, Johnson, Richardson, Fielding, and Smollett as her literary genealogy, she says: "I yet presume not to attempt pursuing the same ground which they have tracked; whence, though they may have cleared the weeds, they have also culled the flowers, and though they have rendered the path plain, they have left it barren." If for Burney there was no longer anything novel about the novel of Fielding and Smollett, for Sir Walter Scott this was because their novels had become old romances.

14. Scott, *Lives of the Novelists* (London: J.M. Dent; New York: Dutton, 1820), 46–70. The Fielding essay is dated 1820.

15. Arthur Johnston, *Enchanted Ground: The Study of Medieval Romance in the Eighteenth Century* (London: Athlone Press, 1964). I am indebted to Professor Linda Georgianna for calling my attention to this book.

16. George Dekker, *The American Historical Romance* (Cambridge: Cambridge University Press, 1987), 24.

Chapter 1

1. Cf. J. Hillis Miller, "Narrative and History," *ELH* 41 (1974): 456; Jean Rousset, "Une forme littéraire: le roman par lettres," in his *Forme et signification* (Paris: Librairie José Corti, 1962), 75. Rousset's essay and Robert Adams Day's *Told in Letters* (Ann Arbor: University of Michigan Press, 1966) are essential to any consideration of the epistolary novel. My discussion later in this chapter is indebted to both.

2. My examples are all English and American novels, but one could easily supply European works—for instance, the importance of gossip in the novels of Balzac and Dostoyevsky, Julien Sorel's "talent" at writing letters, and the letter that brings him to attempt murder.

3. *Emma, The Novels of Jane Austen*, ed. R. W. Chapman, Vol. IV, 3rd ed. (London: Oxford University Press, 1933), 21.

4. *The Form of Victorian Fiction* (Notre Dame, Ind.: University of Notre Dame Press, 1968), p. 88.

5. *Being and Time*, trans. John Macquarrie and Edward Robinson (New York: Harper & Row, 1962), 212–13. I am aware of the wrenching involved to associate "idle talk," *endoxa*, and *sensus communis*, but while there are distinctions, there are also the intersections which interest me here.

6. *Contre Sainte-Beuve*, in *Marcel Proust on Art and Literature: 1896–1919*, trans. Sylvia Townsend Warner (New York: Meridian Books, 1958), 187. Proust's purposes in this essay are of course rather more complex.

7. "From *In Praise of Richardson*" (*Eloge de Richardson*), trans. Howard E. Hugo, in *Aspects of Fiction: A Handbook*, ed. Howard E. Hugo (Boston: Little, Brown, 1962), 12.

8. *The Sot-Weed Factor* (New York: Grosset and Dunlap, 1964), 625.

9. "Hawthorne's Castle in the Air: Form and Theme in *The House of the Seven Gables*," *ELH* 38 (1971): 315. The quotations from Hawthorne's novel are from the Ohio State Edition, pp. 196, 123, 122 respectively. I am deeply indebted to Dryden's discussion of this theme and also for his calling my attention to Max Gluckman's "Gossip and Scandal," *Current Anthropology* 4 (1963): 307–15, and "Psychological, Sociological and Anthropological Explanations of Witchcraft and Gossip: A Clarification," *Man* 3 (March, 1968): 20–34.

10. Cf. Miller, *Form of Victorian Fiction*, 70; Ann Y. Wilkinson, "The Tomeavesian Way of Knowing in *Vanity Fair*," *ELH* 32 (1965): 370–87; Harriet Baylor Press, *Behind the Looking Glass: The Heroine as a Vehicle for Literary and Social Satire in Thackeray's Major Novels* (Dissertation, New York University, 1977), 76–86.

11. *Plato's Phaedrus*, trans. R. Hackforth (Cambridge: Cambridge University Press, 1972), 158 (275 E).

12. Cf. Jacques Derrida, *Of Grammatology*, trans. Gayatri Chakravorty Spivak (Baltimore: The Johns Hopkins University Press, 1976), 136.

13. See Edward Said, *Beginnings: Intention and Method* (New York: Basic Books, 1975), particularly chapter three, "The Novel as Beginning Intention," 79–188.

14. He suggests it often, usually in the context of a distinction between poetry and prose, but as an explicit point in "Poetry and Abstract Thought," *The Art of Poetry*, trans. Denise Folliot (New York: Pantheon, 1958), 64. This is Volume 7 of the Bollingen Collected Works of Paul Valery.

15. Day, *Told in Letters*, 6.

16. "Psychological, Sociological and Anthropological Explanations of Witchcraft and Gossip: A Clarification," 33.

17. "Preface to Familiar Letters on David Simple . . . 1747," as reprinted in *The Criticism of Henry Fielding*, ed. Ioan Williams (New York: Barnes and Noble, 1970), 133. Fielding is defending, by way of preface, an epistolary volume by his sister, Sarah Fielding.

18. *Vanity Fair*, ed. with intro. and notes by Geoffrey and Kathleen Tillotson (London: Methuen, 1963), 182.

19. Jacques Lacan's "Seminar on 'The Purloined Letter,'" trans. Jeffrey Mehlman, *French Freud: Structural Studies in Psychoanalysis*, Yale French Studies 48 (New Haven, Conn.: Yale University Press, 1972): 38–72; and Jacques Derrida's "The Purveyor of Truth," trans. Willis Domingo, James Hulbert, Moshe Ron, and Marie-Rose Logan, *Graphesis: Perspectives in Literature and Philosophy*, Yale French Studies 52 (New Haven, Conn.: Yale University Press, 1975), 31–113 have been important to my thinking on the matters of this essay. Among many other things, both essays involve a theory of fiction.

20. "Reflections on the Letter: The Reconciliation of Distance and Presence in *Pamela*," *ELH* 41 (1974): 375–99; see particularly on this point, 396. Many of the issues I take up cross issues raised by Roussel. Any study of *Pamela* or the letter must take its point of departure from this essay.

21. *Pamela* (New York: Norton, 1958), 4–5, my emphasis.

22. See Leo Braudy's extended analysis of this and other themes in "Penetration and Impenetrability in *Clarissa*," *New Approaches to Eighteenth Century Literature*, ed. Philip Harth (New York: Columbia University Press, 1974), 177–206.

23. *Clarissa*, intro. John Butt (London: Dutton, Everyman's Library, 1968), IV: 157 (Letter LX, Lovelace to Belford, Wed. Morn., Aug.

23) and 212–13 (Letter LXXIX, Belford to Lovelace, Monday Night, Aug. 28–Tuesday, Aug. 29).

24. See Said's argument in *Beginnings*, chapter 4, "Beginning with a Text," 191–275, and in "The Text, the World, the Critic," *Bulletin of the Midwest Modern Language Association* 8 (Fall 1975): 1–23.

25. See J. Hillis Miller, "Fiction and Repetition: *Tess of the D'Urbervilles*," *Forms of Modern British Fiction*, ed. Alan Warren Friedman (Austin: University of Texas Press, 1975), 43–71. Jan B. Gordon also discusses Tess's letter along with the theme of gossip in his "Origins, History, and Reconstitution of Family: Tess' Journey," *ELH* 43 (1976): 366–88.

26. See Dryden's discussion of "The Custom-House" preface at the end of his essay on *The House of the Seven Gables* (317), cited above, and in his book *Nathaniel Hawthorne: The Poetics of Enchantment* (Ithaca, N.Y.: Cornell University Press, 1977), esp. 46, 148, 151–53.

27. I take recourse to the familiar distinction of the Russian Formalists: see Boris Tomashevsky, "Thematics," in *Russian Formalist Criticism*, trans. and ed. Lee T. Lemon and Marion J. Reis (Lincoln: University of Nebraska Press, 1965), 66–78.

28. *The Decentered Universe of "Finnegans Wake"* (Baltimore: The Johns Hopkins University Press, 1976), 125–26.

29. It is a term not completely susceptible of definition and appears throughout his work, but one can see the "Interview" in *Diacritics* 2, 4 (Winter 1972): 37, and *Diacritics* 3, 1 (Spring 1973): 44, and the title essay in *La dissémination* (Paris: Editions du Seuil, 1972).

30. *Coleridge's Miscellaneous Criticism*, ed. Thomas M. Raysor (London: Constable, 1936), 304.

31. The names also raise questions of shifting levels of discourse in their mixture of ordinary, stereotypic, and emphatically allegorical names. The name of the hero himself has a multiple register: it is at once ordinary and "realistic," stereotypic, the name of a the novel, and, of course — wrong.

32. Cf. J. Paul Hunter, *Occasional Form: Henry Fielding and the Chains of Circumstance* (Baltimore: The Johns Hopkins University Press, 1975). One must also note the value of Martin Battestin's superb introduction, commentary, and notes for the novel in the Wesleyan Edition of the Works of Henry Fielding: *The History of Tom Jones: A Foundling*, 2 vols. (Oxford: Wesleyan University Press/Oxford University Press, 1975) as well as his own critical work on Fielding.

33. *Middlemarch*, ed. Gordon S. Haight (Boston: Houghton Mifflin Company, 1956), 302.

34. "Narrative and History," cited above, and "Optic and Semiotic in *Middlemarch*," *The Worlds of Victorian Fiction*, ed. Jerome H. Buckley,

Harvard English Studies 6 (Cambridge, Mass.: Harvard University Press, 1975), 125–45. *The Form of Victorian Fiction* is also concerned with *Middlemarch*.

35. "Optic and Semiotic," 128.

36. The questions I have raised here about *Tom Jones* I will continue in a later chapter.

37. I refer, of course, to Roland Barthes, *S/Z: An Essay*, trans. Richard Howard (New York: Hill and Wang, 1974). The clearest elaborations are in several essays of Frank Kermode; see especially his *The Classic: Literary Images of Permanence and Change* (New York: Viking, 1975) and Jonathan Culler's *Structuralist Poetics* (Ithaca, N.Y.: Cornell University Press, 1975). I should add that the *way* I raise the problem of narrative structure owes more to Kermode's earlier *The Sense of an Ending* (New York: Oxford University Press, 1967) than to the later work.

38. *The Marble Faun*, ed. with intro. and annotation Richard H. Rupp (Indianapolis, Ind.: Bobbs-Merrill, 1971), 90–91. The passage could, incidentally, stand as an almost perfect description of *Finnegans Wake*.

39. I am indebted to the fine discussion of the novel in Edgar Dryden's "The Limits of Romance: A Reading of *The Marble Faun*," in *Individual and Community: Variations on a Theme in American Fiction*, ed. Kenneth Baldwin and David Kirby (Durham, N.C.: Duke University Press, 1975), 17–48, and also for his treatment of origins and failures to end in his book on Hawthorne, cited above.

40. See Eugenio Donato, "Topographies of Memory," in the Acts of the Borges Symposium held in Maine, April 1976, and his " 'Here, Now'/'Always, Already': Incidental Remarks on some Recent Characterizations of the Text," *Diacritics* 6, 3 (Fall 1976): 24–29.

41. Cf. Donato, "Topographies of Memory."

Chapter 2

1. I, 188. All citations of *Moll Flanders* and *Robinson Crusoe* refer to the Shakespeare Head edition (Oxford and New York: Oxford University Press, 1982). Quotations of the third volume of *Robinson Crusoe, Serious Reflections*, are taken from the George A. Aitken edition (London, 1895). Quotations from *Roxana* and from *A Journal of the Plague Year* are taken from the Oxford English Novels series: *Roxana*, ed. Jane Jack (London: Oxford University Press, 1964) and *A Journal*, ed. Louis Landa (London: Oxford University Press, 1969).

2. Actually, Robinson was born under the name *Kreutznaer*, "but

by the usual Corruption of Words in England, we are now called, nay we call our selves, and write our Name *Crusoe*."

3. See G. A. Starr, *Defoe and Spiritual Autobiography* (Princeton, N.J.: Princeton University Press, 1965) and J. Paul Hunter, *The Reluctant Pilgrim* (Baltimore: The Johns Hopkins University Press, 1966).

4. Ian Watt, *The Rise of the Novel* (Berkeley: University of California Press, 1959), 133.

5. At least part of the impulse behind Defoe's fiction is the desire to explore human possibilities in the face of a necessity so harsh as to suspend normal laws. The whole question of natural right has been examined in Maximillian E. Novak's *Defoe and the Nature of Man* (Oxford: Oxford University Press, 1963).

6. The pressures against Defoe's writing these novels seem multiplied when one remembers that Defoe was violating the Puritan ban against realistic fictions. For a discussion of this problem, see Hunter, *The Reluctant Pilgrim*, 114–24. For other accounts of Defoe's ambivalence about "feign'd Histories," see Maximillian Novak, "Defoe's Theory of Fiction," *SP* 61 (1964): 650–68, and the chapter on Defoe in Alan McKillop, *The Early Masters of English Fiction* (Lawrence: University of Kansas Press, 1956). For a discussion of the background of this problem, see William Nelson, "The Boundaries of Fiction in the Renaissance: A Treaty Between Truth and Falsehood," *ELH* 36 (1969): 30–58.

7. See James Sutherland, *Defoe* (London, 1950), 91.

8. Frank H. Ellis has revealed in the introduction to his *Twentieth-Century Interpretations of Robinson Crusoe* (Englewood Cliffs, N.J.: Prentice-Hall, 1969), 12ff., the extent to which Defoe organized this book on the basis of images of devouring.

9. *Confessions*, trans. R. S. Pine-Coffin (Baltimore: Penguin, 1961), Bk. V, Sec. 10, 103. References in the text are to this edition.

10. I make a more extensive comparison with Augustine's *Confessions* later on. Augustine's influence on the Puritans is well known. In addition, however, there are structural similarities between Augustine's *Confessions* and Defoe's "autobiographies." This influence was conveyed, if not directly, by way of the confessions and spiritual autobiographies of the seventeenth century, as Starr and Hunter have shown. On this point, see also Paul Delaney's *British Autobiography in the Seventeenth Century* (London: Routledge and Kegan Paul, 1969).

11. Jean-Paul Sartre, *Nausea*, trans. Lloyd Alexander (Norfolk, Conn.: New Directions, 1959), 58.

12. See Erich Auerbach's essay on "Figura" in his *Scenes from the Drama of European Literature* (New York: World, 1959, rpt. Gloucester, Mass.: Peter Smith), 45.

13. See note 6.

Chapter 3

1. *The History of Tom Jones, a Foundling*, ed. Martin C. Battestin, 2 vols. (Oxford and Middletown, Conn.: Oxford University Press, Wesleyan University Press, 1975), 79. Battestin's edition, with its extensive notes, makes possible a whole new pleasure in reading the book. Citations of the novel will be to this edition and will be identified by book and chapter as well as page numbers to facilitate reference to other editions.

2. The 8th edition of Wood's *Institute of the Laws of England* (London, 1752), from which I quote in the third epigraph to this chapter. I am indebted to the University of Illinois Law Library for providing a microfilm of the relevant passages.

3. Blackstone's *Commentaries*, I, xvi, 459 (Philadelphia: Rees Welsh, 1902), 433–34.

4. See Hugh Amory, "Law and the Structure of Fielding's Novels" (Dissertation, Columbia University, 1964), 278–84.

5. Since *Oedipus Rex* is an Aristotelian "model" tragedy, successful avoidance of incest would clearly indicate a comic property in Fielding's plots. Full discussion of this question would add another level to the analysis in which I engage in this essay. Aristotle's references to *Oedipus* have to do with the discovery of true parentage. The generic "parentage" of Fielding's novels is an old question, too large for me to enter into here. I want merely to refer to one way the question is thematically charged *in* the text. It is worth remembering that the Homeric parent, the comic epic, was totally lost—see Fielding's remarks in the preface to *Joseph Andrews*.

6. Robert Nisbet, "Genealogy, Growth, and Other Metaphors," *New Literary History* 1 (Spring 1970): 354.

7. "Chaine des événements: Chain of Events," in *Philosophical Dictionary*, ed. and trans. Theodore Besterman (Harmondsworth: Penguin, 1971), 111. The third epigraph is from the 8th edition of Wood (London, 1752), 69. Fielding owned an edition of this work, which is the same law book I cite Battestin as quoting below. I am indebted to the University of Illinois Law Library for providing a microfilm of the relevant passages.

8. In addition to his article in note 5, see Nisbet, *Social Change and History* (London: Oxford University Press, 1969) and Frederick J. Teggart, *Theory and Processes of History* (1918; rpt. Berkeley: University of California Press, 1960). My thinking on this question has been stimulated and influenced by Edward Said's *Beginnings* (New York: Basic Books, 1975), particularly chapters three and four, by the opening remarks in Paul de Man's "Genesis and Genealogy in Nietzsche's *The Birth of Tragedy*," *Diacritics* 2, 4 (Winter 1972): 44–53, and by Michel Foucault's "Nietzsche, la généalogie, l'histoire," now translated into English in *Language, Counter-*

Memory, Practice, ed. Donald F. Bouchard (Ithaca, N.Y.: Cornell University Press, 1977). See also Edgar Dryden's essay on *Pierre* in *boundary 2*, Thomas Maresca's *Epic to Novel* (Columbus: Ohio State University Press, 1974), and Ronald Paulson's remarks in "Recent Studies in the Restoration and Eighteenth Century," *Studies in English Literature* 16 (Winter 1976): 517–44. Important discussions of Said's work which touch upon this issue are to be found in the articles of Hillis Miller, Hayden White, Joseph Riddel, and Eugenio Donato in *Diacritics* 6, 3 (Fall 1976). I have earlier discussed the importance of the genealogical theme in my review-article on Said in *Modern Language Notes* 91 (October 1976): 1141–49, and in "The Errant Letter and the Whispering Gallery," *Genre* 10 (Winter 1977): 573–99.

9. The Filmer and the Locke have been usefully edited, introduced, and annotated by Peter Laslett, *Blackwell's Political Texts* (Oxford: Blackwell's, 1949) and (New York: New American Library, 1965) respectively. John Neville Figgis, *The Divine Right of Kings* (1896; rpt. New York: Harper Torchbooks, 1965) is still useful. The medieval origins of the issue have been traced by Ernst H. Kantorowicz in *The King's Two Bodies* (Princeton, N.J.: Princeton University Press, 1957). For the more general importance of genealogy in eighteenth-century historiography, see Frederick Meinecke, *Historism* (*Die Entstehung des Historismus*), trans. J. E. Anderson (New York: Herder and Herder, 1972), and chapter 2 of James William Johnson, *The Formulation of English Neo-Classical Thought* (Princeton, N.J.: Princeton University Press, 1967). For the background on what I discuss below concerning the political nature of English historiographical debate, see J. G. A. Pocock, *The Ancient Constitution and the Feudal Law* (New York: W. W. Norton, 1968), *Politics, Language and Time* (New York: Atheneum, 1973), "Modes of Political and Historical Time in Early Eighteenth-Century England," in *Studies in Eighteenth-Century Culture* 5, ed. Ronald C. Rosbottom (Madison: University of Wisconsin Press, 1976); Isaac Kramnick, *Bolingbroke and His Circle: The Politics of Nostalgia in the Age of Walpole* (Cambridge, Mass.: Harvard University Press, 1968) and "Augustan Politics and English Historiography: The Debate on the English Past, 1730–35," *History and Theory* 6 (1967): 33–56; and Quentin Skinner, "The Principles and Practices of Opposition: The Case of Bolingbroke Versus Walpole," in *Historical Perspectives: Studies in English Thought and Society in Honour of J. H. Plumb*, ed. Neil McKendrick (London: Europa Publications, 1974). For Fielding's interest in historical questions, see Robert M. Wallace, "Fielding's Knowledge of History and Biography," *Studies in Philology* 44 (January 1947): 89–107.

10. *The Ancient Constitution*, 45–52.

11. For this background, see Battestin's introduction to his edition

of *Tom Jones*, W. B. Coley's introduction to his edition of Fielding's *The Jacobite's Journal and Related Writings* (Oxford: Oxford University Press, 1975), and Rupert C. Jarvis, *Collected Papers on the Jacobite Risings*, 11 (Manchester: Manchester University Press, 1972). For important discussions of Fielding's treatment of the '45 in *Tom Jones*, see J. Paul Hunter, *Occasional Form: Henry Fielding and the Chains of Circumstance* (Baltimore: The Johns Hopkins University Press, 1975), 182–86; Leo Braudy, *Narrative Form in History and Fiction* (Princeton, N.J.: Princeton University Press, 1970), 91–212; and Battestin, "Tom Jones and 'His Egyptian Majesty': Fielding's Parable of Government," *PMLA* 82 (March 1967): 68–77; Ronald Paulson, "Fielding in *Tom Jones*: The Historian, the Poet, and the Mythologist," in *Augustan Worlds*, ed. J. C. Hilson, M. M. B. Jones, and J. R. Watson (Leicester: Leicester University Press, 1978), 175–87.

12. The question is debated, for example, in Battestin, "Fielding's Changing Politics and *Joseph Andrews*," *Philological Quarterly* 39 (January 1960): 39–55, Coley, "Henry Fielding and the Two Walpoles," *Philological Quarterly* 45 (January 1966): 157–78, and in the introductions of their editions in the Wesleyan Fielding; also see the discussion in Brian Richard McCrea, "Fielding's Political Writings" (Dissertation, University of Virginia, 1975). For the political background, see John B. Owen, *The Rise of the Pelhams* (1957; rpt. New York: Barnes and Noble, 1971).

13. *The True Patriot* has been edited and annotated by Miriam Austin Locke (University: University of Alabama Press, 1964). The pamphlets are collected, edited, and annotated in Peter Harold Hemingson's "Fielding and the '45: A Critical Edition of Henry Fielding's Anti-Jacobite Pamphlets" (Dissertation, Columbia University, 1973).

14. There is, incidentally, too much suggestion of irony in this passage and too much variety in the ways the narrator has of characterizing his relationships with the text, critics, and readers throughout the novel to take this at face value as a statement of narrative authority. For an interesting discussion of narrative authority in *Tom Jones*, see Hugh Amory's dissertation, cited above.

15. This is an old argument concerning *Tom Jones*, in which Ian Watt's attack on Fielding in *The Rise of the Novel* (Berkeley: University of California Press, 1957) and Wayne Booth's defense of him in *The Rhetoric of Fiction* (Chicago: University of Chicago Press, 1961) represent important stages. Fielding criticism divides itself according to its insistence on the external reference or on the self-referentiality of the novel. On the one hand, roughly, Hunter, Battestin, and Ronald Paulson, *Satire and the Novel in Eighteenth-Century England* (New Haven, Conn.: Yale University Press, 1967) could be placed, while on the other would be found books

like Andrew Wright, *Henry Fielding: Fast and Feast* (Berkeley: University of California Press, 1965) and Robert Alter, *Fielding and the Nature of the Novel* (Cambridge, Mass.: Harvard University Press, 1968) and *Partial Magic: The Novel as a Self-Conscious Genre* (Berkeley: University of California Press, 1975). I have discussed the problem in relationship to *Tom Jones* in statements of the theoretical problem, see Paul de Man, "Semiology and Rhetoric," *Diacritics* 3, 3 (Fall 1973): 27–33, J. Hillis Miller, "The Fiction of Realism: *Sketches by Boz, Oliver Twist,* and Cruikshank's Illustrations," in *Dickens Centennial Essays,* ed. Ada Nisbet and Blake Nevius (Berkeley: University of California Press, 1971), and on the other side of the question, Edward Said, "The Text, The World, The Critic," *Bulletin of the Midwest Modern Language Association* 8, 2 (Fall 1975): 1–23, and "Roads Taken and Not Taken in Contemporary Criticism," in *Directions for Criticism: Structuralism and Its Alternatives,* ed. Murray Krieger and L. S. Dembo (Madison: University of Wisconsin Press, 1977) as well as his *Beginnings.*

16. A similar claim was made against Charles's father, James III. See Amory, "Law and the Structure of Fielding's Novels," 299.

17. I refer, of course, to the concept Roman Jakobson introduced into discussions of the novel in his book with Morris Halle, *Fundamentals of Language* (The Hague: Mouton, 1956). For recent examples of metonymic analysis of the novel in Anglo-American criticism, see de Man, "Semiology and Rhetoric" and Hillis Miller's essay on Dickens cited above, and also Fred See, "The Demystification of Style: Metaphoric and Metonymic Language in *A Modern Instance,*" *Nineteenth-Century Fiction* 28 (March 1974): 379–403, and David Lodge, *The Modes of Modern Writing: Metaphor, Metonymy, and the Typology of Modern Literature* (Ithaca, N.Y.: Cornell University Press, 1977). But see also Jacques Derrida, "White Mythology: Metaphor in the Text of Philosophy," trans. from *Poétique* 2, 5 (1971) by F. C. T. Moore in *New Literary History* 6 (Autumn 1974): 5–74.

18. Richard A. Lanham, *A Handlist of Rhetorical Terms* (Berkeley: University of California Press, 1969), 3. But see also Paul de Man, "The Rhetoric of Temporality," in *Interpretation: Theory and Practice,* ed. Charles S. Singleton (Baltimore: The Johns Hopkins University Press, 1969). For a general discussion of allegory in eighteenth-century English literature, see Victor Harris, "Allegory to Analogy in the Interpretation of Scriptures," *Philological Quarterly* 45 (January 1966): 1–23.

19. For the importance of examples, see the first chapter of *Joseph Andrews* and Paulson's and Braudy's books, cited above.

20. See Henry Knight Miller, "Some Functions of Rhetoric in *Tom Jones: Philological Quarterly* 45 (January 1966): 209–35. Hugh Amory be-

lieves Fielding's novels are constructed as "law cases." The rhetorical organization was part of Fielding's education. See Marvin T. Herrick, *Comic Theory in the Sixteenth Century* (1950; rpt. Urbana: University of Illinois Press, 1964) for typical analyses of comedy by orational patterns.

21. Lanham, *A Handlist*, 68.

22. But see Hunter's different argument, *Occasional Form*, 143–65.

23. See Paulson, *Satire*, 121–26. Hugh Amory discusses the episode of the bird as an "archetype" of the action of the first six books of the novel, "Law and the Structure," 261–75.

24. See Raymond Williams, *Keywords: A Vocabulary of Culture and Society* (Oxford: Oxford University Press, 1976), 226–30.

25. One would need also to explore further the implications of this play of tropes *on* tropes and the unstable relationships between tropological systems and between them and performative and grammatical modes. See Paul de Man's theoretical caveat in "Semiology and Rhetoric" and his analyses of these relationships in texts of Nietzsche and Rousseau. A good example is his "Action and Identity in Nietzsche," in *Graphesis: Perspectives in Literature and Philosophy* Yale French Studies 52 (New Haven, Conn.: Yale University Press, 1975): 16–30. The rhetorical term for what I have been examining is, in the most general sense, *parabasis*, which de Man, by way of Frederich Schlegel, links with irony (see "The Rhetoric of Temporality"). Fielding's test would seem to provide an interesting site for the examination of these problems. In the obvious sense of the term, the narrator's intrusiveness—parabasis—is the most commented upon feature of Fielding's writings, both dramatic and novelistic. On the question of Fielding's irony, see George R. Levine, *Henry Fielding and the Dry Mock* (The Hague: Mouton, 1967) and Glenn W. Hatfield, *Henry Fielding and the Language of Irony* (Chicago: University of Chicago Press, 1968).

26. The term "bastard" was also, curiously, a favorite political term of Bolingbroke's, associated with an illegitimate House of Commons— that is to say, a Walpolian one. See Kramnick, *Bolingbroke and His Circle*, 79 n. 59, 284.

27. One of the narrator's "themes" is his complaint against misrepresentation. A pertinent example for the present point is his lament: "I question not but thou has been told, among other Stories of me, that thou wast to travel with a very scurrilous Fellow: But whoever told thee so, did me an Injury. No Man detests and despises Scurrility more than myself; nor hath any Man more Reason; for none hath ever been treated with more; And what is a very severe Fate, I have had some of the *abusive Writings of those very Men fathered upon me*, who in other of their Works have abused me themselves with the utmost Virulence" (XVIII, i, 914; my emphasis).

28. See Kramnick, *Bolingbroke and His Circle*, 39–83.

29. *Amelia*, 2 vols. (London: Everyman's Library, 1962).

30. The *locus classicus* for philosophical discussions of accident is Aristotle, particularly the *Posterior Analytics*, I, 6, 75a–b; *Physics*, II, 196a–198a, see also 199b; *Metaphysics* 1025a, 1026b. There is almost no historiographer who fails to address the problem—see Teggart, *Theory and Processes of History*, and Lord Bolingbroke's *Historical Writings*, ed. and intro. Isaac Kramnick (Chicago: University of Chicago Press, 1972), for example, 19. Leo Braudy provides a very good discussion of "accidents" in Fielding in his *Narrative Form*, as does Ronald Paulson in his *Satire and the Novel*. Also see Philip Stevick, "Fielding and the Meaning of History," *PMLA* 70 (December 1964): 561–68. In general, for the role of accident in novelistic struction and historiography, see Harold Toliver's interesting *Animate Illusions: Explorations of Narrative Structure* (Lincoln: University of Nebraska Press, 1974). The best representative of the providential argument is, of course, Martin Batestin, "*Tom Jones*: The Argument of Design," in *The Augustan Milieu: Essays Presented to Louis A. Landa*, ed. Henry K. Miller, Eric Rothstein, and G. S. Rousseau (Oxford: Clarendon Press, 1970), 289–319.

31. *Philosophical Dictionary*, 110.

Chapter 4

1. The following remarks are "torn away" from their context in a larger project on *Tristram Shandy*. I chose this text in part because it was one of Eugenio Donato's favorite texts, a pleasure we shared, a text he, Edgar Dryden, and I discussed together in seminars in Buffalo. It was first published in a special collection in memory of E. D. Needless to say, my "scene of reading" here refers constantly, not the least in its difference, to Eugenio's, and especially to those represented by his two texts in this volume.

2. In general, the episode has been treated as one of several examples of "readers reading" in *Tristram Shandy*, "of using the book's characters as surrogates for the reader who can learn about his own responsive process by watching the eccentric (but predictable) Shandean responses" in the words of J. Paul Hunter who has given the most extensive treatment of the episode in his admirable essay "Response as Reformation: *Tristram Shandy* and the Art of Interpretation," first published in *Novel* in 1971, and usefully reprinted in the Norton Critical Edition of *Tristram Shandy*, ed. Howard Anderson (New York: W. W. Norton, 1980), 623–

640. Hunter stresses "the power of context," demonstrated by the episode and the way it is a version of "the whole-as-part-within-a whole" tradition of interpolated tales, plays within plays, and so on. I will refer to these ideas below. I have also made use of the suggestiveness of Richard Macksey, "Alas Poor Yorick: Sterne Thoughts," *MLN* (December, 1983): 1006–1020. I have also found useful treatments of Sterne in a number of Ronald Paulson's works and in Walter L. Reed's chapter on Sterne (particularly his discussion of "displacements" in *Tristram Shandy* and its relationship to institutions and canon formation) in his *An Exemplary History of the Novel: The Quixotic Versus the Picaresque* (Chicago: University of Chicago Press, 1981). I have used here the edition of the novel edited by James A. Work (New York, 1940).

3. Cf. Macksey, "Alas Poor Yorick," 1009.

4. Note the implications in I, xi, 23–25, plus the fact that Yorick, like Tristram, is too tall for his forebears.

5. The authority of the individual conscience was also, of course, an important issue in the Reformation, and the particular institutional issues of conscience Walter and Dr. Slop are most interested in turn out to be explicitly engaged by the sermon.

6. The literature on this question is extensive. Most helpful is George Wesley Buchanan's translation and commentary in his edition of *To the Hebrews* for the Anchor Bible (Garden City, N.Y.: Doubleday, 1972) which I refer to throughout my text.

7. Again the literature is extensive. I quote the text of this second "Essay" of Locke's from Volume VIII of the 1823 London edition of *The Works of John Locke*. See also the slightly abridged "Essay" in John Yolton's collection, *The Locke Reader* (Cambridge: Cambridge University Press, 1977), pp. 10–28.

8. While the Anchor Bible "convinced," the Oxford RSV "are sure that," and the King James (and Sterne) "trust" provide another example of a problem in translation, they also provide a nice summary of the changes Yorick brings with the theme.

9. There are a number of ways besides the general question I develop below in which the sermon episode engages, renews, or anticipates explicit references to Locke elsewhere in *Tristram Shandy*. For example, the possibility that the mind of conscience might "insensibly become hard" (127) reminds one of Tristram's example of "Dolly's red seal-wax," which he uses to explain Locke's theory in chapter ii of the same volume (86), and the play on "wit" and "judgment" in the sermon book foreword to Tristram's internal "Preface" (III, xx, 192–203).

10. Cf. Locke on the confusions of personal pronouns: "the frequent changing of the personage he speaks in renders the sense very un-

certain, and is apt to mislead one that has not some clue to guide him; sometimes by the pronoun, I, he means himself; sometimes any Christian; sometimes a Jew, and sometimes any man, etc. If speaking of himself, in the first person singular, has so various meanings; his use of the first person plural is with a far greater latitude, sometimes designating himself alone, sometimes those with himself, whom he makes partners to the epistles; sometimes with himself, comprehending the other apostles, or preachers of the Gospel, or Christians; nay, sometimes he in that way speaks of the converted Jews, other times of the converted Gentiles, and sometimes of other, in a more or less extended sense, every one of which varies the meaning of the place, and makes it to be differently understood" (*Works* VIII, 6; Yolton, 15–16).

11. For what follows, see J. N. D. Kelly, *Early Christian Creeds*, 3rd ed. (New York: Longman, 1972), esp. 52–61.

Chapter 5

1. Sir Walter Scott, *Waverley or 'Tis Sixty Years Since*, ed. Claire Lamont (Oxford, New York: Oxford University Press, 1986). References in the text are to this edition; references to other novels are as follows: *Old Mortality* (Oxford, New York: Oxford University Press, 1993); *Redgauntlet* (Oxford, New York: Oxford University Press, 1985) (Kathryn Sutherland's "Introduction," Editor's Notes and "Appendix: *Redgauntlet* and Scottish History" are particularly helpful, the "Appendix" for Scott's other Scottish novels as well, but then it is also true that the introductions of all the Oxford Scott novels provide some of the best recent critical essays on Scott); *The Heart of Midlothian* (Oxford, New York: Oxford University Press, 1982), also with a helpful Scottish History appendix by Claire Lamont; *Quentin Durward* (Oxford, New York: Oxford University Press, 1992); *Rob Roy* (London: Dent, 1991). It is impossible to do justice to an increasingly rich body of criticism and scholarship about Scott, and it would be impossible to mention all the writings which have fed the reading to follow, but, in addition to those cited below, it is necessary to mention the following as having the most importance to my argument: Lukács, Johnson, Daiches, Muir, and Dryden. I am especially indebted to Edgar Dryden's reading of *Waverley* in the context of American romance, *The Form of American Romance* (Baltimore: The Johns Hopkins University Press, 1988). Katie Trumpener's "National Character, Nationalist Plote: National Tale and Historical Novel in the age of *Waverley*, 1806–1830," *ELH* 60 (1993): 685–731, changed my way of thinking about

Scott's novels. I am also grateful to her for allowing me to read the manuscript for her forthcoming book with Princeton University Press, from which I profited greatly.

2. Sir Walter Scott, *Lives of Eminent Novelists* (London: Dent, n.d.), 48.

3. See, for example, Scott's review of Jane Austen as well as his essays in *Lives of Eminent Novelists.* "*Emma*: A Novel," *Quarterly Review* 14 (1815–16): 188–201; reprinted in *Sir Walter Scott on Novelists and Fiction*, ed. Ioan Williams (London: Routledge & Kegan Paul, 1968). Further references will be identified by page numbers in this edition. Scott's review is also reprinted in *Jane Austen, The Critical Heritage*, ed. B. C. Southam (London: Routledge and Kegan Paul, 1968). On the issue of the emergent "historical" aspects of the earlier eighteenth-century fictions, see also George Dekker's *The American Historical Romance* (Cambridge, New York: Cambridge University Press, 1987).

4. Jacques Derrida, "Aphorism Countertime," trans. Nicholas Royle, in *Acts of Literature*, ed. Derek Attridge (New York, London: Routledge, 1992), 413–33; see also in this volume " 'This Strange Institution Called Literature': An Interview with Jacques Derrida," 63–67, and "Before the Law," trans. Avital Ronell and Christine Roulston.

5. E.g., J. G. A. Pocock, *The Ancient Constitution and the Feudal Law: A Study of English Historical Thought in the Seventeenth Century. A reissue with a Retrospect* (Cambridge, London, New York: Cambridge University Press, 1987). See also Fiona Robertson, *Legitimate Histories: Scott, Gothic, and the Authorities of Fiction* (Oxford: Clarendon Press, 1994).

6. See, for example, Scott's 1830 "Introduction" to *The Lay of the Last Minstrel* and *The Lady of the Lake*, as well as the first three stanzas of the latter. See also Nancy Moore Goslee's splendid book on the poetry, *Scott the Rhymer* (Lexington: University Press of Kentucky, 1988).

7. Cf. Judith Wilt, *Secret Leaves: The Novels of Walter Scott* (Chicago: University of Chicago Press, 1985). Wilt cites Francis R. Hart's *Scott's Novels: The Plotting of Historic Survival* (Charlottesville: University Press of Virginia, 1966), 249. Both books are indispensable for the student of Scott. The focus on the violent emergence of the modern nation-state not only can be found in the metrical romances and novels but seems to be there for Scott at least as early as what is thought to be one of his first published literary works, his 1799 translation of Goethe's drama, *Goetz Von Berlichten*. See also his preface to this translation.

8. Richard Humphrey, *Walter Scott:* Waverley (Cambridge: Cambridge University Press, 1993), 5. Humphrey has some interesting new things to say about *Waverley* in this short introductory book in Cam-

bridge's Landmarks of World Literature series. I am indebted to Jerome Christensen for first insisting, politely, that I should look into the question of the relevance for Scott and Austen of Napoleon's late itinerary.

9. So dated internally by references to growing problems in the American colonies, another frame of possible reference; see for example Kathryn Sutherland's note for p. 245 (451).

10. Note also Scott's story in his 1829 "General Introduction," about his misplacing, losing, and then rediscovering his manuscript of *Waverley*.

11. The question in modern criticism about the passivity of the *Waverley* hero has its classic discussion in Alexander Welsh's groundbreaking book, *The Hero of the Waverley Novels* (1963), reprinted with additional essays (Princeton, N.J.: Princeton University Press, 1992). I have also found very useful Daniel Cottom, *The Civilized Imagination* (Cambridge: Cambridge University Press, 1985).

12. On this point and many others, including Scott's "manly" intervention with *Waverley* into a current critical debate about female fictions, see one of the most important and informative books in recent years on Scott and contemporary discourse about the novel, see Ina Ferris, *The Achievement of Literary Authority: Gender, History, and the Waverley Novels* (Ithaca, N.Y.: Cornell University Press, 1991).

13. *The Sinews of Power: War, Money and the English State* (New York: Knopf, 1989).

14. *Hegel's Philosophy of Right*, trans. T. M. Knox (New York: Oxford University Press, 1971), 245, addition to paragraph 93.

15. Juliet Flower MacCannell, *The Regime of the Brothers: After the Patriarchy* (London and New York: Routledge, 1991).

16. The Scottish Enlightenment's stadialist theory of the common stages of social/cultural progress has become a staple of Scott and, indeed, of Romanticism criticism. It has been discussed succinctly and usefully in George Dekker's book cited above, but see also Ronald L. Meek, *Social Science and the Ignoble Savage* (Cambridge, New York: Cambridge University Press, 1976).

17. Review of *Culloden Papers*, *Quarterly Review* (January 1816), reprinted in *The Miscellaneous Works of Sir Walter Scott, Bart.*, Vol. XX (Edinburgh: Adam and Charles Black, 1881), 92–93.

18. E. J. Hobsbawm gives a modern historian's analysis not very different from Scott's version:

> The foundation of Highland society was the tribe (clan) of subsistence peasants or pastoralists settled in an ancestral area under the chieftain of their kin, whom the old Scottish kingdom had

(wrongly) attempted to assimilate to a feudal noble, and English eighteenth-century society (even more wrongly) to an aristocratic landowner. This assimilation gave the chiefs the legal—but by clan standards immoral—right to do what they wanted with their "property," and entangled them in the expensive status-competition of British aristocratic life, for which they had neither the resources nor the financial sense. They could raise their income only by destroying their society. From the point of view of the clansmen the chief was not a landlord, but the head of their tribe to whom they owed loyalty in peace and war and who in turn owed them largesse and support. Conversely the social standing of the chief in Highland society depended not on the number of his acres or moorland and forest, but on that of the armed men he could raise. The chiefs were therefore in a double dilemma. As "old" chiefs their interest lay in multiplying primitive subsistence peasants on increasingly congested territory; as "new" noble landlords, in exploiting their estates by modern methods, which almost certainly meant either exchanging human tenants for livestock (which requires little labor) or the sale of their land, or both. In fact they did all these things successively, first multiplying an increasingly pauperized tenantry, and later forcing it into mass emigration. . . . After the Wars [the temporary boom of the Napoleonic Wars] the times of horror began. Greedy or bankrupt landlords began to "clear" their uncomprehendingly loyal tribesmen from the land, scattering them as emigrants throughout the world from the slums of Glasgow to the forests of Canada. Sheep drove men from the hills. . . . the Highlands became what they have ever since remained, a beautiful desert. (*Industry and Empire*, Pelican Economic History of Britain, Vol. 3, *From 1750 to the Present Day* [Baltimore: Penguin, 1968, 1969], 301–3)

19. Cf. Ortega y Gasset's remark: "So it is not only that *Quixote* was written against the books of chivalry [the romance], and as a result bears them within it, but that the novel as a literary genre consists essentially of such an absorption," *Meditations on Quixote* (New York: Norton, 1963), 139.

20. See Philippe Lacoue-Labarthe and Jean-Luc Nancy, *L'Absolu littéraire: Théorie de la littérature du romantisme allemand* (Paris: Editions du Seuil, 1978) and its partial English translation, *The Literary Absolute*, trans. Philip Barnard and Cheryl Lester (Albany: State University of New York Press, 1988). On a more ironic note, see also John Guillory, *Cultural Capital* (Chicago: University of Chicago Press, 1993), 129–33.

Chapter 6

1. Sir Walter Scott, Review of "*Emma*: A Novel," *Quarterly Review* 14 (1815–16): 188–201; reprinted in *Sir Walter Scott on Novelists and Fiction*, ed. Ioan Williams (London: Routledge & Kegan Paul, 1968); also in *Jane Austen: The Critical Heritage*, B. C. Southam (London: Routledge & Kegan Paul, 1968); Scott, *Lives of the Novelists* (London: J. M. Dent; New York: Dutton, 1820), 48, 70, 63

2. Ian Watt, *The Rise of the Novel* (Berkeley and Los Angeles: University of California Press, 1959).

3. Walter Raleigh, *The English Novel: A Short Sketch of Its History from the Earliest Times to the Appearance of "Waverley"* (London: John Murray, Albemarle Street, 1916).

4. David Masson, *British Novelists and Their Styles: Being a Critical Sketch of the History of British Prose Fiction* (Cambridge: Macmillan and Co., 1859; reprinted Folcroft, Penna.: Folcroft Press, 1969).

5. Charles Eaton Burch, "British Criticism of Defoe as a Novelist, 1719–1860," *Englische Studien* 67 (1932–33): 178–98 and "Defoe's British Reputation, 1869–1894," *Englische Studien* 68 (1933–34): 410–23.

6. Daniel Defoe, *Robinson Crusoe*, ed. Michael Shinagel, 2nd ed. (New York, London: W. W. Norton, 1994). One should also consult Pat Rogers, ed., *Defoe: The Critical Heritage* (London and Boston: Routledge & Kegan Paul, 1972) and his Unwin Critical Library volume, *Robinson Crusoe* (London: Allen & Unwin, 1979).

7. Leslie Stephen, *Hours in a Library*, new Edition, with Additions, in three volumes (London: Smith, Elder, & Co., 1892), I: 3–4.

8. And sometimes with the collaboration of Scottish Enlightenment intellectuals who were also apparently the first to "invent" English literature for academic purposes. See Robert Crawford's essential account in *Devolving English Literature* (Oxford: Clarendon Press, 1992).

9. J. R. Moore, "Defoe and Scott," *PMLA* 56 (1941): 710–35.

10. I am referring of course to post-colonial criticism. Minimally, in regard to Defoe one must mention Peter Hulme's chapter on *Robinson* in his *Colonial Encounters: Europe and the Native Caribbean, 1492–1797* (London and New York: Methuen, 1986); Martin Green, *Dreams of Adventure, Deeds of Empire* (New York: Basic Books, 1979), and Pat Rogers's book on *Robinson*, cited above in n.6 are also still valuable starting points for this subject.

11. On Barbauld, see Catherine E. Moore, " 'Ladies . . . Taking the Pen in Hand': Mrs. Barbauld's Criticism of Eighteenth-Century Women Novelists," in *Fetter'd or Free? British Women Novelists, 1670–1815* ed. Mary Anne Schofield and Cecilia Macheski (Athens: Ohio University Press, 1986), 383–97. Much of the detail about these editions that follows is from

the second volume of Michael Sadleir's *XIX Century Fiction: A Bibliographical Record Based on His Own Collection*, 2 vols. (London: Constable and Berkeley: University of California Press, 1951).

12. The best account of the publication and problems of *Ballantyne's Novelist's Library* I know of is in Jane Millgate's *Scott's Last Edition: A Study in Publishing History* (Edinburgh: Edinburgh University Press, 1987).

13. David Hume, *A Treatise of Human Nature*, ed. L. A. Selby-Bigge, 2nd ed. with text revised and notes by P. H. Nidditch (Oxford: Clarendon Press, 1980), 566.

14. An important account of the scholarship concerning the development of the Defoe canon or oeuvre is in P. N. Furbank and W. R. Owens, *The Canonisation of Daniel Defoe* (New Haven, Conn.: Yale University Press, 1988). They develop some of the questions I raise here but still inconclusively. Rogers has interesting short accounts of the publishing and the biographical/critical tradition of the Defoe canon in both *The Critical Heritage* and in his book on *Robinson*. Much of the information that follows comes from these sources.

15. *Librorum ex Biblothecis Philippi Farewell, D.D. et Danielis Defoe, Gen. Catalogus* (1731).

16. Peter Earle, *The World of Defoe* (New York: Atheneum, 1977), xi.

17. Lennard Davis, *Factual Fictions: The Origins of the English Novel* (New York: Columbia University Press, 1983; reprint Philadelphia: University of Pennsylvania Press, 1997). A further decisive move has been made more recently by J. Paul Hunter, *Before the Novel: The Cultural Contexts of Eighteenth-Century English Fiction* (New York: W. W. Norton, 1990).

18. Pierre Bourdieu, *The Field of Cultural Production: Essays on Art and Literature*, ed. Randal Johnson (New York: Columbia University Press, 1993), 179.

19. See for example Anthony Easthope, *Literary into Cultural Studies* (London and New York: Routledge, 1991). For the problems in Easthope's argument, see Bill Readings, *The University in Ruins* (Cambridge, Mass. and London: Harvard University Press, 1996), 97–98.

20. Richard Stang, *The Theory of the Novel in England* (New York: Columbia University Press, 1959); Kenneth Graham, *English Criticism of the Novel, 1865–1900* (Oxford: Clarendon Press, 1965).

21. Dugald Stewart coined this expression. See I. S. Ross, ed., "Dugald Stewart's Account of Adam Smith L.L.D.," in Adam Smith, *Essays on Philosophical Subjects*, ed. W. P. D. Wightman and J. C. Bryce (Oxford: Oxford University Press, 1980), 292–93. See also Alan Bewell, *Wordsworth and the Enlightenment: Nature, Man, and Society in the Experimental Poetry* (New Haven, Conn. and London: Yale University Press, 1989), 59.

22. Maximillian E. Novak, *Defoe and the Nature of Man* (Oxford: Oxford University Press, 1963) and *Realism, Myth, and History in Defoe's Fiction* (Lincoln: University of Nebraska Press, 1983); George A. Starr, *Defoe and Spiritual Autobiography* (Princeton, N.J.: Princeton University Press, 1965); J. Paul Hunter, *The Reluctant Pilgrim: Defoe's Emblematic Method and Quest for Form in Robinson Crusoe* (Baltimore: The Johns Hopkins University Press, 1966).

23. Roland Barthes, "The Reality Effect," in *The Rustle of Language*, trans. Richard Howard (New York: Hill and Wang, 1986), 141.

Index